In the Remains of Progress

Studies in Critical Social Sciences Book Series

Haymarket Books is proud to be working with Brill Academic Publishers (www.brill.nl) to republish the *Studies in Critical Social Sciences* book series in paperback editions. This peer-reviewed book series offers insights into our current reality by exploring the content and consequences of power relationships under capitalism, and by considering the spaces of opposition and resistance to these changes that have been defining our new age. Our full catalog of *SCSS* volumes can be viewed at https://www.haymarketbooks.org/series_collections/4-studies-in-critical-social-sciences.

Series Editor
David Fasenfest (York University)

New Scholarship in Political Economy Book Series

Series Editors
David Fasenfest (York University)
Alfredo Saad-Filho (Queen's University, Belfast)

Editorial Board
Kevin B. Anderson (University of California, Santa Barbara)
Tom Brass (formerly of SPS, University of Cambridge)
Raju Das (York University)
Ben Fine ((emeritus) SOAS University of London)
Jayati Ghosh (Jawaharlal Nehru University)
Elizabeth Hill (University of Sydney)
Dan Krier (Iowa State University)
Lauren Langman (Loyola University Chicago)
Valentine Moghadam (Northeastern University)
David N. Smith (University of Kansas)
Susanne Soederberg (Queen's University)
Aylin Topal (Middle East Technical University)
Fiona Tregenna (University of Johannesburg)
Matt Vidal (Loughborough University London)
Michelle Williams (University of the Witwatersrand)

IN THE REMAINS OF PROGRESS

Utopia and Suffering in
Brazilian Popular Entrepreneurship

Henrique Costa

Haymarket Books
Chicago, IL

First published in 2024 by Brill Academic Publishers, The Netherlands
© 2024 Koninklijke Brill NV, Leiden, The Netherlands

Published in paperback in 2025 by
Haymarket Books
P.O. Box 180165
Chicago, IL 60618
773-583-7884
www.haymarketbooks.org

ISBN: 979-8-88890-564-7

Distributed to the trade in the US through Consortium Book Sales and Distribution (www.cbsd.com) and internationally through Ingram Publisher Services International (www.ingramcontent.com).

This book was published with the generous support of Lannan Foundation, Wallace Action Fund, and the Marguerite Casey Foundation.

Special discounts are available for bulk purchases by organizations and institutions. Please call 773-583-7884 or email info@haymarketbooks.org for more information.

Cover design by Jamie Kerry and Ragina Johnson.

Printed in the United States.

Library of Congress Cataloging-in-Publication data is available.

For Sue and Júlia

Inside, everything was white-walled, moss-tiled and moonlit. Everything smelled of recent rain. The thin priest was asleep on a mat in the raised stone verandah. A brass platter of coins lay near his pillow like a comic strip illustration of his dreams. The compound was littered with moons, one in each mud puddle. Kochu Thomban had finished his ceremonial rounds, and lay tethered to a wooden stake next to a steaming mound of his own dung. He was asleep, his duty done, his bowels empty, one tusk resting on the earth, the other pointed to the stars. Rahel approached quietly. She saw that his skin was looser than she remembered. He wasn't Kochu Thomban any more. His tusks had grown. He was Vellya Thomban now. The Big Tusker. She put the coconut on the ground next to him. A leathery wrinkle broke to reveal a liquid glint of elephant eye. Then it closed and long, sweeping lashes resumed sleep.

A tusk towards the stars.

ARUNDHATI ROY, *The God of Small Things*

Contents

Foreword IX
    Nadya Araujo Guimarães
Acknowledgements XIII
List of Maps XV

Introduction: *In the Remains of Progress* 1
1   Wageless Life 6
2   Structure of Feelings 10
3   Questions of Approach 12
4   Book's Guide 21

PART 1
Ethnography

1 The Sun Shines for Everyone: the New Peripheral Middle Class 28
    1   Utopia in Paraisópolis 32
    2   Middle Class in the *Quebrada* 37
    3   Local Knowledge 42
    4   Possible Goals 45
    5   Strugglers 50
    6   Recognition 57
    7   Onwards 64

2 Between Lights and Shadows: Stories of Suffering and Religiosity 68
    1   Guiltless World 70
    2   Us and Them 77
    3   Mistrust 83
    4   Prosperity 85
    5   Family Ties 90
    6   God Willing 97
    7   Uncertainty 103
    8   Know-How 107

3 Mirages: Utopias of Modernity in Social Entrepreneurship 113
    1   Anti-capitalist 117
    2   Social Impact 122

    3   Two Sides of the Bridge   128
    4   Spreading Wings   137
    5   Powers   140
    6   Competence   143
    7   Peripheral Subject   149

PART 2
Structure of Feelings

4 **Reconfigurations**   157
    1   Family, Community and Social Classes   163
    2   Social Entrepreneurship and the Classless Society   168
    3   From Precarious Labour to Popular Entrepreneurship   174

5 **Utopia and Suffering**   183
    1   Self-Management and Therapeutic Narrative in Two Exemplary Cases   188
    2   The Guiltless World and Its Deconstruction   189

Conclusion: the Moral Economy of Brazilian Wageless Lives   193

References   199
Index   209

Foreword

The year 2020 has passed and, amid a pandemic, a report on entrepreneurship is gaining prominence in the Brazilian media. Conducted by the Global Entrepreneurship Monitor (GEM), in partnership with the Brazilian Micro and Small Business Support Service (SEBRAE) and the Brazilian Institute for Quality and Productivity (IBPQ), it presents some striking figures: no less than 50 million Brazilians say they want to start a business in the next three years. This figure has increased by 75 per cent compared to the previous survey conducted by the same institute.[1]

One might think that such a huge result would be due to the acute economic crisis and shrinking opportunities, deepened by the COVID-19 health catastrophe and related social isolation. Not so much. The survey conducted the following year by the same GEM, when the Brazilian economy was getting back on track, estimated that no less than 43 million adults in Brazil already ran a business (formal or informal) or had taken some action in 2021 with a view to starting a business in the near future. What's more, the expectation of having your own business – ranked third of the main 'dreams' (as the survey asked) of around half (46 per cent) of the Brazilians interviewed – would far outweigh the aspiration to have a successful career in a company – ranked as the eighth 'dream' imagined by no more than a third (32 per cent) of the people interviewed at the time.[2]

Another equally significant finding pointed to the considerable weight of those in the country who say they turn to business 'out of necessity', in other words, because of the lack of alternatives for earning an income. Almost half of the people who were entrepreneurs in 2021 were in this condition. Among the so-called 'nascent entrepreneurs', those who did business 'out of necessity' were 47.9 per cent in 2020 and, a year later, had increased to 49.3 per cent. In other words, even when companies were hiring again, people didn't trust the opportunity to survive on salaried jobs. In the words of the President of SEBRAE, the study's partner organisation, "we can infer that the initial entrepreneurs are very low-income and that a large number of them are potential

---

1   Available at: https://g1.globo.com/empreendedorismo/noticia/2021/10/05/50-milhoes-de-brasileiros-desejam-abrir-um-negocio-nos-proximos-3-anos-aponta-pesquisa.ghtml (consulted 29 April 2024).
2   Available at: https://sebrae.com.br/Sebrae/Portal%20Sebrae/Sebrae%2050+50/Notícias/gem-fev-2022.pdf (consulted on 29 April 2024).

individual micro-entrepreneurs (MEI) or have recently formalised themselves as such".[3]

But the strength of 'entrepreneurship' as an alternative form of economic insertion that marks modern-day Brazil can also be seen in another way, namely in how much space the topic has occupied in the country's print media. Maia (2024) set out to compute the frequency with which the word 'entrepreneurship' appeared over the last fifteen years in one of the main national print media outlets. He found that, from being almost imperceptible until 2009, the term has increased fivefold in the national news since 2012. The most elaborate form – and close to what the Global Entrepreneurship Monitor (2021) calls 'opportunity entrepreneurship' (in distinction from 'necessity entrepreneurship') – is perhaps expressed by the figure of startups. Curiously, and still following the clues raised by Maia (2024), it was only in 2017 that the term began to gain prevalence in the news, and its presence in print media only exploded between 2018 and 2021.

Although sociological analyses have attended to the phenomenon since the mid-1990s (Martinelli, 1994 and Aldrich, 2005 make two exhaustive assessments of the subject), Swedberg (2000: 28) acidly notes that among sociologists, "the subject of entrepreneurship has never been particularly popular".

Among us in Brazil, as a generation of new and creative Brazilian social scientists (Costa, 2022; Fontes, 2023; Maia 2024) have shrewdly observed, 'setting up your own business' and 'working for yourself' have long been expressions of the desired modes of engagement that make up the lexicon of *viração* (Gregori, 2000). These common terms allude to alternative livelihoods adopted by those who needed to survive outside the circuit of regular and protected jobs. Where, then, was the novelty in the face of what had previously been captured with all its ethnographic richness by authors of the calibre of Luiz Antonio Machado da Silva (1971, 2003)?

I would say that works like Henrique Costa's challenge us, firstly, to reject arguments that dilute the current novelty in external determinants, such as the irresistible capacity to forge subjectivities that emanates from neoliberal capitalism. In its simplicity, it's an attractive explanation that relieves those who assume it from the effort to explore and find the multiple mediations that give concrete form to this historical form in different realities.

By immersing himself in the daily lives of these individuals, Costa invites us to face up to the complexity of the determinants that shape the actions of

---

3 Available at: https://sebrae.com.br/sites/PortalSebrae/sebrae50mais50/noticias/pesquisa-mundial-de-empreendedorismo-divulgada-no-projeto-sebrae-50mais50 (consulted 29 April 2024).

these 'popular entrepreneurs'. Thus, if the experience of work is present, the grammar based on difference and conflict between classes does not exhaust the way in which representations are structured and the exit doors for survival are activated; there, other actors such as the family and the community also call the shots. What's more, the periphery appears in all its complex heterogeneity, which includes multiple universes.

In this context, entrepreneurship, far from being singular, appears to be plural, ranging from glitzy and politically engaged 'social entrepreneurship' to successful entrepreneurship, which feeds new ways of life responsible for deepening this heterogeneity, expressing itself, for example, in the condominiums that house a local 'new middle class' to the varied forms of self-employed and small traders operating on the fringes of legality.

Not without reason, there are many discourses that shape and translate these unequal experiences. They can range from Teologia da Prosperidade (Theology of Prosperity), an important vector in this popular entrepreneurship, to advanced forms of self-management under new technological resources. A complex structure of feelings emerges, made possible over the course of five years of ethnographic observation. This, little by little, gives us a glimpse into the codes and markers of a moral economy that governs wageless life, which becomes increasingly clear over the course of the five chapters that make up the beautiful text of this book.

In short, Henrique Costa – and the new generation of interpreters of which he is a part – are offering us a renewed social science, which unashamedly incorporates advances in urban anthropology, the social history of labour, a sociology of emotions and feelings, and well-established Marxism, leaving us with a new vision of Brazilian society and the challenges we must face. These young researchers leave us with the certainty that Brazil, as has already been said, is not for beginners.

Nadya Araujo Guimarães
São Paulo, Brazil

References

Aldrich, H. (2005) Entrepreneurship. In: Swedberg, Richard; Smelser, Neil (orgs.) *The Handbook of Economic Sociology. Second Edition.* New York: Russell Sage Foundation; Princeton University Press.

Costa, H. (2022) *Um lugar ao sol: Utopia e sofrimento no empreendedorismo popular paulistano.* PhD Dissertation. Universidade Estadual de Campinas.

Fontes, L. (2023) Informality, precariousness, and entrepreneurialism: new and old issues of urban labor in Latin America over the last decade (2012–2021). *BIB – Revista Brasileira de Informação Bibliográfica em Ciências Sociais*, 99.

Gregori, M. F. (2000) *Viração: experiências de meninos de rua*. São Paulo: Companhia das Letras.

Machado da Silva, L.A. (1971) Mercados metropolitanos de trabalho manual e marginalidade. Master's dissertation. Universidade Federal do Rio de Janeiro.

Machado da Silva, L.A. (2003) Mercado de trabalho, ontem e hoje: informalidade e empregabilidade como categorias de entendimento. In: Santana, M.A.; Ramalho, J.R. *Além da Fábrica; Trabalhadores, Sindicatos e a Nova Questão Social*. São Paulo: Boitempo.

Maia, M. (2024) Jovem firma procura investidor: como as aceleradoras promovem encontros e moldam startups. PhD Dissertation. Universidade de São Paulo.

Martinelli, A. (1994) Entrepreneurship and Management. In: Swedberg, R.; Smelser, N. (orgs.) *The Handbook of Economic Sociology*. Princeton: Princeton University Press.

Swedberg, R. (ed.) (2000) *Entrepreneurship*. Oxford: Oxford Management Readers.

Acknowledgements

The long road to the publication of this book has not been without the support and teachings of others. There are always more or less Herculean obstacles along the way, but it's precisely because of the interaction with teachers, university colleagues and friends that they are no longer insurmountable. One of them, the COVID-19 pandemic, did indeed prevent some academic plans, but I was also lucky not to go through it alone. Here I express my thanks to those who, with patience and/or interest, have followed the challenge over the five years that the research has taken and the journey to the publication of this book.

In the inconstancies that surround academic work, euphoria and scepticism alternate, and thanks to the guidance of important intellectual references, a synthesis is found. At UNICAMP, I was able to count on the then-coordinator of the Postgraduate Programme in Social Sciences, Angela Araújo, who generously took on my supervision and saw me through to the end. I thank her for the academic and sensitive relationship we built. I would therefore like to thank Vera da Silva Telles and Carolina Catini for their comments during my qualification. On my doctoral committee, I also had the satisfaction of working with Nadya Araújo Guimarães, Cibele Rizek and Taniele Rui. I still have the privilege of having Nadya as my post-doctoral supervisor at the University of São Paulo (USP) and the Brazilian Center of Analysis and Planning (CEBRAP).

I had the gratification of an intellectual interaction and friendship with Pedro Mendes Loureiro during my stay as a visiting scholar at the Centre of Latin American Studies (CLAS) at University of Cambridge. His observations on my work were essential for finalising this book. In Cambridge, I am also grateful for the fundamental support of Chriselia de Vries, the warm reception of David Lehmann and the partnership with Lenon Maschette. In London, I had the chance to share ideas, projects and friendship with Aiko Amaral, Gareth Jones, Mara Nogueira and Deborah Fromm, whom I would like to thank.

I am grateful for the support of the Department of Sociology at USP and CLAS-Cambridge, institutions where I was able to revisit my doctoral thesis and turn it into this book. Also, to David Fasenfest, Alfredo Saad-Filho and Brill for making publication possible. This research would certainly not have taken the direction it did without the dialogue with Paulo Arantes at USP. I would also like to thank André Singer, Ruy Braga and Camila Rocha for their dialogue and valuable teachings at different stages of my intellectual career.

I would especially like to thank all my interlocutors, to whom I would like to give due recognition. People who gave not only their time, but above all their privacy. No amount of acknowledgement will be enough – without them this book would not exist. But this is not a utilitarian thank you. In the months I spent writing this text, I found myself once again immersed in their lives, between anguish and gratitude, moments that transformed me as a researcher and as an individual. A special *salve* to Thiago Vinícius de Paula, who opened a dozen doors for me in the *quebrada*, as well as Fernando Bike and his contacts in Vargem Grande.

Finally, I would like to thank my parents, Josane and Egidio, my life partner, Sue Iamamoto, and my daughter Júlia, whose laughter and tears were always present during the writing of this book. With love.

Maps

1 City of São Paulo 26
2 Zona Sul (South Zone) 27

Introduction: *In the Remains of Progress*

> From the physical intimidation of the fascist state to the agonising repetitions of neurosis, the idea of freedom takes the same temporal form: a sudden perception of an intolerable present which is at the same time, but implicitly and however dimly articulated, the glimpse of another state in the name of which the first is judged. Thus the idea of freedom involves a kind of perceptual superposition; it is a way of reading the present, but it is a reading that looks more like the reconstruction of an extinct language.
>
> FREDRIC JAMESON

∴

The first few times I was in the Zona Sul (South Zone) of São Paulo for the research that gave rise to this book, I held a multitude of assumptions and hunches about the entrepreneurship of the poor. I went to the periphery of this part of the city, home to more than two million people, excited to immerse myself in the vibrant local culture, in the songwriters and poets of the soirees and in the realities that their rappers narrated with the living flesh intensity of their contradictions. On the one hand, I was looking for that sense of revolt against inequality and police violence; on the other, I was dismayed by the reports of a 'pacified' universe, where the criminal world was self-regulating and evangelical churches were managing ever-increasing numbers of precarious workers, in a balance that was always under threat. In fact, these factors were all there, but what slept was a popular culture that brought together these characters among many other unpaid workers living out their uncertainties and dealing with them. These were people with their feet firmly planted in concrete reality and with a sidelong glance at a longed-for emancipation, in which they placed both hope and suffering.

In the popular culture that welcomes it, individualism cradles the aspirations of people like the hairdresser Toni, who, at 41 years of age, finds himself full of satisfaction, married, with a young son, apartment and car of his own – maximum symbols of autonomy in liberal capitalism, which incidentally he flatters with his American flag-print hairdressing capes. He maintains his salon with dignity, navigating the typical exasperations of popular commerce and with emerging competition, but he does not complain, always remembering that 'the sun shines for everyone'. His wife Sueli completes the ideal of the popular enterprising couple with her respect for the institution of family, for which autonomy is its justification and orientation. These two Northeastern immigrants, Christians of flexible religiosity, built a life step by step in São Paulo despite persistently precarious occupations and periods living in *favelas* (slums). As Teresa Caldeira (2017: 6) states, "despite indisputable precariousness and persisting poverty, the processes of transformation of peripheral areas offer a model of social mobility, as they become the material embodiments of notions of progress". And they see, of course, merit in their social ascension.

Trajectories like this have great social and historical ballast. Predictions about the demise of religion due to the advance of secularisation can be mapped throughout modernity, and the family has not escaped condemnation either (Weber, 2004; Hochschild, 2018; Brown, 2019). The fact remains, however, that both institutions persist, and are perhaps stronger than ever in a country in which nine out of ten believe in God.[1] The vertiginous growth of Pentecostalism in Brazil symbolises this persistence, in which, together with devotion to God, recourse to the family proves to be indispensable for the self-management of these individuals. In fact, the anguish, indecision and despair that permeate family relationships, instead of imploding them, intensify situations of dependency and authoritarianism, a result of the reckless public world where the discursive matrix of crime predominates. Young people who deliberately seek to break with parental wisdom, seen as old fashion, find themselves stuck when they can turn to nothing and no one as they themselves become parents.

It is the modernising process itself that erodes these customs rooted in popular culture. The refusal of rationalisation may not be active, as in the nineteenth century English context studied by E. P. Thompson, but it is simply expressed in scepticism and neglect of the oppressive Brazilian reality of the 21st century, in which the conflicts at the heart of the popular are highlighted by the individual's withdrawal for the sake of himself and his family. Thus, workers in the peripheries consider the evasion of salaried work, which increasingly punishes and robs them of time for leisure, for children or even for housework (especially in the case of women), to represent the possibility of governing their own time, even if this implies the loss of labour benefits. These are small and silent individual manifestos that contradict the logic of capital, if not capital itself. A fragmented universe, it is in the challenge to modernisation that these outsiders recognise themselves. As culturally relegated populations,

---

1 According to the Global Religion Survey 2023, produced by the Ipsos institute in 26 countries.

where would one locate the cohesion that was lacking between the different types that populate the margins of large cities? I believe the answer lies in the rise of popular entrepreneurship, the contemporary cultural form of a *wageless life*.

Entrepreneurship cannot be seen as an isolated phenomenon. Above all, it brings with it a utopian sense of freedom, even when this is felt simply as a temporary escape from alienated, poorly paid and possibly undignified labour. Both self-employment and its modern, properly 'entrepreneurial' variant bring together characteristics that are common to popular and peripheral daily life, and which at this moment in history are combined in the formation of a renewed subjectivity. Thus, through ethnography in the streets and popular shops, in religious temples and in the universe of social entrepreneurship, I sought a gradient that ranges from the individual without great ambitions who runs their small business alone, to the young entrepreneur born into this logic who sees therapeutic discourse as a way out of emancipation, far from the conventional labour market. Among them are people saturated with popular experience who struggle, but feel rationalising tendencies compelling them to break with their customs in the name of a promised and, often, unfulfilled social ascension.

Entrepreneurship encompasses ways of earning a living that have their own historical dimension and which contemporary dynamics act to reinforce, in terms of the economic aspect, and to increase, in terms of the moral aspect, shaping a contemporary version of popular individualism. The small traders and self-employed workers who, alone or with their families, run their businesses with determination and cunning, on the edge of survival and a degree of comfort, boast exactly what the modernising discourse tries to subjugate: practical knowledge, attachment to concrete reality and the reward for competence. These are the factors on which these traders base both their customs and the scepticism with which they view intellectual work and everything that is distant from their immediate reality, such as politics. Experiences of prolonged unemployment, unplanned pregnancy, the early death of a family member as a result of police violence or their involvement in the world of crime, addiction to alcohol or drugs, as well as the growing demands for job qualifications, are concrete examples of how uncertainty compounds anxiety and suffering.

For many who have lived through the experience of being employed, certain obligations imposed by employers painfully undermine the values of good work, a sense of responsibility and professional ethics, as Christophe Dejours (1999) observed. Thus, in a world seen as constantly changing, men, women and their families live hanging by a thread (Castel, 2015), in which limited and sometimes threatening horizons accentuate their attachment to customs and their exclusive trust in themselves and in the family, seen as a fortress.

In unravelling the utopian dimension of entrepreneurship, I want to highlight another aspiration of the working classes that for a long time was considered the true Brazilian utopia: that of access to regulated citizenship and the expectation of social protection. Adalberto Cardoso saw Getúlio Vargas' development model as the seed of a social and political identity inspired by this utopia, made possible because real trajectories of social ascension created a yearning among those excluded from the world of rights, "as long as they did it". After all, as part of an authoritarian project, the state circumscribed and regulated this integration, and thus encouraged differentiations within the working class. "Vargas framed, through physical and symbolic violence, the horizon of expectations and the daily lives of workers, limiting them to the petty boundaries of capitalist sociability, by promising access to the world of consumption and the goods of liberal civilisation" (Cardoso, 2019: 226), symbolised by the Consolidation of Labour Laws (CLT) and the Employment and Social Security Record Card (hereafter 'work card').[2] This 'good life' utopia persists, in part. In fact, working class people value a life that isn't exhausting and abusive, but in many cases, even the CLT no longer guarantees this. For their children, low-paying, low-skilled jobs frustrate both them and their parents, who don't see their investments paying off, and the gap between those with 'regulated citizenship' and everyone else becomes smaller and more unstable.[3] It is in the freedom now promised to those who work only for themselves that a new utopia is to be found.

This book is about the practices and lifestyles of people who are poor, but not so poor. These are people whose flexibility is the hallmark of their trajectories, as well as the relationships they establish on both an individual and family level. What really counts here are the concrete conditions for reproducing life on the peripheries of São Paulo, which include the uncertainty and instability caused by new labour processes; the introduction of new technologies into everyday life; violent sociability; the intensification of Pentecostal religiosity; new forms of microcredit and consumption; the omnipresence of the market;

---

2 The Employment and Social Security Record Card (CTPS), known in Brazil as *carteira de trabalho*, is the document that records the worker's professional life and guarantees access to the labour rights provided for by law.
3 As Wanderley Guilherme dos Santos (1979: 75) put it, "all those whose occupation is unknown to the law thus become pre-citizens .... The legal instrument proving the contract between the state and regulated citizenship is the professional card, which becomes, in reality, more than labour evidence, a civic birth certificate".

the expansion of access to higher education and the differential distribution of the state's presence. How do individuals on the margins respond to transformations at the most basic levels of their existence?

Based on these considerations, therefore, wageless life and entrepreneurship are determined cultural forms, not as mechanisms in which content is essentially prefigured, predicted and controlled by a pre-existing external force, in which the superstructure is merely a reflection or imitation of the reality of the base, but in the sense of 'setting limits and exerting pressures' as defined by Raymond Williams. For Williams, the base is not a static and uniform object or an economic abstraction, but a process. Thus, he goes back to the notion of productive forces, emphasising that "the most important thing a worker ever produces is himself, himself in the fact of that kind of labour, or the broader historical emphasis of men producing themselves, themselves and their history" (Williams, 1973: 6). Moreover, as Marshall Sahlins (1976) has argued, the economy is the main site of symbolic production and is a source of narratives to think about the contemporary social world.

For the purposes of this book, the term 'entrepreneurship' requires clarification. In Brazil, as in other countries of the Global South, its spread in popular territories is recent, unlike in the North, where it is reasonably common to refer to the entrepreneurial attitude of individuals in precarious contexts. Ítalo Pardo, for example, researched the centre of Naples in the mid-1990s, where informality was largely dominant among the working poor. His discussion sought to understand these activities as belonging "to the complex interplay of moral themes, expectations and motivations that underlies both these people's distance from industrial values and their combination of different resource domains in their entrepreneurship" (Pardo, 1996: 35). In the Brazilian peripheries, the management of wageless life has this characteristic, but the incorporation of entrepreneurship in daily conversation is associated with owning a business and living by yourself, a 'modern' way of life, organising institutional discourses and individual references. It is not something applied from the outside to individuals without agency, an ideological masking of economic activities considered precarious. It is therefore an attempt by individuals experiencing instability to reinterpret their own history in order to fit into the entrepreneurial narrative, affiliating themselves with a culture seen as modern.[4]

---

4 Accentuating the strongly globalised nature of contemporary discourse, Quentin Chapus (2020) identified in the proliferation of start-ups in Morocco a divergence from traditional business culture, resting on the ideas of innovation and performance. Aiko Amaral (2018), in her research on the Bolivian fairs in São Paulo and El Alto, identified among the sellers'

Thus, the theme of the book derives precisely from this incorporation and provides the foundation from which my main consideration arises. A new composition that emerges as a late impulse of modernisation and de-traditionalisation, in the context of a remote and persistent wageless life, counterposes to popular culture a global wave of affirmation of instrumental rationality with repercussions beyond its economic aspects *stricto sensu* and with a direct impact on popular ways of life. This consideration takes as its inspiration the work of Reinhart Koselleck, for whom "experiences overlap and mutually impregnate one another. In addition, new hopes or disappointments, or new expectations, enter them with retrospective effect. Thus, experiences alter themselves as well, despite, once having occurred, remaining the same. This is the temporal structure of experience and without retroactive expectation it cannot be accumulated" (2004: 262).

1   Wageless Life

The concept of experience applied here combines the Thompsonian sense, which refers to the orality present in historical accounts and its permanence even in the face of increased literacy,[5] with Koselleck's 'space of experience'. In the latter, "many layers of earlier times are simultaneously present, without, however, providing any indication of the before and after" (2004: 260). That is, everything that can be remembered from one's own life or the lives of others, transmitted by generations and institutions, is present simultaneously. For the historian, what distinguishes the space of experience is its quality as a present past, "whose events have been incorporated and can be remembered" (2004: 259).

In Brazilian popular culture, this experience is essentially filled with the normative precedence of a wageless life. For Michael Denning (2010), this experience is defined by the assumption that "unemployment precedes employment, and the informal economy precedes the formal, both historically

---

expectations of social mobility that depend on uncertain economic gains, reinforcing their choice of an urban, dynamic and economically upwardly mobile identity, as opposed to the stereotypes that represent indigenous women as rural, traditional, backward and poor.

5 As Thompson (1993: 21) observed, that is, how "both practices and norms are the slowly differentiating ambience are perpetuated largely through oral transmission, its anecdote and of narrative example; where oral tradition is by growing literacy, the most widely circulated printed products, such as chapbooks, almanacs, broadsides, 'last dying speeches' and anecdotal accounts of crime, tend to be subdued to the expectations of the oral culture rather than challenging it with alternatives."

and conceptually. We must insist that 'proletarian' is not a synonym for 'wage labourer' but for dispossession, expropriation and radical dependence on the market" (Denning, 2010: 81). In *viração, correria* and other uncertain, unpredictable and non-salaried ways of earning a living, working class people change status: they do *bicos* or *frilas* and share situations of transience within the family and neighbourhood, as in the very common case of wage earners who need to supplement their income, who live with the unemployment of their spouse, or of the generational rupture of their daughter who has overcome the barrier of university education and seeks to realize the promise of entrepreneurship. Wageless life is, therefore, a way of life.[6]

Wageless life also means giving up the time management imposed by the employer. This often conflicts with other temporalities of individuals and families, allowing them to be grasped beyond the 'economic' temporality associated with planning, rationalisation and cost-benefit calculations. The 'calculation' can make the interlocutor's reasoning lean towards the security of a job, up to a certain point. Dignity and a less strenuous routine are, for some of them, the right choice.[7] Personal relationships are also highly valued, because when money is tight – which is the norm in the peripheries, with or without a wage – it is channelled towards immediate expenses. Individuals rely on personal relationships in the event of setbacks. People don't tend to save, buying on credit is viewed with suspicion and many are apprehensive about the risk of getting into debt. So, while money is important to support the household and basic needs, family, friends and community recognition may also be important considerations when it comes to resources, security and future problems.

Since the 1970s, Brazilian academic production on urban peripheries has sought to interpret the ways in which working class individuals and families cope with insufficient income and seek better living conditions. The family's project of social ascension, once they own a home, is thus directed towards their children, who are expected to dedicate themselves to their studies and

---

6 These words are common everyday slang in various regions of Brazil. *Viração* appears frequently in this book and refers to the act of *se virar* (getting by), i.e., dealing with an immediate problem, usually of a financial nature. It was first used as a native category by anthropologist Maria Filomena Gregori (2000). *Correria* (rush) has a similar meaning and comes from the idea of a nonstop job. *Bico* and *frila* are slang terms for short-term, one-off jobs; the origin of the term *frila* comes from the English word 'freelance'.

7 Marilena Chauí (2001: 69) made a similar observation about Luiz Antonio Machado da Silva's work on *botequins*, in which he identifies in the regulars an incapacity for projects and plans as a result of a rigid routine obscuring the perception of time. For Chauí, we should ask whether "for such men, [time] would necessarily have to have the same meaning that Benjamin Franklin gave it".

"move on to a non-manual or manual job with high qualifications, or another, even more difficult job, starting a 'business'" (Durham, 1988: 187). By the way, in Teresa Caldeira's (1984) study, self-employment was seen in a positive light, even though the 'reality' – society's obstacles – opposed the 'model' – no longer working for others. At that time, however, the author observes that the belief in the possibility of working for oneself was reiterated only by those few success stories that permeate the imagination of the lower classes, those that describe "someone who has already climbed the ladder".

In popular experience, there is a subtle but not irrelevant difference between wanting to be a boss and wanting to not have a boss. The legitimate desire for autonomy cannot be confused with an exotic 'neoliberal reason' that would govern the individual's choices.[8] As Benoît de L'Estoile (2020) observes, this freedom is related to a power differential, in other words, a longed-for ability to 'govern time', which can result in a disposition towards insubordination. This is not only because the Brazilian self-employed worker, and even the small businessman, often have no capacity or intention to employ staff, but because their individualistic ethics are saturated with a popular experience and historically based on the need for subsistence, characterised by minimal or miserable standards of living (Candido, 2017; Mello; Novais, 1998; Cardoso, 2019).[9] The

---

8   The current trend has dealt with the issue from the perspective of a 'neoliberal rationality', inspired by an interpretation of the concept of 'governmentality' from the centre of capitalism (Foucault, 2004). Laval and Dardot (2013) see neoliberalism as the generalisation of competitive logic, a political rationality that operates directly on subjectivities, transforming individuals into 'companies of themselves'. For them, neoliberalism is not just a set of economic measures applied by the state, but a political construction and a technology of control that induces populations to spontaneous actions of self-government. A similar position is held by Veronica Gago (2015), for whom a "neoliberalism from below" is formed in the popular economy, in which a network of practices and knowledge operates, and in which 'calculation' becomes the primary subjective matrix. Wendy Brown (2019) revisits the neoliberal and ordoliberal theses on which the policies to dismantle welfare states are based. In this case, intellectuals such as Hayek, Von Mises and Friedman, in proposing the 'demassification' of society, have provided theoretical instruments so that, through the 'entrepreneurialisation' of workers, practices of 'family self-provision' could be re-established.

9   In the early days of the economic decline of the Brazilian countryside and the advance of industrialisation and urbanisation, Antonio Candido (2017) noted the final imbalance in the way of life that characterised it. He observed that migration to urban centres was marked "not only by a relative conservation of traits, but true regressions, which show the vitality of traditional culture". The culture of the cities is absorbing the 'rustic cultural varieties', increasingly playing the role of the dominant culture, "imposing its techniques, standards and values". This implies, among other things, a painful adaptation to the new situation "by means of material and social techniques that had been elaborated for a vanished general situation" (Candido, 2017: 252–256). From the 1950s onwards, immigration from the Northeast towards São Paulo intensified, due in part to the city's

reference to cosmology in the oral accounts we see here goes back, albeit in a mitigated way, to this timeless past, which endures in popular language. From this, the expectation of redemption or the end of times in the Catholic sense are derived, firmly anchored in tradition and in an ethic that is hostile to capitalism as a rational and impersonal machine (Löwy, 2014).

In the characters who circulated the streets of Brazil at the beginning of the 19th century, Antonio Candido identified forms of socialisation typical of a universe of social outcasts. Ways of circumventing both work and the lack of it shaped the possible arrangements in this 'guiltless world', which Candido contrasts with American puritanism and its strict morals and regulated conduct. In this 'dialectic of order and disorder' that organises the social life of free and poor individuals in the 18th and 19th centuries in Brazil, a kind of balance between good and evil manifests, typical of a "vast general accommodation that dissolves the extremes, takes away the meaning of law and order, manifests the reciprocal penetration of the most disparate groups, ideas and attitudes, creating a kind of moral no-man's-land, where transgression is just a nuance in the range that comes from the norm and goes to crime" (1970: 87). It's no coincidence that in everyday popular language the verb 'to struggle' is often used to recognise a permanent challenge.[10]

In order to deal with uncertainty, the popular subject's hope for better days is always present and in Brazil they almost invariably turn to God, because His plans are mysterious and the future is up to Him. Thus, these precepts also appear in an evangelical-marginal version through the rap of the group Racionais MC's, in which "the one who speaks, narrates or retells the story is on one side or the other, is in battle, has adversaries and works for a particular battle" (Hirata, 2011: 199). It is in the idea of *proceder* (proceeding), the 'correct' behaviour of the brother in battle, that the struggler/battler is highlighted, who tries to remain dignified even while drowning in a logic based on consumption, from those who seek money at any cost, in other words, the traitor, the coward and the stingy person.

---

rapid industrialisation. Around 39 million people migrated from the countryside to large and medium-sized cities between the 1950s and 1980s. "What brought them all together, whether they were permanent wage earners, small landowners, squatters or partners, was the misery or extreme poverty in which they lived" (Mello; Novais, 1998: 576).

10 For Tocqueville (2002: 574), "individualism is a mature and calm feeling, which disposes each member of the community to sever himself from the mass of his fellow-creatures; and to draw apart with his family and his friends". This is an "erroneous judgement" rather than depravity, he says. It is precisely the belief in the absolute self-sufficiency of the individual spirit that makes each person close in on themselves and, from there, set themselves up as an implacable judge.

The lifestyles of these *batalhadores* (strugglers) show choices informed by the experiences of subalternate subjects, willing to make a living with the alternatives they have at hand. This uncertainty makes this world a place for both the *vida loka*, whose existence is marked by risk and contingency and presents illegal ways out, and the *zé povinho* and their aversion to deviance.[11] The imposition here is the same, that of earning a living as honestly as possible while dealing with the contingency and risks of a wageless life.

2 Structure of Feelings

Popular culture exists based on residual cultural forms and the impositions of the present. Social relations are always dynamic and emerging cultural forms make popular culture a constant field of tension. As Stuart Hall (1981: 229) observes, "there is no separate, autonomous, 'authentic' layer of working-class culture to be found. Much of the most immediate forms of popular recreation, for example, are saturated by popular imperialism. Could we expect otherwise?"[12] Entrepreneurship appears here as an emerging form, which emanates from the dominant culture and impinges on that residual *ethos* of wageless life with new rationalising constraints, specially intertwined with and justified by therapeutic discourse. Of course, "'rationality' and 'self-interest' are not pregiven self-evident categories of social action", it is codified and institutionalized in pervasive ways as "emotional life became imbued with the metaphors and rationality of economics; conversely, economic behaviour was consistently shaped by the sphere of emotions and sentiments" (Illouz, 2008: 60).[13]

---

11 *Zé povinho* is a popular expression that denotes, in a derogatory tone, the simple person, from the people, adept at gossip and envy and therefore seen as mediocre. *Vida loka* is generally used to refer to forms of behaviour in the periphery marked by instability and almost always risky or illegal strategies for dealing with it.

12 Willis (1981: 59) also noted that "themes are *shared* between particular manifestations because all locations at the same level in a class society share similar basic structural properties, and the working-class people there face similar problems and are subject to similar ideological constructions. In addition, the class culture is supported by massive webs of informal groupings and countless overlappings of experience, so that central themes and ideas can develop and be influential in practical situations where their direct logic may not be the most appropriate."

13 Williams (1973: 10) defines residual as "some experiences, meanings and values which cannot be verified or cannot be expressed in the terms of the dominant culture, [that] are nevertheless lived and practised on the basis of the residue – cultural as well as social – of some previous social formation".

Phenomena that are linked to practical consciousness are social not in the institutional or formal sense, but because they represent the changing present, and "do not have to await definition, classification, or rationalization before they exert palpable pressures and set effective limits on experience and on action", Williams (1977: 132) points out. Entrepreneurship manifests the structure of feelings through its ability to encompass a series of elements typical of contemporary times, such as recourse to self-help and labour self-management in the various forms in which it appears.[14] Perhaps surprisingly, popular entrepreneurship is not the result of the consecration of *homo economicus*, but rather the massive propagation of therapeutic discourse.

The search for self-recognition is a basic human aspiration, but in the face of concrete historical events, it falls on the individual, reduced to himself, his family and his social reproduction. This is a symptom of the narrowing between the space of experience and the horizon of expectations in the contemporary world, which the events of the second half of the 20th century, including the dismantling of welfare states in the centre of capitalism and the collapse of economic modernisation projects on its periphery, the environmental crisis, the threat of nuclear war, the productive restructuring of capitalism and the increasing mechanisation of the work process, have subverted the idea of continuous progress, lowering expectations and stimulating a culture of narcissism (Arantes, 2014; Lasch, 1991).[15]

This ambition for self-recognition has the potential to transform to scepticism towards the public world and its institutions, which fills the context in which a popular sector becomes 'entrepreneurial' and crosses the real and

---

14   Incidentally, in mental health, the dizzying growth of demand for psychologists and psychiatrists and self-help techniques in the 20th century turned therapeutic culture into a global phenomenon of pathologising and remedying disorders, with the aim of maintaining the work functionality of individuals who are increasingly pressured by exhaustion and competition (Illouz, 2007, 2008). If, on the one hand, the phenomenon of self-help strengthens the individual's burden in the search for their own cure, "in a 'throw-away' society, where the rule is the search for the satisfaction of momentary pleasures, self-help is gaining considerable ground, as it answers individual questions simply and quickly, giving the feeling that it is feasible to achieve the desired changes in a short space of time" (Martelli, 2010: 217). Elaine Leite and Natália Melo (2008: 42) saw self-help literature as a source of propagation that would have naturalised the term. The authors assessed that "in this way, the idea of the entrepreneur and the successful man, linked to the rich man, is being formed in Brazil".

15   For Arantes (2014), the rupture caused by modernity, inventions, the great navigations and the French Revolution meant that the space of experience saturated by the Christian eschatological vision – waiting for the end of the world – no longer responded to the expectations opened up by these innovations.

metaphorical bridge that separates the outskirts of São Paulo from its centre, always in a position of subalternity, even when it has very different expectations. From the domestic worker who comes from the backlands of Bahia, who sews for others and would like to have her own business "not to get rich", but to have more time for her young son, to those who see themselves as 'peripheral subjects', who don't conform to any kind of submission and who negotiate their interests, the contradictions of remaining on one side of the bridge are revealed, metaphorically describing the divide between tradition and modernity.

Hall, in his work between the turn of the 1970s and 1980s, notes that despite entrepreneurship's manipulative character, "then it is because, alongside the false appeals, the foreshortenings, the trivialisation and short-circuits, there are also elements of recognition and identification, something approaching a recreation of recognisable experiences and attitudes, to which people are responding" (Hall, 1981: 233). Thus, entrepreneurship is an essential part of a culture that contains a utopian paradigm. It needs to respond to people's real needs not as an empty distraction or mere 'false consciousness', but by transforming social and political anxieties and fantasies into an effective presence in cultural commodities, so that they can later be managed or repressed, as Fredric Jameson (1992) observes. Entrepreneurship re-signifies a dream of ideal work and at the same time an escape from the reality of degraded labour. On the one hand, it stimulates the agency of the individual, caught up in the deep desire to live on their own. On the other hand, it re-establishes the centrality of work by emphasising the negativity of wage-earning, replacing it with a fantasy of individual satisfaction.

Popular entrepreneurship embodies a utopia of a life without subjection, in dialogue with both the *malandro* (scoundrel) of popular culture and the contemporary celebrity, who don't sell their work but their lifestyle. These characters draw the substrate for their utopia from the 'guiltless world', in the expression coined by Candido (1970).

3   Questions of Approach

On a Wednesday morning in February 2020, a few weeks before COVID-19 spread across Brazil, I arrived by bus at the Terminal Campo Limpo, in the Zona Sul of São Paulo, in the drizzle and bitter cold of the season. A few days earlier, a huge storm had caused destruction and disruption in the city, and as the rain was still threatening, a certain amount of caution was warranted. My appointment that day was to attend *Pitch Day*, a course organised by Projeto

Rede for aspiring entrepreneurs.[16] I had already visited Rede a few times, which describes itself as "a non-profit organisation that welcomes and supports families living in poverty in the Campo Limpo region". It was founded in 1968 and runs an entrepreneurship and income generation centre, coordinated by Felipe.[17]

I met Felipe a year earlier, at the pre-carnival meeting of *coworking da quebrada*, a social entrepreneurship agency that I'll discuss more later. While in Pinheiros, a middle-class neighbourhood in the West, the streets were filled with revellers and marching bands, in Campo Limpo the atmosphere was the same. At the agency, DJs took turns and the sound ranged from rap to reggae, with some soul and funk. The crowd was small, ranging from 20 to 30 people, all from the region. João Vicente, the agency's founder and a social entrepreneur, had done his usual publicity on social media, but the expected audience from the wealthy Zona Oeste seemed confounded by his street party and didn't turn up. However, partners who had been important throughout his life were there, like his former teacher Felipe, whom João thanked for having taught him "everything". A light-eyed man with a beard and abundant grey hair, he was carrying the book *Managing Knowledge Networks* by the consultant and self-help writer J. David Johnson, and told curious stories about his life between spiritual retreats, macrobiotic food and entrepreneurship.

With an appointment for 10:00 am, I arrived at Rede's headquarters a little late, but the event was yet to begin. In a laboratory room, built with sponsorship from the Ray-Ban sunglasses company, preparations continued, where nine people I had yet to identify were waiting with their laptops ready for the pitch – a short, direct presentation aimed at selling the business to an investor. Eventually, jokes about 'unicorns' relaxed the atmosphere, and seemed quite natural to everyone.[18] At the head of the table, three chairs were set up: one for Felipe, one for Rede's institutional coordinator, and the last chair for me. When I entered the room, Felipe introduced me and informed the participants that I would be part of the 'panel', i.e., my presence there was justified by what I could contribute to the presentations based on the 'experience' of someone who has followed good and bad examples of entrepreneurs. At the rectangular

---

16   The name of the institution has been changed.

17   The names of the interlocutors have been changed to protect their privacy. In the case of the interview transcripts, they were minimally edited when they helped to improve comprehension, especially regarding the excessive use of slang and expressions which, in written form, may hinder reading. However, I did my best to maintain the spirit of what was being said and the characteristics of everyone.

18   Financial market jargon for startups valued at over 1 billion dollars.

table, men and women, black and white, alone or in couples, deal with their presentations: a vegan version of *acarajé*, pot cakes, pies and 'healthy' or 'ancestral' lunchboxes. All of them were presenting essentially popular gastronomic knowledge, but with environmental or identity-based adornments, reflecting precisely how the course had taught them to be innovative and, in addition, acquire the label of 'peripheral' – much more than just a geographical reference.

Unsuspecting, I tried to figure out how to get out of the situation without causing embarrassment to everyone involved, and I realised that there was nothing else to do: the pitch went ahead, and my opinion was asked at the end of each presentation, which would also be filmed. Finally, I mediated the situation by giving generic impressions, while remaining genuinely concerned about the fate of those people with almost always precarious trajectories, wageless workers who were investing time and money in the dream of not just making *viração*, but of becoming successful entrepreneurs.

Even though the situation described reveals the unusual and causes me great embarrassment, moments in which would-be entrepreneurs seek empathy and validation for what they do are frequent, indications both of the expectation they place on their own entrepreneurial initiative and of their insecurity about the steps to be taken. The role of the 'expert', however, exposes a contradiction. On the one hand, in the case of entrepreneurs by necessity – those who have given up looking for stable jobs, spending a lot of time idling or just getting by – the expert becomes a reliable interlocutor who can present solutions and ways forward – not by chance, this figure is a constant presence at social entrepreneurship events. On the other hand, specifically when in contact with the peripheral subject,[19] there is a mistrust of the specialist, the one who is seen as expressing opinions without knowing the local reality, regardless of their academic knowledge. In both cases, you must deal with symbolic violence.[20]

As well as the discomfort of being there to fulfil another stage of the research and act as an expert in a procedure that I had only recently learned about in

---

[19] From here on, I use the adjective 'peripheral' to refer specifically to those who identify themselves as such in reference to peripheral culture, and popular for all other interlocutors.

[20] Particularly in interviews, the relationship that is established between unequal subjects is reminiscent of Pierre Bourdieu's observation (2012: 694). "Although the research relationship differs from the majority of ordinary exchanges, since its purpose is mere knowledge, it remains, in spite of everything, a *social relationship* that exerts effects (variable according to the different parameters that can affect it) on the results obtained."

practice, I feared that I wouldn't meet the expectations of both Felipe and the participants. Knowing how much these people need help to start breathing (even if just a 'like' on their social media page) and not feeling authorised to do so, imposes constant reflections on the ethnographic exercise. The episode narrated above is thus the culmination of a long process of reflections, disappointments and redefinitions of the research problem, and marked the moment when the pieces finally began to fit together. From the popular to the peripheral, a diverse range of self-employed workers, small traders and entrepreneurs would pass me by on the streets, at entrepreneurship events, in their shops and homes. As the interactions went on, which with the peripheral workers took months to consolidate, they loosened up a bit, but the laconic speeches were still recurrent. My presence at the promoted activities, even if motivated primarily by research, ended up becoming a sign of 'being together', which is part of the informal code of ethics of the *quebrada*. 'Broken' is the affectionate way in which young people from the periphery refer to their neighbourhoods, while still acknowledging their precarious reality. In other words, 'running together', always guided by 'what's right', is an extremely valued lesson that can be seen in popular ways of life. This is fundamentally what makes this type of research possible.

• • •

The sheer size of São Paulo's southern zone cannot be put into perspective, nor can the inequalities within it. You don't even have to be in the centre to realise the impressive scale of the commute, which by bus can easily take two hours, sometimes more. With the recent extension of the 5-Lilac underground line, journeys have become more comfortable and faster, but this doesn't reach all of the periphery. In those cases, the São Paulo Metropolitan Railway Company (CPTM) trains go a little further, and even then, there's still a lot of ground to cover until you reach the extreme edge of the city, only about 70 kilometres from the São Paulo State coast. My trips to the field were therefore planned very strictly, as I had to consider these routes and any delays in transport. Arrivals at appointments were planned, but returns were limited exclusively by the public transport timetable, when the return journey often took place in the early hours of the morning. To take part in the *vivência* at the João Vicente agency, for example, I got up at 4:00 am in a storm that was sweeping the whole city. Luckily, the rain stopped during the morning activity in Campo Limpo. A return journey from Jardim Ângela took two and a half hours. It's important to recognise at this point that, despite often being frowned upon, São Paulo's public transport has proved valuable and reliable.

The periphery is the centre, as many in the *quebrada* say. In fact, the Zona Sul has several centres, sometimes not even in the capital itself. From the Cratera de Colônia, on the edge of the city, still considered rural and home to indigenous reserves, to the neighbouring municipality of Taboão da Serra, passing through Campo Limpo, Grajaú, Jardim Ângela and Paraisópolis, the city that was born and grew 'from the bridge to here' in a few blocks separates a *favela* from a condominium, social projects from an organic food store, politicised soirees from evangelical churches, but whose communicating vessels form a network that is both dispersed and interdependent and which holds a multitude of enterprises. In 2019, of the 660,000 individual microentrepreneurs (MEI) formalised in the capital, according to the Secretariat for Economic Development and Labour, the region covered by the Campo Limpo sub-prefecture concentrated 26.870, fewer only than Sé, the central region (Fonseca, 2019).

The data on developments in Campo Limpo was one of the criteria for my choice of the Zona Sul of São Paulo. I already knew the region because of a long period of party activism, and above all because part of the ethnography I conducted in my master's research was in the Largo Treze region, a popular shopping area and location of the campus of the private university where some of my interlocutors studied (Costa, 2018). I also visited Capão Redondo and Jardim Germânia for short pre-field visits. The decisive aspect, however, was the interest aroused by the rich cultural scene in the Zona Sul: in addition to the hip hop scene that produced groups and rappers like Racionais MC's, Sabotage, among others, there were also soirees (Cooperifa's, Binho's) and various public and private facilities inaugurated since the 2000s, such as Unified Educational Centres (CEUs), Fábricas de Cultura and a unit of the Social Service of Commerce (SESC-SP), an important network of cultural centres concentrated in São Paulo and maintained by the powerful commerce association.

I attended these centres and a few others between 2017 and 2021. At first, I followed where the entrepreneurship took me. I'll explain: my first intuition when I started preparing my fieldwork was to look for people who stood out in social entrepreneurship, which was already very much in vogue in the mid-2010s. The axis of a global phenomenon of 'ethical capitalism' and – especially relevant to this analysis – social entrepreneurship is part of initiatives aimed at promoting 'small worlds of development' on the premise that the poor are inherently entrepreneurial.[21] New sources often describe these social

---

21   The concept of microcredit was developed by Bangladeshi economist Muhammad Yunus. His bank, the Grameen Bank, focussed on income generation and the smooth repayment

entrepreneurs in a somewhat messianic way as those who find their own means of generating income in the periphery without waiting for the government, using their 'vocation' to find creative ways out of the economic crisis. While reading these accounts, I came across my first contact, João Vicente, and his social entrepreneurship agency in the Campo Limpo neighbourhood.

During the months that I was in frequent contact with him, I received a dozen invitations and referrals from João to entrepreneurship events all over the Zona Sul. On each of these occasions, which took the form of fairs, workshops or large forums, I met new contacts who recommended others to me, and so I mapped out an ecosystem that operated on the outskirts of São Paulo around social impact businesses, which were based on current trends in ethical capitalism and the valorisation of a certain 'ancestry'.[22] What they had in common was the ostentatious presence of corporate foundation logos, which sponsored and even named these events where the discourse always referred to progressive ideas (sustainable, anti-racist, feminist, etc.).

Except for those who attended these events as guests – among them, social entrepreneurship success stories, business school researchers and the coordinators of the promoting organisations – there was anxiety and incomprehension among the public, sometimes even nonconformity, which seemed to disrupt the atmosphere of harmony and optimism that the organizers sought to create. Despite being highly politicised, they were totally oblivious to the economic and political mood, marked by the government of far-right president Jair Bolsonaro. The larger and more impersonal these meetings were, the more people there were who wanted to change their lives but felt insecure and lost in the terms and prescriptions of a group engaged in the world of social impact business. In reality, there is no magic formula for success, and there was a sense that success depends on various factors that are not always within the

---

of such loans. But as Ananya Roy (2010: 24) notes, "although Yunus frames his vision of microfinance in the language of human rights, his ideas are in fact concerned with entrepreneurialism rather than redistribution, with opportunity rather than equality. His fierce emphasis on self-reliance creates a model of poverty alleviation that is simultaneously poor-centric and anti-welfare". Roy traces a genealogy of microcredit policies that leads directly to the initiatives implemented by the World Bank in the mid-1990s, when the 'poverty agenda' took centre stage at the bank. Its main result was the inclusion of the poor in the financial market, even reformulating several of Yunus' premises by advocating the concept of 'minimalist microcredit'.

22   For the purposes of this study, the terms 'social entrepreneurship' and 'social impact business' will be treated in an approximate manner. 'Peripheral entrepreneurship', on the other hand, is that which dialogues directly with peripheral culture.

reach of people who lack economic, social and cultural capital. Not everything is a question of mindset.

So, I decided to look for the entrepreneur who had not yet earned this epithet, that is, the self-employed or even salaried worker who has decided to change his or her life, and who has seen in the plethora of uplifting messages scattered around his or her world a way of overcoming the exhausting routine, precariousness and social devaluation. These messages invariably point to entrepreneurship, present in schools, NGOs, companies, the media, bar conversations and family lunches, and touch on a very relevant feeling: a willingness to be autonomous, which is part of an *ethos* that I have identified in this research, with the help of sociological, historiographical and anthropological literature. But in order to understand this *ethos*, it was necessary to refute, even temporarily, the 'neoliberalism' that appears with such emphasis in academic understandings of entrepreneurship and entrepreneurs. In Brazil, salaried work guaranteed by the rules of the state has always been an exception, so it is non-salaried labour that has historically defined the Brazilian working masses, long before or totally indifferent to the great thinkers of neoliberalism such as Hayek, Von Mises, Friedman and their colloquiums in the Swiss Alps.

By clearing the space, the popular subject emerges. In the narratives of the aspiring entrepreneur, often marked by wageless life, there is a remarkable measured hope for a new world that opens up, where the possession of credentials is the differentiator and no longer the know-how. However, another question then arises: Why use the label entrepreneur, if the *ethos* was so ingrained in popular culture long before the term escaped from offices and human resources agencies? So, I left the self-declared entrepreneur environment for a new stage of ethnographic incursion into the popular shopping streets of the Zona Sul and other meeting spaces, notably Pentecostal churches, where I went to follow the so-called 'prosperity cults'. My timing coincided with the COVID-19 pandemic. While this imposed obvious difficulties – apart from a few exceptional situations, I made all my journeys by public transport – and a constant obsession with hygiene, it opened up new layers of dialogue with the interlocutors, which helped to shed light on the workings of their *ethos,* and details emerged that only extraordinary situations can evoke.

Here, in addition to the masks, the politically correct speeches from social entrepreneurship environments also disappeared. Compared to the peripheral culture, a very different reality emerged, in which scepticism structured opinions that were often prejudiced and cynical about political and social dynamics, but also generous and hopeful. Stories of lives suffered, sometimes told with tears in their eyes, sometimes with the use of jokes. On my side, armed with a tape recorder and a semi-structured script, I combined curiosity with a researcher's humour, reduced interventions as much as possible, opened up space for the interlocutors to let their stories be saturated with spontaneity, and invested in trust between the parties. Arlie Russell Hochschild (2018) insists that we cross the 'walls of empathy' when we engage in fieldwork, especially with those who are so different from us.[23] I am convinced that this research could only reach the results I am presenting through a judgement-free path.

Between one appointment and another, certain paths sometimes seemed to be points of no-return, like when I was approached by a First Command of Capital (PCC) *disciplina* at the entrance to an alleyway in Paraisópolis.[24] Inadvertently wandering around the *favela* with my mask on my face and my rucksack on my back, after dozens of similar incursions, my overconfidence would receive a warning. Unlike other researchers accustomed to the world of crime, which I only knew from reading about, I was taken aback by the intimidating approach of this figure who controls the flow in the *quebradas* in the name of the *Comando*, maintaining a certain order in the chaos. A few centimetres from my face, I was asked to prove that I was a researcher linked to the university and not a policeman, to tell him where I lived, what my research was about … This round of questioning seemed eternal, and I tried to mentally prepare myself for the worst, a more 'rigorous' interrogation, and for the less negative outcome, contracting COVID-19. Not entirely persuaded by my story, the *disciplina* called in a colleague, who took a good look at me, checked my ID and gave his opinion.[25] "He said he's doing a survey of the shopkeepers," said the first. "Yeah, he's got a good face," nodded the second with a debauched smile.

---

23   In a curious passage in her book, a case study of the base of the new right in Louisiana (one of the poorest states in the United States), she tells of being told by one of her interlocutors that "we Cajuns like to laugh. I hope you do". I often found myself laughing during the conversations I conducted in my research, partly spontaneously and partly in search of empathy. In fact, that was my first feeling when conducting this work.
24   The criminal organization PCC emerged in 1993 among inmates at the Taubaté House of Custody and Treatment in the state of São Paulo. According to Karina Biondi (2019: 49), after a massacre during a football match between rival factions, some prisoners in this maximum-security prison had the objective of "organising themselves to try to avoid the mistreatment they claimed to suffer in the prison system, while at the same time regulating relations between prisoners so that the mistreatment didn't come from themselves. The opinion was that they had to unite (because, after all, they shared the same situation) to then demand what they considered to be dignified treatment in the prison system."
25   In the hierarchy of the First Capital Command (PCC), the *disciplina* (discipline) is responsible for ensuring compliance with the rules drawn up by the faction. According to Biondi (2010), discipline is synonymous with ethics for the 'thieves' and is related to 'right', which is never defined in advance.

Finally convinced, they offered to call me an *uber*. Life goes on: the entrepreneurial thing gave me another nod.

⋯

Raymond Williams (1989) once said that culture is ordinary, whether it's produced by ways of life and their common meanings, or that which comes to us through the arts, knowledge and creative endeavours. In all these incursions, the profusion of cultural manifestations revealed an impressive scenario of textures, sounds, smells and images, from *tecnobrega* to James Brown's funk, from vegan *feijoada* to pot cake, from the Northeastern, gaucho or Spanish accent of a Mexican interlocutor to the religiosity of Pentecostals, Catholics and *Candomblecistas*, which I'll discuss throughout this book. I also watched police programmes, soap operas and reality TV shows that evoked the theme of entrepreneurship and, finally, I stayed connected to the virtual environment, as many of my interlocutors advertised their products and services on YouTube channels, Instagram, Facebook and WhatsApp profiles, which I constantly monitored, both to complement the ethnography and to seek out new contacts.

I tried to characterise their lifestyles, seeking a dense description of representations and opinions; therefore, themes such as family, work and politics appear here not as generalisations, but from those realities that are reproduced on the outskirts of the Zona Sul of São Paulo. As well as participant observation, I carried out 46 interviews in total, 40 of which make up the core of the research with self-employed workers, small traders and entrepreneurs, and six with interlocutors who helped me understand the context of popular entrepreneurship.[26] In the case of some qualified interlocutors, I paid special attention to their life stories, which are covered in the following pages. I reached out to other interlocutors using the snowball method.

In the relationship between researcher and interlocutor, there is only the tape recorder and a field notebook. As Teresa Caldeira says, each interview is a unique experience. The testimonies, as much as they refer to everyday life, are not trivial events. What is said there is filtered through systematised considerations that are not expressed in this way in everyday situations. "Daily life is the ordinary and what is lived immediately is fragmentary; in it, the comments, observations, opinions that are being elaborated are inevitably glued to the

---

26 Due to the COVID-19 pandemic, some interlocutors (six) asked to be interviewed by telephone.

parts, there is no way to distinguish between them and no way to escape the immediacy and fragmentation" (Caldeira, 1984: 44).

When taken out of everyday life, the interlocutor tries to rationally put together what was fragmented when faced with unfamiliar topics, relying on the memory of stored images that are rarely used. Thus, interpreting testimonies requires attention to other important elements that take into account the ambiguities that often characterise these occasions. In other words, analysing the contexts in which each statement was given becomes fundamental for meaning to emerge and comparisons to be possible. One example is precisely the way in which the term 'entrepreneurship' is used by different interlocutors, in spaces ranging from small businesses on a normal working day to events sponsored by millionaire foundations. However, contexts are also part of a whole, and they refer to experiences that are collective, that unfold at a specific time and in a specific place, which are apprehended and interpreted both by participant observation and by theory and historiography. The data collected in detail, which is often disorganised in a chaotic sequence of pages in a field notebook or in an account recorded by the researcher himself, is essential for mapping those symbolic aspects of working class lifestyles that are precisely important for interpreting and categorising them in this way.

In this book, I have tried to construct a theoretically informed ethnography, as Paul Willis and Mats Trondman advocate, recognising "the way in which experience is woven into the flow of contemporary history, both broad and narrow". The theory mobilises works in favour of ethnographic evidence, helping to understand social phenomena; at the same time, it is fundamental to challenge the textures of everyday life expressed in purely descriptive ethnography. Likewise, culture appears not as strictly discursive, but "in the broad sense of the growing imperative for all social groups to find and construct their own 'lived' roots, ways and meanings in societies undergoing profound processes of restructuring and de-traditionalisation" (Willis; Trondman, 2008: 212–214).

4 Book's Guide

This book is organised into two parts, in addition to this Introduction and the Conclusion. In Part 1, I detail the fieldwork I conducted over five years in the southern zone of São Paulo, as well as the dozens of trajectories that I analysed to build this narrative arc. I divide this part into three chapters. In the first chapter, I present relatively successful experiences of entrepreneurship *per se*, i.e., people who see themselves as entrepreneurs and have set up relatively stable businesses. They are micro and small entrepreneurs, not always formalised, but who have managed to keep their accounts and families afloat and make concrete plans for the future. Work experiences tie these narratives together, but other dimensions of wageless life appear here as well, such as merit, both in the popular sense of recognising competence and in its more contemporary version of those who stress the value of accumulating credentials. Other habits are incorporated and relate to the new ways of life that become part of the peripheries, from condominiums to restaurants built for a local 'new middle class'. Among them, entrepreneurship is also on the horizon as an alternative way for the country to face its crises. The biggest concerns of these interlocutors relate to the de-bureaucratisation of the state and the tax burden, as well as affinities with the Bolsonaro discourse.[27]

Chapter 2 focuses on a more precarious context, in which small traders and self-employed workers share experiences of *viração*, commercialise products with low economic value added and eventually combine legal and illegal ways of earning an income. In general, they preserve a modest way of life, and their main aspiration is to avoid exhausting work, with the right to one day off a year to visit their distant relatives. If they produce residual forms of locality, especially in the more peripheral regions, they also resent the rationalising pressures and assaults on customs that they see challenging their children's upbringing, feelings that intensify when they reach adolescence. As these stories slip into accounts of exploitation, abuse and family conflicts, the experiences of suffering reveal dark aspects of popular reality. One of the main vectors of popular entrepreneurship, Teologia da Prosperidade, is addressed here, both through participant observation and the trajectories of interlocutors.

Chapter 3 concludes the empirical section with the ethnography of social entrepreneurship. Here I bring together the fieldwork I carried out at forums, lectures and workshops held by the social impact business ecosystem, which brings together social organisations, business foundations and protagonists of peripheral culture. Among the young people from the periphery who have been at the forefront of the Zona Sul's cultural effervescence over the last three decades, activism brings hearts and minds together with the emerging structure of feelings. They see entrepreneurship as the final horizon of integration in the face of the implosion of the Luiz Inácio Lula da Silva's project of inclusion through consumption and social programmes.[28] The relationship

---

27 See also Costa (2019b).
28 According to André Singer (2012), the regular adjustment of the minimum wage, the accelerated expansion of credit and the increase in the formalisation of work at growing levels, as well as access to new public policies such as the Bolsa Família and the University for All Programme (Prouni), would have displaced the 'subproletariat', previously hostile

between therapeutic discourse and advanced forms of self-management is particularly prominent here.

In Part 2, I summarise my findings and conclusions, linking empirics with theory to answer the hypothesis regarding the formation of popular entrepreneurship in São Paulo. Chapter 4 reconstructs the forms of wageless living in the face of reconfigurations in the world of work and in the space of experience, as well as the mediations and contradictions of the categories of work, family, community and social classes that cross popular daily life. Chapter 5 moves towards the structure of feelings to which entrepreneurship is linked, exploring in the light of ethnography the vectors that determine contemporary self-management, such as therapeutic discourses and new technological resources.

In the Conclusion, I try to answer some questions about how popular entrepreneurship exposes a moral economy of the wageless life, adjusts to the convergences and conflicts between popular individualism and entrepreneurship in the periphery, and aggravates the generational clashes in popular territories, seen under the mediation of scepticism.

---

to the PT, to become the party's main electoral base, configuring the phenomenon known as *Lulismo*.

PART 1
Ethnography

MAP 1   City of São Paulo

ETHNOGRAPHY

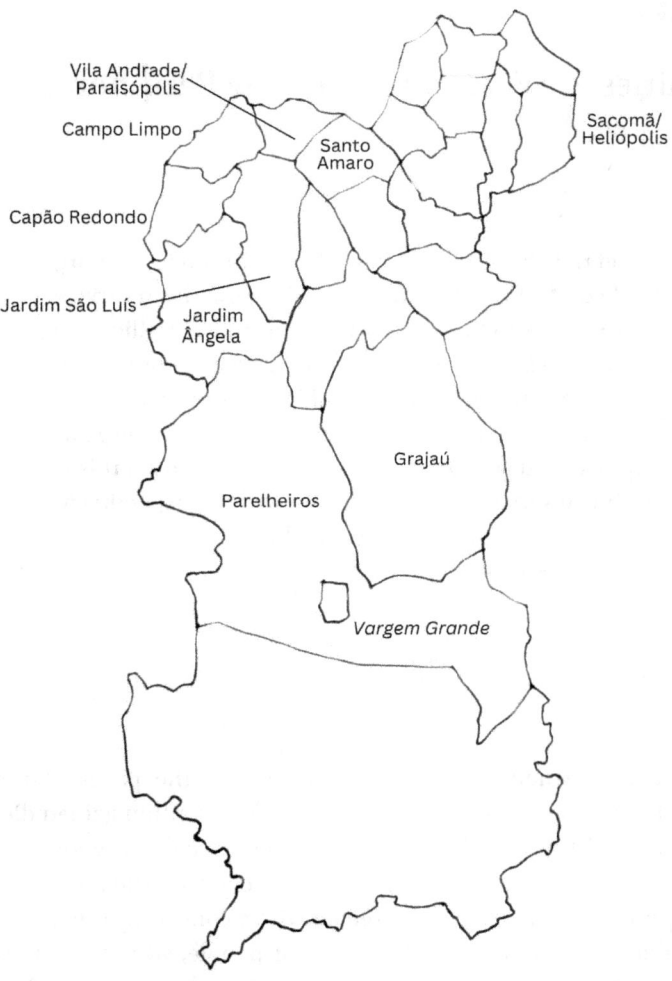

MAP 2   Zona Sul (South Zone)

CHAPTER 1

The Sun Shines for Everyone: the New Peripheral Middle Class

> I don't want to get rich, but I want to have the minimum of comfort, the minimum of comfort I want to have, right? So that I can survive well, so that I don't have to be so tight, but I don't have millionaire pretensions, because it's good to keep your feet on the ground. You have to have expectations that you can fulfil, not something that's impossible, right? So, the goals must go up slowly, you set small goals and as you improve, you set something higher. But for now, this is the goal: to be able to survive on my trade, but without expecting to be rich from it. To live as comfortably as possible.
> SUELI, 37, domestic worker

∴

It was November 2008 when Paraisópolis appeared on the pages of the prestigious British newspaper *Financial Times* (FT). The mention gained disdainful exclamations of third-world solemnity in the journalist's report: the opening of a Casas Bahia store in the São Paulo *favela*, chosen to be the first to receive the very popular retail chain, was greeted with a concert by the samba group Exaltasamba and excitement of hundreds of people, who danced "as if there was no tomorrow" (Wheatley, 2008). From that day on, instead of facing a trip of more than an hour to the nearest store, customers living in the *favela* would have a Casas Bahia right there to pay for their tickets and a multitude of goods to enjoy during their visit. The prosperity of retail chains, even after the economic slowdown during the recessive years of 2015 and 2016, demonstrates that the sector maintained its pace even with the rise in unemployment and other negative indicators.[1] The FT article also reported that the store's expectation was for continued growth. This was confirmed, by

---

1   In 2019, according to IBGE data, retail sales grew by 1.8 per cent, the third annual increase in a row.

the store's continued presence there twelve years later, despite the country's repeated economic and political crises.

The popularity of Casas Bahia grew along with the myth of its founder, the businessman Samuel Klein. One of Gabriel Feltran's interlocutors, a young man who at the time worked as an electrician for the retail chain, believed that Klein had fled Nazism, had never worked for anyone and had started his career selling door to door. "Entrepreneurship is what Casas Bahia is all about", he said (Feltran, 2011: 103).[2] So, the simultaneity between the opening of the store in Paraisópolis and the success of the narrative that supports Klein's myth (which will appear again in this chapter) brings together the transformations that occurred in the periphery with the contemporary structure of feelings.

On the way to the Zona Sul of São Paulo from the city centre, taking the bus along Avenida Marginal or the train via the Esmeralda line, you can see the bridges that adorn the Pinheiros river. During much of the journey, mirrored buildings, multinational headquarters, international chain hotels and temples of luxury consumption are reproduced in the unusual landscape of one of the largest cities in the world. Around June 2019, the exhortation *Bora empreender, Brasil* (Let's get entrepreneurial, Brazil), a campaign by Santander bank, was printed on the facade of one of these buildings, visible from many kilometres away. As can be noted while traveling in public transport, the black and brown population grows proportionally during the journey.[3] Especially in the train carriages, the delirious alternation of informal workers offers everything from seasonal fruits to cell phone chargers, and when more than one of them slips into the crowded wagon at the same time, it is hoped that solidarity between the dispossessed overcomes need and competition.

When you reach the Transamérica bridge, where the Pinheiros river divides to form the Jurubatuba and Guarapiranga rivers, the traveller's view begins to perceive the city that grew up on the margins, and which is home to more than two million workers. It is the periphery of the Zona Sul approaching, with its cluster of autoconstructions and *favelas*, now with condominiums scattered among them. The small businesses that once dominated the landscape

---

2   Lula also contributed to this myth. In 2006, while campaigning for re-election, the former president attended the inauguration of a distribution centre for the chain in São Bernardo do Campo and praised his 'conception' of partnering with the poorest. In front of Klein, Lula declared that "although I'm not president of Casas Bahia, I'm president of Brazil, my conception of how to treat this country is the conception that you had of establishing your partnership with the poorest part of the population" (Scinocca, 2006).

3   This impression is confirmed by the 2010 Census, in which the districts of Jardim Ângela, Grajaú and Parelheiros appear to have the largest black and brown populations in the city.

alternate between bank branches and large retail chains, such as Casas Bahia and Magazine Luiza. There are also private universities, fast food chains and countless evangelical churches scattered along the main roads.

Continuing to the Marsilac district, on the edge of the city and approximately 50 kilometers from the city centre, it is clear that the inequality, even within the periphery, is appalling. In the heart of some districts, such as Jardim São Luís, bars and small shops are linked together in the chaos between narrow streets, and stray dogs and cats dominate the ground. Not far away, you reach Campo Limpo, a neighbourhood with a good structure of public services, condominiums, transport and public and private facilities. Far away, further south, around the Grajaú train station, the confusion of informal commerce cannot be confused with the order and cleanliness of the Capão Redondo underground station. In the damp alleys of Jardim Maria Sampaio, on the border with the neighbouring town of Taboão da Serra, the impression of precariousness and abandonment is absolute, given the dirtiness of the local *piscinão* (water retention reservoir) and the control of the flow in the *favela* by the PCC, also noticeable in some entrances of Paraisópolis.

Essential to the formation of the periphery was the 'logic of disorder', in which the principle of accumulation (extraction of profit) would clash with that of speculation (the extraction of income from land), producing a chaotic occupation due to the lack of planning, at the mercy of private economic interests (Kowarick, 1980). In São Paulo, the 1960s and 1970s were years of intense industrialisation and, concomitantly, of great growth in the working population, with continuous flows of internal migration. Faced with the regulation of subdivisions and the incorporation of the periphery into the formal service structure, important improvements arrived, resulting, as a side effect, in more uncertainty among the popular classes, as the value of housing increases with the construction of new urban facilities (Caldeira, 2000).

Between the 1970s and 1980s, the chaotic occupation that had begun around 30 years earlier by workers expelled from the central regions and due to the intense migration towards the city – a result of its robust but uneven and centrifugal economic development – began to take hold on the outskirts of São Paulo. It was through autoconstructing on irregular plots that this dispossessed population settled in areas lacking in urban infrastructure, basically served by dirt roads at the time. Without financing or government aid, this was the pattern of peripheral expansion in the metropolis, where, driven by the dream of home ownership, thousands of workers used their free time and meagre savings to gradually consolidate an aim of progress and citizenship (Holston, 2008). For those who managed to settle down, owning a house represented the completion of a long-awaited family project. Eder Sader (1988), among others, perceived this essential motivation in the drive for autoconstruction,[4] which spread throughout the periphery of São Paulo in the 1970s. The sociologist argued that the sacrifices that these workers made for the dream of owning their home were based on 'instrumental reasons' – avoiding rent and thus having a reserve of value – and expressed by deeply rooted cultural values – "the search for stability against the uncertainties of unwanted changes, security for family cohesion, the power to organise your own space" (Sader, 1988: 111). The result of these choices is closely intertwined with the context exposed above. Home ownership, which once represented a series of personal and family sacrifices, today allows children to study, delay entry into the job market and to experiment with entrepreneurship.

In this chapter, I highlight a set of experiences of self-employment and entrepreneurship *per se* that I followed in different neighbourhoods in the South of São Paulo, and which see self-employment as the realisation of an ideal. These are individuals who have achieved a certain stability and even envision greater successes, but who pay a high price for this. Namely, they face an accumulation of occupations and strenuous hours and difficulty reconciling them with leisure and family, in situations driven by the increasing presence of technology of self-management and intensification of work. These individuals cling, however, to an individualism rooted in popular culture, in which their practical sense and feet firmly planted on the ground define their options and establish tangible objectives. As one interlocutor warns, those are 'possible goals' – of 'projects' and not dreams, as another says. This *ethos* of hard, gradual work defines success, which will be achieved one step at a time.

However, this excessive attachment to tangible results limits the imagination. Evidently, when acting within very narrow margins, the possibility of a false step is considerable, always reminding you how a part of your destiny is not under your control. To paraphrase Fredric Jameson (1974), none of this has anything to do with entrepreneurship itself, which is rather a distorted reflection of individual dreams and feelings about non-alienated work.

---

4 In using the term 'autoconstruction' for the deep-rooted process of residents building their own houses, I chose to follow Caldeira (2017), Holston (2008), among others, and emphasize the Latin-American term for it.

1   Utopia in Paraisópolis

The bus route to Paraisópolis, from the city centre, is certainly one of the most notable demonstrations of inequality possible to be observed in São Paulo. Crossing the Morumbi neighbourhood, the vehicle passes by decadent mansions and condominiums in neoclassical style, the Palácio dos Bandeirantes – the imposing and kitsch headquarters of the São Paulo government – as well as high-end hospitals and clinics. The scenery is only momentarily interrupted by the São Paulo Futebol Clube stadium, designed by the architect João Batista Vilanova Artigas, an example of São Paulo modernism, and its surroundings occupied by street vendors selling everything from drinks and quick meals to, of course, football shirts, all duly falsified. A few more kilometres and you reach one of the roads that separates the upper-middle class neighbourhood, its narrow sidewalks desolate, from Avenida Hebe Camargo and the intense circulation in the streets and alleys of the city's second largest *favela*. Home to more than 150,000 people according to projections by Seade População,[5] it was even the subject of a soap opera on Rede Globo at the beginning of the end of the Lula period.

On the avenue named for a pioneer television presenter, the profusion of small businesses already conveys the message of the *favela's* 'vocation', resulting from a failed allotment in the 1920s. The construction of the stadium and the Albert Einstein Hospital in the nearby neighbourhood would attract many construction workers from the 1950s onwards, whose population would continue to grow with Northeastern immigration in the following years. This vertiginous urbanisation was never accompanied by the necessary infrastructure, though in no way resulted in a lifeless neighbourhood. In Paraisópolis there are bank branches and microcredit shops, the occasional large store, community facilities generally associated with non-governmental organizations (NGO) and social organisations, basic health units, a public educational centre and a state technical school. The core of the *favela* is dense, the narrowness of its streets can be oppressive, but a feeling of ordered chaos prevails there. Bare bricks dominate in a landscape of autoconstructions lined up side-by-side, their slabs erected in a way that defies engineering: there are three, sometimes four floors, many hosting some commercial enterprise on the ground floor. Circulating on foot involves extra attention, as only a few metres of sidewalk are free for pedestrians, forcing them to invade the street and become the potential target of a motorbike crossing through gridlocked traffic. On the main roads, the

---

5   Available at: https://populacao.seade.gov.br/evolucao-populacional-msp/.

sequence of stores selling clothes, accessories, electronics, cakes, religious items, grocery stores and bars is overwhelming, and in front of them hundreds of street vendors occupy part of the streets, selling fruits and vegetables, CDs and DVDs, pen drives, cigarettes and football shirts. Improvised second-hand bookstores established on some sheets laid on the ground display self-help, computer and English workbooks and novels of questionable taste. Unlike other important commercial addresses in the city centre, such as Praça da República, there is no worry about the *rapa* here.[6]

The characterisation of Paraisópolis as a hub for popular entrepreneurship relied on two stimuli that would not exist without each other, based on the traditional local *viração*. First, the increase in income and access to microcredit during the first Worker's Party (PT) terms in the federal government (2003–2016); and second, the cultural industry's approach to needy communities, in the process of renewal with the advent of the so-called 'new middle class'. At the height of this period, the Brazilian Institute of Geography and Statistics's (IBGE) national household sample survey (PNAD-Contínua) reported an unemployment rate of 6.2% in the fourth quarter of 2013, the lowest level in the survey series. Portrayed no longer only through the lens of violence, but also in the exaltation of their creativity and perseverance, the *favela* lived between euphoria and disappointment with the interruption of economic growth from 2015 onwards.

Exhibited that year by Rede Globo, the biggest television broadcast of Brazil, the soap opera *I Love Paraisópolis* is still present in the neighbourhood: references to it can be seen in the graffiti and decoration of bars in the Vila Madalena style, the bohemian neighbourhood far away from there. For its part, there was an effort from Globo to cast the *favela* as a symbol of racial mixing.[7] The show was one of the biggest television hits of the decade, on average present in more than 1.6 million homes in Greater São Paulo alone (Botto, 2015). To this end, it told a well-known story, that of the working class young girl who falls in love with a rich and well-intentioned young man, then delved into the complications brought about by their forbidden courtship and the intransigent refusal of the relationship by the boy's snobbish family who lives in Morumbi, but overlooks the neighbouring *favela*.

---

6 "Rapa" is a slang term for the street surveillance carried out by the police against illegal or smuggled products.
7 In the first verse, the singer refers to the station's historical stance of exalting an essentially Brazilian and mixed-race identity, shouting that "black, white, brown, coloured; Caucasian, all in a cry of no; To prejudice, long live miscegenation; Mixture of races, we are the colour of Brazil". See also Hamburger (1998).

What made the soap opera notable was not the banality of the script, nor even the setting of the precarious neighbourhood – which, in fact, was reproduced in the broadcaster's studios in Rio de Janeiro. In fact, it celebrated the rise of the new middle class that was emerging there, its entrepreneurial virtues and the outcomes of the previous years' economic growth. In the first episode, young Marizete and her best friend arrive in New York City looking for work and trying to escape the hardships of their wageless life on the periphery. Between blatant merchandising, a sunny aerial shot of Paraisópolis fills the screen and the protagonist's voice-over narration in flashforward says that "if we got this far, built a city within the city, it's because we deserve a chance". But the next scene subverts the cliché: looking at the trinkets of a street vendor in the middle of Times Square, the friends are surprised by a kind of New Yorker *rapa*, which produces a commotion typical of big Brazilian cities and causes them to lose their bag with money and passports. The staging immediately brings us closer to the reality of the Global South and suggests a tangible 'Brazilianisation' of the world, reversing the direction of Ulrich Beck's (2014). In São Paulo or New York, we have all the 'same' problems, as well as the same solutions. The soap opera continues with the redemption of the girl and the thousands of young dreamers she purportedly represents. In the story of comings and goings, the 'learnings' ultimately lead her to set up a restaurant in Paraisópolis and let go of the illusions of regular jobs.

Despite all the symbols exposed above, Paraisópolis has countless trajectories that share Marizete's aspiration. New ventures in the *favela* no longer have the traditional precarious appearance and have gained more refined adornments, such as a local famous bar in a large room in the upper storey, carefully decorated with waiters in bow ties presenting a craft beer menu. It was there that I took shelter on an afternoon of heavy rain and observed the local rising class take over a large part of the area. The view offered is of the *favela*: a cool island in the middle of a sea of precariousness. But this feeling was probably mine alone.

Both the soap opera and other products of the cultural industry open a new chapter in relations with poor communities. The president of the influential Union of Residents and Commerce of Paraisópolis (UMCP) is Gilson Rodrigues, known there as 'Mayor' due to his intense activity inside and outside the community. He heads the G10 Favelas, an initiative that resulted from the first Slum Summit, held in 2019 and which brought together representatives from the ten largest *favelas* in the country.[8] Today, G10 has its own bank based on the Yunus

---

8   The G10 Favelas defines itself as "a bloc of *favela* leaders and social impact entrepreneurs who, like the wealthy countries (Germany, Canada, the United States, France, Italy, Japan and the United Kingdom) of the G7, have joined forces in favour of economic development and

model, G10 Bank, of which Gilson is the CEO. The bank offers loans of between 1,000 and 15,000 reais to small entrepreneurs, charging an interest rate of 0.99 per cent per month (Cesar, 2021). At the 2021 edition of the Slum Summit, Rodrigues led the initial public offering (IPO) event in Paraisópolis for the creation of the first 'unicorn' from a Brazilian *favela*, the logistics startup Favela Brasil Xpress, which specialises in ensuring that purchases made online by residents of the region reach their final destination (Rossi; Oliveira, 2021). He is also a member of the judging panel for *Comunidades a 1000*, a social impact reality show created by fashion entrepreneur Cris Arcangeli, whose first season evaluated five businesses conceived and run by women from Paraisópolis and selected by Rodrigues. All the participants received mentoring to accelerate their businesses, but the winner received a cash prize and in-person oversight, rather than virtual oversight like the other contestants did.

Before *Comunidades a 1000*, Arcangeli was a judge on another reality show for aspiring entrepreneurs, *Shark Tank Brasil*, whose origins lie in Japan under the name *Dragon's Den*, with different versions appearing in various countries around the world. The programme consists of the following structure: five well-known businesspeople and investors in the country form a judging panel, in which they are introduced to businesses devised by aspirants from a variety of backgrounds and social situations. Called 'sharks', the panel decides based on the pitch model whether the proposal is economically viable, then makes business proposals if they see potential, usually taking the form of an equity stake. The candidate can make a counter proposal, which increases the sense of tension and expectation for those watching. The majority, of course, leave empty-handed, but not without gaining at least one piece of advice from the panel. The candidate's unpreparedness is often punished with a certain sadism disguised as rigour.

Experiencing humiliation and overcoming it is, as is well known, an important sign of building the image of a successful entrepreneur. On *Shark Tank Brasil*, when the aspiring entrepreneur already has a reasonably established business and is looking to expand it, the risk of humiliation can pay off even when the pitch doesn't succeed. In the 2020 season, the reality show focused on social impact businesses, especially anti-racist, peripheral and gender-inspired ones. In this season, Robson and Tássio, partners in a hamburger restaurant in

---

community activism, with a view to the economic and social development of these urban areas". The group is made up of the *favelas* Rocinha (RJ), Rio das Pedras (RJ), Heliópolis (SP), Paraisópolis (SP), Cidade de Deus (AM), Baixadas da Condor (PA), Baixadas da Estrada Nova Jurunas (PA), Casa Amarela (PE), Coroadinho (MA) and Sol Nascente (DF). Available at: http://www.g10favelas.org/.

Paraisópolis that had only been running for a year, took the chance of attracting the attention of the programme's producers. Excited but struggling to disguise their nervousness, the two quickly presented their burgers and their proposal to expand, initially to two more units, for which they were asking for an investment of 250,000 reais in exchange for 20 per cent of the restaurant. They talked about the dietary 're-education' they were promoting and the 'differential' that was their blend of meats, something unheard of in the *favela* according to them. They also promised that it would be a "tool for social inclusion", using the new kitchens to train chefs for their own restaurants.

The programme's editing, with its suspenseful soundtrack and the suspicious expressions of the evaluators, accentuate the dramatic tone, the outcome of which is usually the dreaded "That's why I'm out!" response, preceded by some kind of justification from the investors and an expression of their regret or disappointment. That's exactly what happened to the two entrepreneurs from the *favela*, who failed to convince the five evaluators: The most common reason was that their business wasn't 'scalable'. In other words, it wasn't capable of growing quickly, an *ad hoc* argument that, if it were always used, would leave almost no hope for any candidate.[9]

The effort of the hundreds of participants who have already been through the programme is to adapt to the expectations of the 'sharks'. This means that terms like scalable, competitive edge, appetite appeal and valuation, in an unjustifiable English accent, abound, regardless of the size of the business, the social background of the candidates, their 'disruptive' potential or their experience of the corporate world. This is acknowledged to a certain extent with words of encouragement, but their quest is really for the promotion that *Shark Tank* offers: In addition to the television programme, excerpts from the pitches are edited and published later on the programme's online platforms, and the candidates themselves make them available on their social networks. In the case of the burger restaurant, a year later the video of their presentation on YouTube had nearly 500,000 views, one of them mine, which led me to the two entrepreneurs and their new partner.

---

9 Silvia Vianna (2013) highlights this random aspect of contemporary reality shows in relation to the traditional fledgling programmes of the hegemonic era of free-to-air television, where some notion of justice was present in the judges' debauched 'analyses' of successes and failures. In reality shows, on the other hand, it's all about 'subjective' evaluations. In Vianna's argument, the issue is the 'criteria' of the labour market itself, which are increasingly less objective and which, as we will see below, are consented to by the dominated themselves, who renounce the measurable, i.e. practical knowledge in the first instance, and credentials (especially the diploma) in the second.

2   Middle Class in the *Quebrada*

In a relatively concealed position, on a side street in the lower part of the *favela*, you'll find the restaurant run by the two friends, a small but well-appointed saloon with urban-appeal decor: black-painted walls with friendly handwritten messages ('I love bacon', 'burger is life', 'dream big', 'live life, be intense', among others) and red synthetic leather seats. But the highlight of this interior is the graffiti on one of the side walls, with the Joker character holding a menu and a stylised New York landscape in the background. Eating there has its unexpected aspect, as the surroundings look nothing like the interior of the salon, except for the television tuned to football that distracts Robson while the conversation goes on.

Wearing the same model of black T-shirts that they wore on the reality show, Tássio and Robson welcome me very kindly, but my initial contact had been with Ivan, the guy who manages the burger restaurant's social media. The three of them have known each other since childhood, but Ivan joined the business after the programme's repercussions, investing in the expansion and becoming responsible for the administrative side, as he has a degree in Business. The two founders have several things in common, apart from their affinity with cooking and their origins in the Northeast. Tássio is 33 years old and has lived in the neighbourhood since 2001. He came from Alagoas with his parents when he was around six years old and settled in Carapicuíba, in Greater São Paulo. Robson is also 33 and migrated as a child, in his case from Piauí straight to Paraisópolis, which he never left. He remembers well when he arrived in the *favela* at the age of five with his siblings, "in the drizzle, in a dilapidated bus", living on favours until his mother, after six months working as a *diarista* (day labourer), managed to buy the shack where they lived until they were able to build their current house. "So [the house] started out in wood, my parents working, building little by little, building one room, we'd go to that room, building another, we'd go to another room." Tássio especially remembers the three-day journey and his amazement at the city's main bus station.

The initiative to open the restaurant, seen in retrospect, seemed predestined in the words of these two entrepreneurs. They both started in the food business at around the same age, around 17. Leaving high school with no prospects, Robson got an odd job as a waiter's assistant and apprentice, worked his way up and changed restaurants. Tássio would have had a similar career path if he hadn't worked as a bricklayer from the age of 10, selling fruit at the open market or in front of the railway station. But a real job, "with uniform and everything", he only had at McDonalds.

They speak with great enthusiasm about the *quebrada* where they live, excited by what they see as a major economic transformation in the area that seems to be progressing steadily, despite the economic crises and even the COVID-19 pandemic, when demand grew dramatically. At the time, they only operated by delivery, accepting WhatsApp orders that they delivered themselves – the apps operate precariously in the *favela*. On one of my trips to the restaurant, the three of them were waiting for a visit from an architect, who arrived and immediately opened her projects, taking up one of the tables. They were preparing to open a new, larger shop, located around Rua Ernest Renan, one of the main shopping streets in the neighbourhood.[10]

The duo's opinions on the changes in the neighbourhood over the past two decades link entrepreneurship, which they see as a local vocation, with the rise of a 'middle class' that doesn't appear in the statistics. This identity connects to habits that residents have incorporated and that give new meaning to their experiences. For Robson, Paraisópolis has recently become a place of business. "Some residents had this discernment in the beginning and are still running their businesses today, and we're talking about more than 100,000 people, so there are a wide range of businesses in Paraisópolis alone." Tássio also suggests a direct consequence of home ownership is the explosion of these businesses, a new chapter in autoconstructing through the verticalization of the *favela*. "If there weren't so many people living here there wouldn't be this, it would be the same as it was before, more or less flat, everyone with their own little house, their own little slab. Not today, today there are five or six storey houses here."

Based on their sensitivity to the local reality and their cultural references, Tássio and Robson elaborate on a phenomenon also noted by researchers, the theme of Brazil's 'new middle class', which came to light in the work coordinated by economist Marcelo Côrtes Neri (2010). In 2012, the segment reached 44.19 per cent of the population, an increase of 17 per cent in six years.[11] Neri, who was president of the governmental Institute for Applied Economic Research (IPEA) during the Dilma Rousseff's government, sought to identify the average income of society, but his point of view would be influenced both by the federal government under Rousseff and by the media, as we have seen in the case of soap opera and reality shows.[12] However, the structure of feelings

---

10   The plan ended up succeeding, and the burger parlour was a success a year later with stand-up comedy shows.

11   The fundamental substance for the growth of this segment was the recovery of the labour market, and the expansion of consumption in the period was also the result of the increase in certain types of personal credit (Neri, 2010).

12   Among those who opposed the thesis are André Singer (2012), Ruy Braga (2012), Marcio Pochmann (2012) and Jessé Souza (2010). Although with important theoretical and

appears when Robson declares that, in Paraisópolis, "more than 60 per cent are already middle class", based on his intuition regarding the consumption potential of the local population. For Tássio, it is success stories like his hamburger shop that reinforce the legitimacy of entrepreneurial initiatives, in a virtuous circle of job creation and new ventures within the *favela*.

Tássio and Robson didn't go to university, a traditional symbol of social distinction in Brazil. The knowledge they use in their burger restaurant has all been absorbed in practice, which they acquired working in restaurants in the Zona Oeste. Thus, in the burger restaurant you can have something close to a middle-class 'experience', adjusted to the social conditions of the *favela*. The partners emphasise that Paraisópolis can provide everything this new middle class needs, and this consideration only superficially refers to the standard of consumption. It's in a renewed way of life that they really aim to 're-educate' the neighbourhood's tastes.

They are well aware that we live in a 'dictatorship of comparison' (Krastev, 2017), with information technologies symbolically reducing national and class boundaries, and they saw this as an opportunity that has paid off. "We said 'man, we won't have any competition if we make a different product', so our competitor was ourselves," commented Robson. By turning to the neighbourhood, they have managed to circumvent the biggest obstacle faced by these popular subjects, who may have economic capital but are vulnerable when faced with the *habitus* of the global city, contradictorily reinforcing the endogenous logic that has always prevailed in peripheral communities. In the street, the incessant noise of motorbikes deafens, and when night falls over Paraisópolis, the 'middle-class experience' is invaded by samba in the street, and the owners themselves sit on the pavement with their beers for a game of *truco*, while the newly hired employee prepares the burgers and the *motoboy* (motorbike courier) makes deliveries to the edge of the *favela*.

However, it is in their ambition to grow that the contradictions also lie. Even though it was Tássio and Robson's experience in the food business that really got the restaurant off the ground, and that led them to the reality show, the leap forward seems to rely too much on an expertise that is, in the end, theoretical. Ivan, the venture's latest partner, arrived sometime after the interview and began, and from then on, to take centre stage in the conversation. He is a nice guy, fluent in the language of administration, and seemed to intimidate the other two, who began to reduce their appraisals based on practical

---

methodological differences, they saw the mobility of a group that, due to its characteristics as a labour force, would still remain part of the working class.

knowledge that had abounded until then, instead making pointed observations on the young administrator's speeches. Ivan gives well-informed opinions on the periphery, the economy and politics, and proposes an organised script for defending human rights without forgetting to take a stand on racism, gender inequalities and the prejudice he sees against the *favela*. "Bro, the kids have, I've always said, the product, the brand, everything, but today they're very focused on the product itself and don't have the time or even the baggage that I had. I worked in a bank for five years, so I've seen a lot of this, even from customers, research, various things, opportunities that we have to transform the burger restaurant," he says. While Tássio and Robson's emphasis was on entrepreneurship and the potential of the periphery, Ivan seemed less interested in it.

He was born in São Paulo to parents from the Northeast and was 30 at the time of the interview. As well as being a partner in the burger restaurant, he worked as a data analyst for Via Varejo, the company that controlled the Casas Bahia chain. "For us to really have this data vision, because with that we can leverage a lot of things, bring a lot of business insights", he says. He has also lived in Paraisópolis all his life but is less attached to the community: he says that he has achieved what he has "despite being from here" and admits that he wants to leave, "to really improve his life, to be more comfortable". His experience on the other side of the bridge, by the way, is quite different from that of his colleagues, who have only worked there in occupations that initially required little qualification. Ivan, on the other hand, went to the traditional university in the upper-middle class neighbourhood of Perdizes and worked in non-manual jobs. It is remarkable how the three of them, gathered in the same room and with the same surroundings that they recognise so well, express the well-known separation between conception and execution that has been present since the work of Harry Braverman (1980), in that their positions in the 'production process' establish arbitrary hierarchies. Ivan speaks proudly of the university education made possible by University for All Programme (Prouni)[13] and, unlike the young people I followed in my master's research (Costa, 2018), he says he had a fruitful experience at the Pontifical Catholic University (PUC).

---

13   Prouni is a federal programme that has been offering scholarships at private universities since 2005. Prouni's full scholarships are reserved for students with a per capita family income of up to 1.5 minimum wages, while partial scholarships (50%) are for students with a per capita family income of up to 3 minimum wages. The programme also offers scholarships to those who declare themselves black, brown or indigenous at the time of enrolment, and there is also a requirement that the student has attended secondary school in public or public schools on a full scholarship.

He made a lot of friends there, which he attributes to the fact that he studied in the morning, when young people don't usually have to combine studying with work. In a way, Ivan makes a mistake by preaching that if everyone had this 'opportunity' they would prosper like him, which was definitely not the case for Tássio, who was also a beneficiary of the same scholarship programme at Colégio Porto Seguro.[14]

One aspect that remains intact between the three is the inevitability of family destiny. Tássio gets emotional when he talks about his mother, whom he holds up as a great example of life. My interlocutors were almost unanimous in saying that it's their parents who inspire them. "If you go into a community, the story will always be the same. There are some variations, but it's always the father and mother from the Northeast who came here, worked hard and did everything they could to educate. It's very strong, because we saw everything that happened," says Ivan, receiving the consent of the others.[15] Tássio has a six-year-old daughter, Robson has a seven-year-old son and sees him as a mirror of what happened. "Now we understand our parents, right? It's not easy, it really isn't, but now we value our parents more than ever." They admit that the routine of working in the burger restaurant, which also involves the daily logistics of buying supplies, as suppliers don't usually deliver to Paraisópolis, is detrimental to family life, and they joke about the fact that they chose to set up their own restaurant in order to have more time for their children, and at the end of the day, they're just as drained as before, working up to 15 hours a day on the busiest days.

So even with all the obstacles they see to starting a business in the *favela*, they are doing very well and believe that some sacrifices are necessary at this time of stabilisation. This doesn't stop them from complaining about inequalities: Ivan gives the example of Itaú, the big bank he worked for, and says he's proud of the 'social management' implemented there with 'empowerment' policies, but doesn't spare the institution, which at the same time imposes demeaning conditions for granting credit to micro and small businesses. (The government, specifically in relation to its role in implementing public policies, barely comes into the conversation). Ivan is equally sceptical about the soap opera inspired by Paraisópolis and the 'legacy' that will make

---

14   Colégio Visconde de Porto Seguro, founded 144 years ago as a German school, has had a scholarship programme since 1966. Currently, around 1,600 low-income students receive full scholarships divided between basic education and education for young people and adults, most of whom come from the neighbourhoods of Paraisópolis and Vila Andrade.
15   This native use of *community* refers mainly to a territorial circumscription, without necessarily encompassing significant social relationships from there.

the neighbourhood remembered in future reruns. For him, "They made their propaganda, they looked good in the media, and they didn't really do anything here. So that's why I say, how do you change that?"

The not-so-thinly veiled purpose of the soap opera, as well as the reality show and the whole contemporary cultural industry, is to encourage microentrepreneurship by re-signifying popular experience, banishing traditional knowledge and practices, 're-educating' its subjects and thereby creating social distinctions. When asked about taking part in *Shark Tank*, Robson and Tássio's eyes sparkle as they describe the anxiety of relatives and friends in the days leading up to it and the 'surreal' situation of being among entrepreneurs who have done 'magnificent things', which is what they want to achieve. So, what has the soap opera done for the neighbourhood?, asked Ivan rhetorically, with the same disdain he expressed for the reality show a few minutes later, when the conversation had already changed direction. It was Robson himself, who was listening to his friend's speech from the side-lines while sharing his attention with the football on TV, who untangled the contradiction, agreeing and at the same time – involuntarily? – correcting him:

"We're doing a lot more, right?". It is in Robson's intuition that the soap opera's legacy emerges: Stimulating the modernisation of Brazilian capitalism through private initiative.

3 Local Knowledge

Across the dirt streets of Vargem Grande, a paved avenue cuts through the neighbourhood with the bustling of local business. That's just as well, because endogenous life there is the rule: except for a few backpackers and tourist excursions to the exuberant remaining Atlantic Rainforest vegetation in the surrounding area, all the commerce is geared towards its residents and the shopkeepers are themselves the consumers of the neighbouring establishments. There are supermarkets, butchers, opticians, pet shops and trinket shops, but the biggest local complaint is the lack of a bank branch. When I was in the neighbourhood in 2020, some streets were being paved and banners thanking the politicians in charge adorned some houses and businesses – after all, it was a municipal election year (none of them seemed to have been homemade).

The area located in the far south of the city, within the Parelheiros district, has a unique characteristic. It is situated over the Cratera de Colônia, a geological heritage site 3.6 kilometres in diameter and around 300 metres deep, caused by the impact of a meteorite more than 5 million years ago. Part of an environmental protection area (APA) and the Billings reservoir, it is the subject of a dispute, as the state government has long been interested in the tourist potential of the site, which is populated by squatters and is home to around 50,000 people.

I was greeted there on a hot day by Renato, the owner of a bike shop he has run for 25 years. Married and the father of two grown-up children, he disguises his 46 years with a soft voice and youthful expression, which he jokingly attributes to his brown skin. In the flat where he lives, the large garage holds tools and maintenance machines, as well as the instruments he uses for his second job as a locksmith. Next to the dining room, Renato proudly shows off his bookcase, and expresses particular admiration for the biography of Samuel Klein, the founder of the Casas Bahia chain. With his parents, he left Paraná at the end of the 1970s and settled in a *favela* on the edge of the Zona Sul. His father disappeared when he was seven, fleeing threats and trouble with neighbours. His mother stayed where she was and Renato moved to Parelheiros, where he married and had children. But first he had to endure many hardships: the neighbourhood had no infrastructure, and his parents were illiterate, which he attributes the fact that he didn't start school until he was 11. By coincidence, it was at the same age that he started working as a helper in a bike shop, a dream that was sparked by poverty. Renato's family couldn't afford to give him a bike, so he learned how to assemble them himself from usable parts of discarded bikes.

Renato has an exceptional knowledge of the periphery. As well as being a shopkeeper for many years, he has been a candidate for councillor on three occasions, making him a recognised figure in the neighbourhood. He wasn't elected, despite getting a good amount of votes – he has a history of party activism in the Socialism and Freedom Party (PSOL) and PT and based on this repertoire he locates a peak for his bike shop under Lula's government and the decline in the period that followed, already in the agonising final years of Rousseff's term. He himself used to have four employees in the shop and at the time of the interview he only had two. His wife is the one who spends the most time there, running the business, while he supplements his income by campaigning for the PT mayoral campaign, scheduled for a few months later. Combining political sagacity with familiarity with popular commerce, Renato mentions several examples of traders who have closed their doors in recent years and describes their survival strategies.

Renato's comments draw attention to the way he associates popular commerce in the periphery with a virtuous way of life, engaging community relations and a certain quality of life that the routine of salaried work deprives the resident of, making the neighbourhood just a dormitory. "You're negotiating with your neighbour, with nice people, you give a credit because the guy sells on credit, this is very common in the periphery and people are faithful to pay, except for one or two (we get a few defaults), but on the whole you manage to receive from the majority, you create a bond similar to a family one." Luiz Antonio Machado da Silva (2018), for example, is suspicious of the practice of *fiado* (selling on credit), associating it with the mere petty calculation of the shopkeeper and acts of 'pity'. In the perception of the owner of the bike shop in Vargem Grande, attitudes like this are not only essential for local sociability, but also represent a virtue based on the trust that only proximity and recognition can provide. While class identity is based above all on the process of working in the factory environment, a different, typically popular production of locality is suggested here.

Although he considers himself more of a 'social activist', Renato isn't reticent when he says that what has strengthened him to carry on with the bike shop has been entrepreneurship. As an example, he says that he and his wife took part in courses run by the Brazilian Micro and Small Business Support Service (SEBRAE) a few years ago: 'Top quality customer service'.[16] He has already had a formal job, but he has a sceptical view of salaried work. This scepticism is based, for example, on the difficulties imposed by precarious transport, which for a long time hampered the lives of workers on the periphery. For Renato, the advantage brought by certain benefits of the CLT, such as 30 days holidays and a guarantee fund, is cancelled out by the lack of freedom and the impositions of the employer. Not by chance, he believes that entrepreneurship is a way out of Brazil's endless crisis. "I think the number of entrepreneurs will grow because we have a lot of unemployed people. The question is how to get a line of credit to make the investment and kick-start it, but I imagine this is the way forward." In the years that followed, his assessment proved to be correct.

As we'll see with other interlocutors, maintaining a local trade, even in goods with little added value, brings advantages within a popular conception of quality of life, such as those mentioned by Renato. Of course, these choices are quite limited, because the tightrope of wageless life brings with it uncertainties that even an apologist like him prefers to anticipate. Although he was discouraged from studying by his family and struggled through formal

---

16 SEBRAE was founded in 1972 and was part of the federal administration until 1990, when it disengaged from public power and became an autonomous social service. It serves micro and small businesses – those with annual gross sales of up to 4.8 million reais – with a focus on entrepreneurship and accelerating the formalisation process through partnerships with the public and private sectors, training programmes, access to credit and innovation, encouraging associations, trade fairs and business roundtables.

education, Renato is keen for his children to take university seriously and reinforces his confidence in education as a tool for social mobility.

4   Possible Goals

Toni and Sueli had high expectations when they left the *sertão* (backlands) of Bahia at the end of the 1990s. In the region near the dam that covered the historic village of Canudos in 1969, the drought comes and goes, revealing in its most extreme appearances the ruins of the old town built on the hill where Antônio Conselheiro, a messianic preacher, gathered thousands of peasants, indigenous people and freed slaves, and which was destroyed by the Army in the late 19th century. In the rural area of Euclides da Cunha, a municipality of 56,000 inhabitants, the two of them spent their youth working from sunup to sundown harvesting corn, manioc and beans. Sueli studied in her spare time. At the age of 12, Toni went to the city to polish shoes and earn his own money. When he was 18, he headed for São Paulo and worked at everything, 'thank God'. He bought a *barraquinho* (shack) in Sapopemba, on the Zona Leste (East Zone), when he started dating Sueli. They both went to Bahia to get married 'religiously', since they both come from Catholic families, and returned to São Paulo to continue a life that, in his account, was one of continuous progress.

His first job was selling chocolate outside the Armenia metro station, one of the busiest in the city. He then sold fruit in the city centre, worked as a kitchen helper, a garment maker, a baker, a *motoboy*, and finally as a hairdresser, which he has been for 12 years with his own salon in Vila Monumento, near the Museu da Independência. With so many *viração* experiences, it seems surprising that Toni discovered an affinity with the craft of hairdressing. At the time of this discovery, he was working in a bakery in the Cambuci neighbourhood, between the centre and the South, facing several salons where he made some friends and kept them in his memory. Sometime later, as a *motoboy* in the Avenida Paulista area, he kept a day job and attended a hairdressing course at night from Monday to Saturday, for three months. He says that his first steps in the profession were quite difficult but emphasises the experience he gained on a daily basis, since the course "was just to learn how to start".

Since the approval of Law 13.352 in 2016, known as the Partner Salon Law, hairdressers, barbers, manicurists, beauticians, and make-up artists can be employed as legal entities (PJ), so that the 'partner salon' is authorised to retain a percentage of the service performed by the 'partner professional', without registering him as an employee. In Toni's case, the transfer amounted to 40 per cent. "Weak people give up because they get scared," he says. "I stayed there for seven months, but it was hard. You cut two hairs, then one ... then four, then on Friday you cut eight ... on Saturday I'd cut ten, twelve, and I thought it was too much". But his perseverance proved to be unshakeable: after that he went to a better salon, until he got some money together to set up his own business. Today, he works as an individual microentrepreneur (MEI).

Aged 41 at the time of the interview, Toni doesn't seem to have many complaints. His move to São Paulo meant leaving the rest of his family in Euclides da Cunha, but he still visits those who stayed there every year. His adaptation to the metropolis, moving between precarious occupations, is recounted with a certain satisfaction at what he left behind. Today, enjoying some stability, he has no doubts about the choice he made. "It was good, right? Everyone who's there wants to come here. It's hard there, man! It's just about surviving, trying to eat, you know? In the *sertão* of Bahia. So, everyone who's getting older wants to come here, to work here. To get their own things, right?".

A few years ago, he moved out of his rented flat and bought his own flat through the Housing and Urban Development Company (CDHU) in Heliópolis, where he lives with Sueli and her eight-year-old son. "But it's a nice little place, well located, it's not in the middle of the noise", he says, after living 'further in' for eight years, referring to the *favela* of the same name. He proudly tells of realising his dream of a brand-new car, which he believes he achieved through hard work. "Thank God it's like that here, you work honestly, you know? God blesses you. And He sees everything we do. And everything works out. My partner has always been a hard worker too, she helps a lot. Thank God, everything we have is the fruit of our labour," he says.

Toni is the author of the phrase 'the sun shines for everyone', which appears in the Introduction and in the title of this chapter. The context of his speech mixes elements typical of wageless life in the periphery, such as popular religiosity and the reward for hard work, all sprinkled with a good dose of moderation, which shows up in his slight annoyance at the new competition in the neighbourhood. He points to the younger generation's lack of experience, who are seduced by the supposed ease of learning a profession like hairdressing through tutorials on YouTube. "I think it's become fashionable all over São Paulo. Little barbershops, the more retro kind, you know? There are a lot of clients who go for the price, and you must look at the situation we're in too. I've never turned a blind eye to anyone either, the sun shines on everyone." Toni understands that the country's economic situation creates not only precarious work, but also the demand for it.

In the area where the rented property is located, storage sheds, small businesses and pubs supply Toni's clientele, who were charged 27 reais a cut in mid-2020. As much as he absorbs the legitimacy of the competition, this means that relatively established schemes need to change eventually. This is another essential characteristic of anyone who wants to maintain their business: one must be prepared for changes brought about, in this case, by economic dynamics. As a branch that has expanded greatly in recent years,[17] salons and barbershops attract a huge number of young people with few qualifications working in very small spaces, requiring established professionals like Toni to lower the value of their work, or invest in a service that allows them to stand out in a market that is becoming increasingly pulverised. His plan was to "give the salon a facelift" as soon as the pandemic of COVID-19 allowed: "I'm going to paint it all over, I'm going to change the worktops here, the glass, I'm going to put in two with individual frames. I'm going to change it. I'm going to see if I can find a professional to work with me who does women's cut. I only do men, I'm on my own here".

In the simple but spacious and organised salon, nothing stands out, with one exception: an extravagant US flag stretched across one of the chairs. Toni explained that a few weeks earlier he had bought a pair of capes, the kind that cover the client and protect them from the hair that falls during the cut, which had the immediately recognizable print of star-spangled on a blue background and red and white stripes. As I passed through the salon, I saw his two sunny morning clients wrapped in the American flag, having their hair cut over it. The unusual scene combines ambiguous aspects of popular culture that I tried to explore with Toni. His first explanation for the event was solidarity with the colleague who often passed by the salon selling these capes. Toni thought it would be a good time to help him. But why choose those capes, specifically? Between brief reflections and laughter, he again mentioned the fashion for retro barbershops, which are identified by the blue, white and red totem on the façade, but he realised, thinking to himself, that perhaps this wasn't enough of a justification. So, he recognised: "Because everything outside is prettier! Everything from outside is better, right? From the United States. Couldn't it be from Brazil? It's complicated. But it's beautiful. It's chic, even the customer likes it. So, I bought two straight away."

The story suggests that in his *ethos* as a self-employed worker there is a desire for success rooted in popular individualism, which both he and his competitors pursue, and whose sovereign symbol is the "American dream", replaced in this case by stability in São Paulo, which is closer to his reality, just as the fashionable haircuts that Toni praises are those of *sertanejo* singers and

---

17   According to a report by the Euromonitor agency, the male beauty market grew by 70 per cent between 2012 and 2017. Available at: https://www.euromonitor.com/brazil.

footballers. Clinging to this realism, his aim is not to get rich, but to live well, summarised in his own flat, a car, one day of leisure a week and an annual visit to distant relatives. "Look, I can say that everything I have has come from this profession, you know? I realised my dream, which was to buy a new car. A four-door, red, brand-new car! I paid 42,000 in cash," he laughs. Once again, it's a practical sense that anchors him to solid ground, a tangible goal that can be achieved with perseverance. Of course, the very idea that "everything that comes from outside is better", said so casually, applies to this practical sense a scepticism about the reality of the country that can be paralysing, numbing, and can narrow the horizon of expectations for the individual and the family. Health is guaranteed by going to the gym in the morning and having a private health plan. Only his son's school is public. He, if Toni has his way, will be a hairdresser like the father.

Often punctuating his thoughts with the expression 'it's complicated', Toni nevertheless deals with life quite simply. He doesn't like getting into debt or paying rent. He works from Monday to Saturday, and on Sunday he cleans the lounge before going to the football match. His routine intensifies as the week goes on, culminating on Saturday, the day he says he feels most tired, but he doesn't complain. On the contrary, he justifies playing football on Sundays not for leisure, but because "in this profession, you have to take care of yourself, otherwise your belly grows a lot", suggesting that even though he spends a lot of time in the salon, it's not a very physically demanding routine.

Escaping exhausting work, even when it means losing labour rights, is not easily admitted by self-employed people who have voluntarily left the security of the CLT, as this falls outside of the narrative of advancing through hard work. But it is precisely this revelation that emerges from certain decisions, which some characterise as being about a certain 'quality of life'. Toni shows great consideration for Sueli – who, however, he doesn't seem to help much with the housework. He speaks proudly of his wife, emphasising just how much of a 'struggler' she is, listing the tasks she accumulates throughout the day, with and without pay – cleaning was her main source of income at the time of the interview. At times, he even gives the impression that he thinks his work is less intense than hers, and that he respects her for it.

Like her husband, Sueli's career in the world of work, which began at the age of 15 on the farm in Euclides da Cunha, makes her value the present. She says she likes the 'hustle and bustle' of São Paulo, where she intends to live all her life, and that she can't stand visiting her relatives in the *sertão* for too long because she finds "everything too slow". The centrality of work in these people's lives is unavoidable, but subjection to intense labour is not. Sueli's case is even more striking in this respect: She worked for 12 years in a shopping centre restaurant until she became a manager. After four years in the job, she quit because of the stress. "I left the shopping centre because there wasn't much quality of life there, right? I worked Monday to Monday. After my son was born, I didn't have any time for him, so I preferred to leave and stay there, as we say, doing odd jobs". At the time, she worked six days a week, with one Sunday off a month. Her first option to avoid having no income at all was to try her hand at her husband's profession. She took a hairdressing course and stayed in the field for a year, long enough to realise that working 'for yourself' can be even more difficult being a microentrepreneur. "Because we delude ourselves, right? We think that hairdressing is a good business, that it provides a good income. Actually, it doesn't. If you have your own salon, it's fine, but not if you work for others."

It's a crossroads where poor but not so poor workers live, always walking a tightrope where they must choose between stability, income and quality of life, and it's hard to reconcile everything at the same time. In the beauty business, Sueli has learned that contracting as a PJ is nothing more than subordination in disguise, at a more intense pace and with even fewer guarantees. For Toni, who was still young, childless and unqualified, it was tolerable until he got his own salon, but Sueli was not in this situation. In any case, despite listing her many obligations, including sewing odd jobs, she doesn't complain too much. She says she works around seven hours a day, obviously not counting the household chores. "Then I can be with my son, I can work, I can look after my things at home too". She accepts with resignation that the change from the CLT to self-employment wasn't financially positive, but she thinks it was worth it for the quality of life and the time she gets to spend with her son. The interview, by the way, was interrupted several times by the boy, who always received a reprimand when he asked for her mobile phone password. We were in the middle of the COVID-19 pandemic at the time, and schools were still closed. When he walked away with a grumble, Sueli gave him a discreet smile.

Sueli does not deny the fact that the housework is divided unequally between the couple, nor the fact that she has ruled out a secure job. These details don't seem to bother her because her priority is not her professional life, but her family, the place where the pieces fit together, which provides her with the security of a stable life to which her future is tied. "Family is everything, right? Family is our foundation, it's who we can count on when we need them, who we can celebrate when we have an achievement, so we work in favour of family." Sueli emphasises this when she asks rhetorically, "What can we be without family?". Of course, within this symbolic construction God appears again, but it's not the divine figure who imposes her obligation towards a religious denomination. She no longer considers herself Catholic, but she hasn't given up looking for a religion she feels good about.

Her convictions regarding what is worthwhile are influenced by another aspect, which makes her still more exalted and justifies her search for counselling in a church, that is, the uncertainty brought on by life in society. When Jair Bolsonaro comes up in the conversation, she first laughs with embarrassment and politely speculates that "He doesn't like the poor very much, does he? I don't know". Toni, a few metres away in a cape and hood doing hair treatment on a client, didn't seem to be paying attention to the conversation, but his presence may have intimidated his wife. After all, at the time of my first visit to the salon, he considered himself a *bolsonarista* (Bolsonaro supporter). The figure of the then-president didn't seem to inspire the same admiration in Sueli, but they agreed on a certain degeneration of the public world, for which Bolsonaro was not at all responsible. She praised the emergency aid for the pandemic as a kind of generous concession from someone "who doesn't like the poor", and if things aren't going well in politics and the economy, it's because the people haven't done their part. "I don't blame poverty, because there are a lot of people who are poor and have character, you know? I think people want things to be much easier, I don't know if we're bringing up our children wrong, if we give them everything they want, even if they don't need it, and they grow up with that", she speculates.

Veena Das (2004) observes that state power is exercised through the differential distribution of its presence, and not through omnipresent sovereignty. Its legitimacy is always at stake in its practices, in which the intelligibility of the state's presence is felt by the participants who find themselves caught up in those frictions. Sueli even expects something from the state institutions when she reflects that education, health and security are not adequately provided for the poorest. Her husband doesn't even make these considerations and has no expectations of public policies, but they converge in the belief that the government has no relevant role in the success of their business, which is attributed solely to individual initiative, certainly with the help of God. This set of values goes back to the messianism of Conselheiro's time and rests somewhere in the consciousness of the popular subject, especially those with a background in rural areas.

5   Strugglers

When the term 'struggle' appears in this book, traders and wageless workers emphasise the ability to change when necessary, to think of alternatives when the situation demands it. This doesn't just apply to the most precarious, poorly educated and professionally unskilled workers, but also to the petty bourgeoisie who, faced with the uncertainties of the contemporary world, are seeing stable socio-economic situations turn upside down. Changes in the population's consumption standards and even large-scale health crises (most notably the COVID-19 pandemic) shake up family budgets that are always very tight and subject to unforeseen shocks. Contingencies can shake up people's lifestyles, but it's in the ways of life that a society of individuals reveals the most significant changes. This is notable, for example, in new forms of spatial production in the peripheries, where 'fortified enclaves' are proliferating, restoring, on the one hand, lost community relations and, on the other, security dynamics typical of traditional middle-class condominiums. Thus, a new middle class is producing locality at São Paulo's periphery (Fontes, 2022; Blokland, 2003).

The verticalisation of Campo Limpo is a good example of a peripheral region that has metamorphosed in recent decades. Developments with more than one tower were built there during the Lula period, basically financed under the government's programme, My House My Life (MCMV). The district was the leader in residential unit launches between 2013 and 2017 in the city of São Paulo, with flats averaging 49.3 square metres. According to the partner of a real estate developer, in 2019 all his clients in the region had financed the property through the housing programme, because "our client probably wouldn't be able to buy through a private bank" (Ferrasoli, 2018). The accelerated change in the district's landscape also saw the construction of a Line 5-Lilac metro station in 2002.

Fernanda, who lived all her life in Interlagos – further south – resided in one of those condominiums in Campo Limpo with her husband and daughter. She started working at the age of 14 in shopping centres. We talked about the cake shop she opened when she was 30, an occupation she shared with the nursery school where she was a teacher. Her watchword is 'opportunity': that's how she has more than once overcome difficulties and, as they say, turned lemon into lemonade. For example, six years earlier, she found herself pregnant. Costs were rising, and she took advantage of her maternity leave to learn cake recipes online. She took what she had in the house where she lived, set up a structure in the garage and involved her husband in the endeavour.

When she came back from leave, Fernanda could no longer cope with work and the baby and had to take a break from baking. After all, she was still burdened by household duties with her husband working away. She returned to the cakes in 2016, selling to acquaintances, but still couldn't fully commit. The couple then decided to take 'a bigger step' and her husband left his job as a salesman. Fernanda jokingly says that she had already tried to sell 'various things' and had never succeeded, which increases her feeling that she is now in the right place. "So, deep down, I think I've always had this desire ... that thing of 'oh, since I was a child, I've always said it'. Today we already have future projects, but at the moment I think it was more born out of a necessity." In addition to SEBRAE, she once again turned to the internet to structure her business. This gave her enterprise, along with many millions of other businesses around the world, the dynamism it needed.

Even though she works part-time at the school, it's baking cakes that takes up the most of her time – 10 hours a day, from Sunday to Sunday – and she's already decided to give up her day job to focus entirely on the business. "I now like entrepreneurship more than teaching, so I was very much looking for the balance – what do I like more? Teaching or entrepreneurship?" However, far from putting her on an equal footing in the labour market or implying a sizeable solidarity network, going out on her own is a risk, since according to SEBRAE itself, 35 out of every 100 businesses that open don't make it to the end of the first year, 46 don't make it to the end of the second and 56 don't make it to the end of the third (Tommasi, 2015). In the case of Fernanda and her husband, they seem very committed to the business. They know what they need, and don't go overboard with their ambitions. Their inspiration is the owner of Sodiê, a large Brazilian cake franchise, who "slept in the shop waiting for customers to arrive", and who in 2021 had more than 300 shops across the country.

So, there is a sacrifice involved. Fernanda says that the family's standard of living improved after the shop, but the exhausting pace required the inspiration of a promising future. She says they are "super tired, super tired. We learnt to accept it a bit, we work a lot because I think that's how it is. I think that's also how it is when you also start an enterprise from scratch, without having a structure, without having any support, without having anything." However, at no point does she think about going back, and suggests that working at the school no longer brings her much satisfaction. Returning to the excitement in her speech, she again quotes her mantra when she tells us about the new shop, they are going to open in partnership in the prized neighbourhood of Brooklin Novo. Even with the pandemic, she quickly looked for a way to continue selling her cakes. "We saw an opportunity to look for these apps, so we could have a new strategy and it worked out really well, so we deliver via the Ifood app," she says, mentioning the market-leading app in Brazil.

Trajectories of this kind have multiplied in the urban peripheries in recent years, with the threat of individual and family catastrophe felt as a result of the health isolation measures. Some of my interlocutors, self-employed workers who have been directly affected by the pandemic,[18] believe that it was through entrepreneurship that they reinvented themselves and overcame the difficulties, a desire that has always been part of their way of life and which was challenged by non-trivial events. These are stories of relative success, in which need was added to previous practical knowledge and some years of experience in a field. As much as having their own business was a goal, it wasn't the ambition that pushed these people, who enjoyed a certain degree of economic stability, into entrepreneurship, demonstrating that this stability was relative and vulnerable to unforeseen and unpredictable events. Thus, even when the business 'works out', you realise that there is no romanticism or glamour, but rather hard work and great sacrifices that don't end with a project's realization, but rather accompany them throughout their lives.

This was partly the case for Mercedes, a 34-year-old Mexican from Monterrey who had been living in Campo Limpo for seven years with her Brazilian husband and their two children. She was studying Business and working in marketing in Mexico, where they got married. They moved permanently to Brazil to realise their desire for their own business and today have a chain of food supplements in three popular shopping centres in São Paulo. After some initial difficulties with the Portuguese language, she began to work in the first shop and the franchise seemed to take off. At the beginning of 2020 they were in Mercedes' country and the unforeseeable happened: The borders began to close in a global move to try to contain COVID-19. Her husband had just signed the contract for the third shop, which he couldn't go back on. That's how, back in Brazil, she began to prepare her favourite Mexican dishes at home while husband delivered them to their condominium, an initiative that would prove essential to keeping the household accounts up when the shops were closed due to lockdown measures.

Like Mercedes, thousands of workers, especially in the peripheries, have mobilised in this direction, as was also the case with Raphaela and Eduardo. They are 'exemplary citizens', with many of the contradictions that this characterisation carries in a classed society. She was 42 and he was 51 when they told

---

18 In addition to the more than 100,000 deaths caused by COVID-19 by mid-August 2020, the country had an unemployment rate of 13.1% at the end of June of the same year. By the first fortnight of June, 716,000 companies had closed their doors, according to the *Pulso Empresa Survey: Impact of COVID-19 on Companies*, carried out by the IBGE. Of the total number of businesses closed temporarily or permanently, 40 per cent (522,000 firms) told the institute that the closure was due to the health crisis. Between March and July of that year, 600,000 workers became MEIs, an increase of 20% compared to the same period in 2019.

me about the Italian food venture they were starting at the time. They also took a ride on one of the pandemic's main forms of business, the delivery service, he as a chef and she busy with the administrative side, serving the condominium where they live in Campo Limpo and the surrounding area. It was an intuitive step for both, as Eduardo had been working in the kitchen for over three decades and Raphaela had management experience.

Eduardo is from Porto Alegre and graduated with a degree in gastronomy from the National Commercial Apprenticeship Service (SENAC), later working in an Italian restaurant whose clientele was made up of the elite of the prosperous shoe industry in the Brazilian Southern region. Buying supplies for the restaurant where he worked in the countryside, he met Raphaela, who worked as a cashier in the supermarket. After that, she moved into administration, and he was invited to help start a new venture in São Paulo.

They had a difficult start in the capital of São Paulo State, where their adaptation problems ranged from the climate to the cultural aspects of the metropolis. His daughter began to suffer from respiratory problems due to the pollution. At a young age, Eduardo says he was dazzled by his first impressions: he immediately rented a flat on Avenida Paulista, the most famous road of the city, but his fantasy was short-lived. Raphaela, on the other hand, fell straight into the harsh reality of the outskirts of São Paulo, and doesn't disguise her irritation with the 'penthouse' that her husband got in Valo Velho, a neighbourhood that belongs to the Capão Redondo district and is close to some of the most precarious *favelas* in the Zona Sul. Time passed and they adjusted, had a second daughter, and moved to a condominium in Campo Limpo which, according to them, guarantees their daughters a childhood like the one they had, with space to run around. Although it is not exactly the same, since they have a green area, a playground, a gym, a party room and everything else that minimises leaving the condominium, especially given the efficient security system. "This is an oasis within the reality of the region ... We live in an oasis, but we know the reality out here, in the neighbourhood, is very heavy ... but there are wonderful people," Eduardo says.

Raphaela and Eduardo are very fond of the condominium they live in and believe they can replicate the quieter life they had in the Southern countryside, with security and space for the girls to play. The couple also value community relations, but what the fortified enclaves offer is a misrepresentation of this. As for Mercedes, it was precisely the precarious social interaction intensified by social isolation that had been making the delivery restaurant successful. Condominium life, as much as it divides individuals and families into refractory cells, creates forms of interaction that convey an illusion of community that is quite adequate in these cases. These practices are similar to Toni's, in relation to the street vendor selling capes, but here this logic only works for those inside. "After all, the condominium implies an attempt to create certain public rules and norms, within the limits of private life, but always as a space of exceptionality, erected as a defence against external barbarism" (Dunker, 2009: 3).

Raphaela and Eduardo pooled their experience, added specialised courses and went into business for themselves; after many years, they were well acquainted with Italian cuisine and the potential public around them, "making a difference here in our region, in our condominium", as he puts it. The trajectory of the two would seem to be one of continuous success, from the *laje* (slab) in Valo Velho to the pleasant condominium, a situation made possible by the entrepreneurial initiative of a couple with well-defined objectives. But that wasn't the case. They were both employed in 2020 when the worsening health crisis caused the restaurants where they worked to close down. There was a climate of tension in the house: The first to be dismissed was Raphaela, and Eduardo followed soon after. "As we joke, [in São Paulo] we open a door, a window, you can sell anything, right? So, we were seeing this before the pandemic, starting to plan, but at a slow pace," says Eduardo. They did indeed have plans to open a business, but the ideal situation for those living on tight budgets never usually arrives – the unexpected takes over before it does. Raphaela, who had been in the same job for ten years, had nowhere else to go during the pandemic. "Come on, let's reinvent ourselves then, start planning what it's going to be like", she said.

In these circumstances, their ability to see danger was decisive for them, and they turned adversity into the realisation of a family project. This is not about a dazzled for bosses or even a vehement denial of wage labour, but about having one's feet firmly planted on the ground and using acquired knowledge. The idea is not to get rich straight away, but to get back on track with their lives, which, as Raphaela knew, would not return to its previous standard any time soon without being shipwrecked first. They attribute their success to relying on their practical experience and familiarity with their audience, showing "people who are here in the region that yes, you can eat something from a good restaurant at a fair price", he indicates. Instead of reinventing the wheel they gave the local public, which has risen socially in recent years, what they wanted.

Raphaela is very strict about the bureaucratic aspects that can help or hinder their business. For now, they are hoping to qualify for MEI status. Asked if they opened the restaurant as a dream, Eduardo corrected me with his moderate tone: "A project, right, mate. I had to set up a structure. I often say that dreams are good in bed, the problem is that you wake up." So today they work around 14 hours a day. "One day we have to go to the market, run there, it's closed at 2pm, run, change clothes, go to the market, buy the inputs, look for the cheapest meat and come back, then put everything in place ... by the time you see it's time to open again, that's from Tuesday to Sunday." Raphaela and Eduardo's colleagues tried the same thing and 'couldn't cope', they say. They don't complain and allow themselves few illusions, they don't minimise the difficulties of working on their own and even share them with their daughters. The eldest, 15 at the time, was already helping with deliveries inside the condominium.

It is in these episodes of relative success, however, that one of the most notable characteristics of popular entrepreneurship emerges: confidence in merit, strengthening the imaginary that prosperity is achieved by those who work and prepare. Although they are aware of the obstacles to starting their own business and are in solidarity with those who don't have the same experience, Eduardo sees the government as having the priority role of "reducing bureaucracy, simplifying, facilitating" and reducing the tax burden, while Raphaela objects to the "lack of control with public money" that she saw in the distribution of pandemic emergency aid, referring to cases of fraud that she saw on TV and even among acquaintances.[19] They believe that, as the old saying goes, "there's no point in just giving them the fish, you have to teach them how to fish", and that the government can't afford to keep handing out money indefinitely. But as citizens who see themselves as conscientious, they extend the same logic to the Judiciary, which was claiming new benefits at the time. They also make a curious comparison with racial affirmative actions, which they oppose on principle. "We're black here in my house. I'm not going to lie to you, the quota service – even though I'm against it – I think it's necessary, because within our reality, if there are no quotas, there won't be this inclusion", says Eduardo.

---

19 All those interviewed after the start of the pandemic supported the emergency aid initiative but with the same reservations: the aid has to be paid to those who "really need it", indicating among them a rancour against those who supposedly take advantage of the benefit without needing it. Luís Alberto, for example, thinks that there are a lot of *nóia* (drug addicts) in the queue for the benefit, but he was receiving the benefit because he was 'unemployed' – the petshop is in his wife's name and the bar is not a legal entity. Another notable contradiction is the fact that these businesses continued to have customers because some of them used their emergency aid to buy superfluous products, as Diego admits, commenting on the increase in sales at his gift shop. Delei was heading in the same direction: "I'm not going to say it hasn't helped because the guy who gets 600 reais can pay a water bill, an electricity bill, he can do something, buy something. I'm not going to say it hasn't helped, but I'd rather be working because if you work, you know what you can achieve, and depending on others isn't nice."

"They should succeed on merit," interrupts Raphaela. "I think even those people in Santo Amaro, who stretch out a blanket on the ground and sell clothes, right? All these people, everyone who is informal, if you talk to them, they want to be formal", she adds, pointing to bureaucracy and high taxes as a barrier to these informal businesses being able to stand on their own two feet. For Eduardo, entrepreneurship is 'the way out' of Brazil's economic crisis, as long as there is less government, not more.

Both are very cynical when it comes to politics, and Eduardo likes to compare the country to his family's favourite football club, the Internacional. They were Bolsonaro voters in 2018, but say they regretted this and criticised him sharply. The development of reasoning, however, doesn't assuage scepticism. "Then you look at the [reserve] bench and you want to cry: it's better to leave who's on the pitch for now and try to bring in someone new from outside, even though we know it's difficult, because who we have on the reserve bench – my goodness! – is to be relegated, isn't it?".

Talking about merit has two functions in popular entrepreneurship. The first function is that it serves those who have achieved some mobility to set an example for those who have fallen behind. The second function is that those who have not yet achieved mobility come to resent this when the promises of inclusion and ascension through education have not been fulfilled for the majority, as we will see below.

6 Recognition

At the age of 36, Diego opened his gift shop in Santo Amaro in the middle of the pandemic. This wasn't his first – he has three other shops in Jardim Ângela, close to where he lives: a clothes shop, a flower shop, and another gift shop, like the one I visited. Present not only in peripheral neighbourhoods, shopping streets also survive in former working class territories such as Lapa, Tatuapé and Vila Mariana. The district of Santo Amaro, in the Centre-South region of São Paulo, was an independent municipality between 1832 and 1935, when it reached as far as the southern zone. Incorporated into the capital, it was subdivided into several districts, as it is today. An important industrial hub in the 20th century, it was served by labourers from the Northeast who settled there and in neighbouring regions. Gradually, with increasing deindustrialisation, it became a commercial centre with popular appeal, in contrast to luxury condominiums occupying entire blocks, shopping malls for the wealthy, and skyscrapers overlooking Parque do Ibirapuera with views of the city in the background and intense real estate speculation. In the interstices between fortified enclaves, some areas remain well-known to São Paulo residents from all over, such as the Largo Treze de Maio.

Diego's shop nearby was the result of 'daring and planning', he says, praising himself. According to him, there isn't much competition in his field in Santo Amaro, because "the wholesalers and retailers are only in the centre, so because of everything I've studied and planned, I think it can't go wrong". In fact, at least up until the time of the interview, Diego claimed to have increased his turnover during the pandemic, selling via WhatsApp and Facebook while the clothes shops remained closed. He kept the four employees of the Jardim Ângela shops at home, paying them half their wages, but he didn't sack anyone. He made the deliveries himself, up to five kilometres away. Exuding optimism, he seemed to radiate the feelings printed on the heart-shaped cushions that surrounded him, as well as other decorative objects common in the homes of lower-class families. Accustomed to the deprivation of Jardim Ângela, around nine kilometres away, Diego was experiencing a sense of social ascension provided by a conviviality in a more central neighbourhood, where salaries are better and the public, to whom he sold his products at a higher price and without having to bargain, is more impersonal. "Today we have a product here for 100 reais, the person pays quietly and rarely asks for a discount. There I have the same product for 70 reais and people still ask for a discount, so there's very little added value in the neighbourhood," he says.

About five years ago, he left his job as a shop manager at a well-known technical assistance and automotive products chain, where he had a CLT contract and only one complaint. Diego says he already had the venture 'lined up' because he saw in it a 'greater capacity' for his knowledge. He has a degree in Human Resources and a postgraduate qualification in Psychology from the same private university located nearby, in Largo Treze. He completed his studies without any grants or funding by choice, as he was able to apply for them. Although he doesn't work in the profession, he believes that his university education is fundamental for dealing with people and getting to know future partners. What's more, he values the knowledge he has acquired, because "nobody can take it away".

As Eva Illouz (2008: 7) put it, knowledge formations "constitute an important aspect of cultural action in contemporary societies" simultaneously professional and popular. The value Diego attaches to his degree today is inversely proportional to the thought that went into choosing it: he assumes that he 'fell into it' because of the preference of a cousin who was applying for the same course. She admonished him, to which he simply replied, "it doesn't matter, I just want to study". As for psychology, he says that while he was still studying for a degree in human resources (HR), he took a course in this area. "The teacher was explaining, I didn't understand anything, and when I started to understand and comprehend, I ended up becoming interested in the human mind. 'I think I'm going to study this a bit more', I thought, which is very important for the sales area". I observed a similar case in my previous book, in which one of my interlocutors was simultaneously taking two courses with practically identical curricula. One he didn't pay for, because he had a Prouni scholarship, but, like Diego, the choice hadn't been made by him, but by his girlfriend, who pushed him towards higher education (Costa, 2018).

For Diego, the university degree represented above all a gain in self-esteem that, for the time being, drives him towards entrepreneurship with remarkable, perhaps excessive, confidence. It's hard for him to explain why being a trader would be better than the stability he had before as a manager, employed in a medium-sized company that was well-established in the market. He didn't feel 'valued' – the investment in his human capital wasn't paying off as he'd imagined. Diego didn't just want to remain competitive and employed – he wanted more, a kind of narcissistic personal satisfaction that subordinate labour was no longer able to provide. "In the company I was in, my salary was really good, but I just felt that they didn't value me the way I felt I should be valued, I was supposed to be on one level, and I was on another, and not for lack of knowledge," he reflects.

Having lived in Campo Limpo for around 20 years, Maicon, 35, from São Paulo, has followed the transformations that have taken place there as services have multiplied and local consumer power has increased. He is a computer technician and was laid off when the college where he worked was sold. In 2019, he decided to turn his fond family memories into an entrepreneurial asset, adding technical knowledge to his repertoire: "But it was very cool for me, because it was within IT [Information Technology] that I managed to get a lot of knowledge to put into using Instagram, using Facebook. Because I used to take care of the company's social media, right?", he says of the opportunity that opened up with his dismissal. Since then, Maicon has sought to insert himself into the emerging gastronomic scene in the periphery, and while he doesn't have the capital to open his own business, he livens up his social networks in his spare time by visiting restaurants in the neighbourhood and posting his impressions. His activity as a digital influencer was still in its early stages, and his strategy was to give visibility to these ventures which, according to him, were just as good as those on the other side of the bridge. "Twenty years ago, it was like that. You didn't have much here. For example, here on the avenue there wasn't a restaurant, today there are three. Gastronomy has evolved here in the neighbourhood," he says, mentioning cases of entrepreneurs who have sought 'knowledge' to open their own businesses.

In 2020, Maicon, who has an MBA in Information Technology Management from Anhanguera University, signed up for Projeto Rede's entrepreneurship course on gastronomy, which he did all online due to the pandemic. As well as preparing for the pitch, he continues to look for courses and credentials that, according to him, can give him even more knowledge. "I've done three burger certifications, I've watched the videos, there's another one I bought that I haven't even finished yet. It was a hobby that's almost turned into a living," he says. However, he still does IT work, which is what actually pays the mortgage on the flat he bought with his wife after moving out of his parents' house. He doesn't feel down about being unemployed, and again emphasises his relentless pursuit of knowledge: at Rede, he learned about sustainability and the use of unconventional food plants.

The passages from Maicon's life that he most likes to emphasise contain a romantic vision of gastronomy, 'on the emotional side'. He likes to tell us that, when he was six or seven years old, he helped his great-grandmother in the kitchen, that his parents cook very well, that his sister is very good at sweets and that his best family memories involve conversation and food. He paints his story in very vivid colours, which matches his goal of having an 'affective cuisine' restaurant, a trendy concept in São Paulo gastronomy that seeks to "bring back nostalgic sensations through the palate" (Öberg, 2018), in other words, transforming popular dishes that are familiar in Brazilian homes into valued assets with *gourmet* appeal. So, although family memories justify his attachment to gastronomy, it is one of the famous exponents of affective cuisine who inspires him, the Brazilian celebrity chef Alex Atala, owner of well-known restaurants in the upmarket Jardins neighbourhood. "A sensational guy, he's a very good entrepreneur," Maicon praises. "There are some classes he gives on gastronomy on YouTube, and he even gives lectures at universities. I always like to watch him because he's very innovative and seems to be a very good chef, a very good person."

In fact, Maicon has little experience in the gastronomy business. Not all of the interlocutors I highlighted in the previous section have had a lot of experience in their lines of business, but they are focussed on the demand they observe. They make little speeches and avoid risk as much as possible, evaluating one step at a time. Maicon relies heavily on the stories he has to tell, which for the time being are enough to build up an audience for his virtual platforms. He also invests a lot in certificates but has a moment of insecurity when he regrets not having had face-to-face training on the Rede course, which could have provided the practical experience that he feels he is lacking.

"Innovation. All the ideas we have are never discarded, we have to take them, write them down and, like, always innovate, do something new," enthuses

Maicon, dreaming of creating a 'revolutionary dish'. In fact, it's this dream that makes him give up the benefits of a formal job in favour of his own business. Symptomatically, to start building his restaurant, he doesn't follow the 'affective' recipes in his great-grandmother's notebook but fills in the narrative he has created for himself. He prefers to mimic the heroes printed in the ideology of 'good' entrepreneurship like Atala, a mirage that mixes up real life and fantasy, a trap of the "culture of narcissism" that Christopher Lasch (1991) examined in his book of that name.[20]

As for Maicon, Keila also worries about inheritance. She used to work in the aesthetics business and about a year ago she rented a townhouse in an elegant part of Chácara Santo Antônio, between chic restaurants and corporate buildings, and struggled to keep it running with a professional partner. This was quite different from the reality she saw in Campo Limpo, where she had a business before deciding to move neighbourhoods. This move was only for work, as she still lives on the periphery with her daughters and husband. Her parents are also there, workers from the countryside.

At just 31 years old, Keila exudes the astuteness of someone who started work early, had three children, the first of whom never met her biological father, and has been running her own business for a few years now, combining it with beauty courses and a degree that was paralysed during the pandemic. Her broad smile conveys a remarkable optimism that contrasts with the difficulties she had been experiencing, especially because of the isolation measures, which resulted in fewer clients. But she is dedicated, convinced of her chosen profession and has ambitions that she doesn't expect to fall from the sky. Her opinions also reveal a certain scepticism, when her mood changes. She believes in herself and her family, holds her parents as an inspiration, is not very close to the neighbourhood and has the moderate religiosity of someone who was brought up Catholic, went through Umbanda and Pentecostalism, but has concluded that she has a "very strong communication with God", and that's enough for now.

Keila idealises the past, when she used to play in the street and come home alone from school, but she believes that her children will never be able to do

---

20   The cult of personal relationships, as contemporary managerial rationality insists, thus conceals a total disenchantment with personal relationships themselves, and it becomes more and more intense as the hope of political solutions recedes, as Lasch (1991) describes. These are pathologies that, for Richard Sennett (2012), are linked to work. The exaltation of risk in this new capitalism, imposing on younger people an ethic of constant mobility, of impermanence in the same job or company, also exacerbates anxious reactions in the previous generation, who see their acquired experience devalued as inert knowledge.

the same. "My children will never have the chance to play tag, hide and seek, cops and robbers in the street," she laments. She condemns what she sees as indiscriminate drug use on the streets of the neighbourhood and attaches extemporaneous importance to the strict upbringing she had from her mother. "I often say that youth began to go wrong when the child stopped respecting father and mother at home," she said more than once during the conversation, which partly took place in the presence of her husband, who had come to pick her up and was waiting on his mobile phone, with headphones perhaps explained why he ignored the many times she complimented him.

Her career path in the world of work, until she found herself in the field of aesthetics, was in a less appealing area. Keila worked for nine years in the call centre sector, until she could no longer stand the stressful routine and personal dissatisfaction. Despite sparing the companies she worked for, she admits that her hours were always calculated and exhausting. However, demonstrating that she has learnt the entrepreneurial logic well, she says that "the problem wasn't the company. Today I realise that the problem was me because I didn't like what I was doing". At the time, she had already taken a course in eyebrow waxing and got it into her head that she would do it for life. She started a technical course in aesthetics in neighbouring Capão Redondo, and continued her search for qualifications, queuing up one specialisation after another. "I did my first degree in aesthetics, left that [call centre] company and started working in the little salons near my house, and then I realised that it wasn't enough for me," she says about the lack of "feedback from the people in the neighbourhood", who she says only value what comes from outside and prefer to be in the shopping centre.

Keila's entrepreneurial logic carries applies to two areas of her life, the personal and the professional, where, as in a house of mirrors, the practicality of one is reflected in the other. Her physiotherapy degree, which was on hold at the time, followed the same criterion: the choice of aesthetics was not a profound culmination of her talents and dreams, but based on the needs of the 'here and now', to which she applied her experience as a sister, as a mother and as a woman. This identity functions to organize her domestic life, marital relationship, her judgements on femininity and entrepreneurial ethics. As a summary of this reasoning, she mentions the classic Brazilian samba-song *Ai, que saudades da Amélia* as the representation that an enterprising woman like her should reject. "I always say that there are women who are Amélia, who don't like entrepreneurship, and there are entrepreneurs who don't like being Amélias."[21]

---

21   The chorus of the song states: "Amélia didn't have the slightest vanity, Amélia was a real woman".

Keila is 'engaged in the MEI' and her speech is in tune with the entrepreneurial *ethos*. She doesn't disguise the difficulties she is going through, but they don't come up immediately in conversation. Firstly, there is the family element, which justifies her quest for autonomy, to make her own timetable and have more time for her children. "I wanted to be my own boss, but it's not that nice," she says with melancholy interspersed with loud laughter, making statements she doesn't usually make in her day-to-day life. "It gives me a sense of autonomy with the challenges, so I like to be entrepreneurial." When asked to elaborate on her difficulties, she relativises individual responsibility, as when she suggests that she took a finance course too late, which could have given her a better foundation to run her salon. "I think that here in Brazil financial education should come from primary school, but the government doesn't want Brazilians to be intelligent, so." This reflection doesn't stop her from praising herself.

The ambition for recognition challenges practical sense. What is the reason that governs her destiny, if even her job at the call centre didn't seem so bad, in her words, insofar as it guaranteed good benefits, in addition to the advantages of a CLT contract? And even in her self-employed career, these are choices that, from a strictly economic point of view, don't seem to make sense. For example, when explaining why she wanted to stop working in Campo Limpo, she points to the clientele, who in the outskirts like to haggle and complain about the price of the service, while in Chácara Santo Antônio there is an etiquette that wouldn't allow this kind of behaviour. But the fact is that she has fewer customers in the upper-middle class neighbourhood and her costs are higher, and even the blow of the pandemic doesn't seem reason enough to start again. "I've already taken the place in the pandemic, so I haven't been able to realise that dimension, right? But I know that the salons in the neighbourhood are usually busy at the weekend. Here, you can open on the weekend, and you won't get any business, there's basically no public to go to on the weekend."

Richard Sennett sees in the culture that proclaims short-term change, in its episodic and fragmentary nature, a 'test of character' in which "the important thing is to make the effort, to risk your luck, even when you rationally know that you are doomed to fail" (2012: 24). The feeling of devaluation in the face of the size of Keila's ambition is what makes going back to work in her peripheral neighbourhood an almost unbearable alternative. The belief in entrepreneurship, emerging from the exhausting reality of the call centre and the promises of social mobility through the continuous search for professional qualifications, led her to a dead end. This might also be said of Diego and Maicon at different times in their lives. Entrepreneurship as a structure of feelings manipulates these anxieties and stokes them with small victories to reinforce its mirage of inevitability. For Keila, the investment in her human capital will only pay off when she finds herself among the elegant women she served at Chácara Santo Antônio. It's no longer possible to go back without greater frustration, to retreat to the place that her new *ethos* has recoded as degraded and unworthy of her training efforts. Her perception seemed overly sustained by the merit she believed she had, and by the first signs of resentment at defeat, reaching a level even deeper than Diego's case, for example.

The past in Campo Limpo idealised by Keila legitimises her current rejection. It is also contemporary with that narrated by the Racionais MC's, who lived in the neighbouring *favela* and saw it as a holocaust long before the social programmes and inclusion through consumption were avenged by *Lulismo*.

In any case, Keila prefers the *feminejo* of singer Marília Mendonça.[22]

7 Onwards

No one seeking autonomy can do without knowledge, but it's not easy to identify what is appropriate or achievable when it comes to the structure of feelings. The competent discourse serves, to a large extent, to legitimise relations of domination, which leave the sphere of injustice to rest on the merit of the subject who has 'education'. Situations in which subaltern individuals explain their own adversities, as well as the fortunes of others, by the fact that they have less formal education, are painfully common among my interlocutors. Those who seek social advancement through great sacrifice and an insistence on qualifications discover the hard way that competent discourse is just discourse. Leticia was not fooled by this chimera, but she had to pass many tests before her merit could be properly assessed. From an early age, she realised a fundamental flaw in competent discourse: inequality is at the root of social reproduction. She saw this early perception materialise in her own quest for recognition.

Letícia was born and raised in Taboão da Serra, but today "she's from the world". She was 26 at the time of the interview, had a degree in Economics from PUC and a Masters in World Political Economy from the Federal University of ABC. Ever since she was a little girl, she would help in any shop that was set up

---

22   *Feminejo* has been successful in Brazil as a branch of *sertanejo*, the local country rhythm, with female performers exalting their empowerment.

in the house, "not a big shop, but to sell ice-cream, make-up, Tupperware, lingerie, cosmetics, that sort of thing". Letícia says that when she wanted a pair of trainers, her mum would help her, but on one condition: the shoes had to cost no more than 70 reais and if she wanted more expensive ones, she would have to work. She decided to follow her mother's advice, and at the age of 14 she went to be a young apprentice at a company in Interlagos, which took a toll on her health. Her day started before 6am – she took a bus, a metro, a train and a van, then three more buses to Morumbi, where she attended school from 5:00 pm to 10:00 pm. She got home around midnight, exhausted and ready to start all over again the next day.

This routine didn't last long, and she soon decided to prioritise finishing secondary school. Incidentally, it was at school that she learned her first lessons about inequality, but not from books. In the early 2000s, her mother decided to stop being a seamstress and took a course to become a security guard. She worked for a few years in a shopping centre and then at Colégio Porto Seguro, which gave her children the right to try for a scholarship there. In the fourth year of primary school, Letícia became a student at one of São Paulo's elite schools. As a black girl on a scholarship, she has no doubt that this was 'the big turning point', in other words, the moment when she realised who she was in the world, that the possibility of having a privileged education came with the brutal realisation of inequality and institutional racism. There, in her words, she experienced the best and worst things that ever happened to her: the incentive to continue studying and a few years of therapy. "But it was this school that enabled me to take the entrance exam and get a full scholarship at PUC, you know? So, I'm very grateful too."

The confrontation with inequality made her want to become a judge, but as fate would have it, her second choice on Prouni was Economics. She admits that she barely knew what it was and was terrified of what she thought would be her future as a bank teller. But encouraged by one of her teachers, she persisted and quickly discovered an affinity with the subject. After a disappointing spell in the financial market, when she was passed over for a promotion, she decided that her knowledge deserved to be valued. "It's not for me, but black women, when they study this moment, they need to understand what kind of empowerment we are experiencing," emphasising this interview as a 'historical record'. Since 2018, she has run a company specialising in education and financial planning courses, of which she identifies as 'founder and CEO'. This was a way for Letícia to circumvent both racism and sexism and the uncertainty of the labour market.

Aimed at black and peripheral audiences, the platform she coordinates has already issued more than 4,000 certificates to people who have listened to its message of 'economic empowerment'. No less important and certainly fundamental to any project of individual affirmation, getting the household bills up to date is one of the pillars of the company's proposal, as it "points the way to overcoming the difficulties that most Brazilians face in balancing their budgets and amortising the effects of the historical inequality experienced in the country", as the website states. With a creative methodology that uses the songs of the Racionais MC's as a bridge for dialogue with the students, "issues related to consumption patterns, techniques for negotiating and settling debts, new approaches to relationships with money, investment mechanisms and prospects for the future" are addressed.

Her gamble of leaving the labour market at an early age to take the plunge into self-employment could have gone wrong, as with any business venture, but Letícia identified a real problem for the country's poor – debt. Talking to her, her ability to articulate her intellectual preparation with her sensitivity to the difficulties of the popular economy is remarkable, and for this she credits readings by Francisco de Oliveira, Florestan Fernandes and, more recently, Wendy Brown. On this point, she doesn't seem to lose focus on her perspective: the financial autonomy of people constantly harassed by creditors and banks. "People have a very weak financial mathematical basis, and then when they go to take out an overdraft, which grows by 300% a year, they don't calculate, you know? And then it snowballs." Her aim is to give people 'tools' so that they "can avoid the pitfalls of the financial system", because Letícia has no doubt that, in the contemporary world, indebtedness is relative. "Debt slavery no longer theoretically exists", she claims.

Leticia also has a very pragmatic view of entrepreneurship, which she doesn't mix with survival tactics for people in precarious situations. "For example, *favelas* that don't have a post office. If you have a *favela* community initiative that is going to solve the problem of people not receiving mail, that's an enterprise, because it's solving a problem in a certain context". Letícia sees entrepreneurship as 'innovation', very different from commerce, which she believes is not entrepreneurship. "Buying cheap and selling more expensive is not entrepreneurship, it's reselling to others," she explains.

She is moved by the stories she receives about people who have paid off their debts, managed to pay for a postgraduate course or renovate their house after going through the courses her company offers. With great emphasis, she attacks the hypocrisy she sees in debates about ostentation in the lower classes, of "thinking that black people can't consume certain things, that the *favela* always has to accept what's bad, what's not good", but she doesn't get distracted from her aim of pointing out the 'commodity fetish' that ultimately leads to debt, and which is the main focus of her social concerns. Leticia sees the big picture, but especially the people who are getting by within it.

CHAPTER 2

Between Lights and Shadows: Stories of Suffering and Religiosity

> I make it with grated coconut, coconut milk, boxed milk, cassava and sugar. It takes four eggs, three tablespoons of butter or margarine, no wheat, but there are some who add wheat, a cup of sugar, four tablespoons of butter, coconut milk, boxed milk and grated coconut, it's very creamy. I'll show you here on my mobile. Guys, I'm nervous, where is, my God? It's my daughter, she sells, we're getting by, you know? Because she works in the bakery and my son-in-law used to work in the restaurant in Vila Mariana, but it closed down because of the pandemic, so he was unemployed, but ... and my daughter works in the bakery, she works on the front line dispatching in the bakery. Bread, serving at the counter. Now she's selling children's clothes and so on, right? Until God blesses us even more and we set up a business for ourselves, I hope one day I'll set up something for myself, one day I'll set up a restaurant, I don't know when, even if it's in my house.
> ESTELA, 61, cleaner and cook

∴

In Brazilian social sciences, the way the poor perceive themselves in comparison to the rich has been analysed countless times. Often, the rich are seen as exploiters of other people's labour. After all, they are the owners of the means of production, while the situation of the poor is very much described like the fated, inescapable rhythm of mere social reproduction. In Teresa Caldeira's study (1984), it was the beginning of the 1980s when a certain fury in the eyes of those people from popular movements on the peripheries of São Paulo saw a society firmly anchored in the division between classes. More remarkable, however, was the way they saw themselves: 'we' who need to work for our own living (since the owners, the real rich in this scenario, don't need to work). There were the poor, but there were also the 'poorest of the poor', who lived under the overpasses and scavenged through the rubbish for food. There was, in the opinion of others, a 'middle class', who also need to work, but live better, and finally those who live better simply because they have 'education'.

As Caldeira says, "for the interviewees, the social world is not only made up of oppositions; it is also a world of differences between equals and from this point of view the 'we' is diluted. ... The category of those 'between' is the most fluid in the representations" (1984: 160–162). Here the role of lawyers, bankers and politicians is blurred. The owner of a small business, in the popular imagination, is on the side of the labourers, because on the opposite side are the rich (or their archetypes), who don't need to work.

There have been sharp transformations in the structure of feelings from time to time. A decisive moment in the formation of 20th century English working class culture was recorded by Richard Hoggart in his classic 1957 work, *The Uses of Literacy*. In that context, he questioned whether recognisable values of the working class in the North of England, such as tolerance (symbolised in the expression 'live and let live'), a sense of group and the need to live in the present, could be degenerated by progress, above all by the growing presence of mass culture in everyday life, despite the improvements in material life brought about by that same progress. For Hoggart, material temptations, especially as they appear in mass publications, tend "towards a gratification of the self and towards what may be called 'hedonistic-group-individualism'; they create techniques of mutual indulgence, to the extent that "traditional sanctions were removed or, in popular belief, proved irrelevant" (2009: 151), thus weakening the communal bonds that sustained those values. The scepticism that emerges from this serves as an armour against a suspicious world.

In the previous chapter, experiences of wageless life and of entrepreneurship were brought together to highlight ambitions and mobility projects, made at the cost of much effort, family support and scepticism about the public world, but whose protagonists were aiming for achievements for themselves. In the text of this second chapter, we see trajectories without the same enchantment or optimism, and some frankly full of anguish, uncertainty and discouragement. In the popular way of life, I have highlighted situations ranging from precariousness to small businesses, more or less stable at a certain level of survival, passing through businesses turned upside down by the COVID-19 pandemic and finally reaching workers on the brink of shipwreck. Unlike the characters highlighted earlier, who see entrepreneurship above all as a project for the future, here they are looking for an escape from a present saturated with losses, wounds and abuse brought on by a modest existence.

A fundamental vector for the self-management of suffering in the lower classes, Pentecostalism is presented here as a driving force behind entrepreneurship in its direct relationship with its faithful and, in the specific case that I will analyse below, as a structuring part of its discursive matrix. In the Universal Church of the Kingdom of God (UCKG), an individual's financial health is constitutive of their happiness, and debts are manifestations of evil and directly affect family relationships, without which receiving the Holy Spirit is impossible. Overcoming them means renouncing temptations and subjecting oneself to sacrifices in the name of God; becoming a 'servant' is a condition for such prosperity. To this end, UCKG has a special day of worship on Mondays, where the Holy Fire promises the expulsion of the devil (and debts). The success of 'neo-Pentecostal' denominations, especially among the poorest, comes from their totalising discourse, in which financial life is the result and condition for happiness in all its dimensions, and from the certainties it imbues in a secular world marked by uncertainty (Mafra, 2002).

In addition to participant observation on these occasions, I spoke to evangelicals from different denominations. The messages of 'don't give up' and 'you will win' that echo through church loudspeakers and pastors' speeches resonate through these individuals in different ways, in part by stimulating their ambition, but especially by pointing to individual and family management of material and spiritual precariousness.

1   Guiltless World

In the city of São Paulo, the commerce sector is responsible for around 1 million jobs,[1] so that its shopping streets are sustained as much by history as by necessity. The extraordinary size of the Zona Sul imposes unfeasible distances for most residents on the peripheries, who rarely have access to supermarkets and wholesalers, and more immediate consumption is guaranteed by small neighbourhood businesses, even when their products are more expensive. Certain non-essential items such as mobile phone accessories, toys and decorative objects are also cheaper because of their origin. These are Chinese products bought in Paraguay and resold on Rua 25 de Março or Rua Santa Ifigênia, two famous shopping streets in the old town (Pinheiro-Machado, 2008).

---

1   Precisely 864,000 in 2020, according to data from the Seade Foundation. Available at: https://trabalho.seade.gov.br.

The price to pay for a less stressful life can be felt in the pocket, but it is also felt in other, non-monetary ways. In Delei's small shop, the collection of hundreds of pirated DVDs accumulated on the shelves, from action films to *forró* shows, is striking. On the other side of the shop, among mobile phone chargers, superhero dolls and cloth masks hanging on the wall, sits the 50-year-old Northeastern, who has lived in Vargem Grande for 20 years. Delei left Aporá, in the North of Bahia, when he was 18. At the age of five he started working in the fields, doing 'softer work' such as planting corn and beans, and didn't think about moving away even when he saw his fellow countrymen coming back from São Paulo 'wearing different clothes'. In the small town, which today has less than 20,000 inhabitants, Delei says it was common to hear fireworks when one of them went to visit the family who had stayed. With his curiosity piqued, he headed for the South, planning to stay for just one year, as "he was brought up with a family from the countryside, but they were not destitute". He spent seven years in São Paulo without even communicating with his relatives. When he returned to Bahia, he could no longer adapt.

Before starting his own business, Delei was a security guard at an apartment block, a job he quit to become a street vendor in Santo Amaro with his wife. There he sold beer, toys and peanuts. As the crackdown on street vendors increased around the CPTM station where he travelled, he began to trade near his home in Vargem Grande. Although he decided to leave his job even against the wishes of the condominium, he considers that the registered job had advantages. His working hours went from 6am to 2pm and, when the holidays came, "I'd spend 25 days in Bahia, come back and start again. Something that was secure. Not here, you have to work every day". He admits that his time in Santo Amaro was very difficult, but he adapted to the trade in Vargem Grande and managed to rent the location where he is today.

The way Delei justifies his choice is confusing, as his comments about the guaranteed salary at the end of the month, as well as his idea that as a street vendor you work much harder and the return is much more uncertain, suggest that formal work left him feeling complacent. "Because if you owe something today and you don't give it back, you go broke, you have to invest. If you sell one thing, you have to buy two, for example. If you sell one SIM, you save the money to buy two, and if you're a registered worker, you don't." Even if the choice doesn't work out financially, Delei 'feels' that, with experience and "thinking about things differently", he was able to find ways to stabilise himself after the most difficult period of getting by. "And I did well, I feel I did well," he says, as he watches the passers-by in front of him, compulsively adjusting the loose mask on his face. 'Doing well', in this case, doesn't refer primarily to his living standards, but to something complicated to explain, which is "growing financially and mentally".

In a sense, working for yourself unleashes the capitalist spirit, but it doesn't thrive when you're just surviving. It's curious, though, how the shop has kept going, offering goods with very little value, and still with some competition in the neighbourhood. From Monday to Monday, Delei is in the shop from 9:00 am to 8:00 pm, practically without deviation, except when he goes to the centre to pick up more products. His wife, who also used to be a street trader, only helps out in the mornings. It's been seven years since his last holiday, when he spent 15 days in the Northeast. His work in the shop isn't exhausting, he says. "Mentally you get a bit worn out, but the body is fine," he says with sense of humour. In fact, Delei spends most of the day sitting on his stool, checking his mobile phone and occasionally being interrupted by a customer. It's quite different from his routine fleeing the *rapa* at Santo Amaro station or on the farm in Bahia, when his parents "used to teach us how to do things. Taking milk from the cattle, from the cows, fetching the animals from the pasture to bring them to the corral. We'd get up early, put our boots on our feet, get our clothes all wet from the wet grass". For them, it was "first you work, and then you study". Delei follows a certain pattern in his answers, which is to minimise the difficulties he has gone through, to not appear to be complaining.

Talking about his weekly routine, he once again confuses the researcher regarding which was the most troubled moment in his career, whether it was as a shop owner or as a street vendor, since in the latter case, "you don't have to pay for water, you don't have to pay for electricity, you don't have to pay for rent. If you want to go to work for a week you do, if you don't you stay at home. If you have a shop, you have opening hours and closing hours." The determining factor here is that wageless life, among the poorest, is inevitably defined by uncertainty, but that, with the exception of situations of misery and deprivation, it can be worth it for the challenge, for the purpose that seems to exist in the pursuit of self-employment. Delei feels that during this period he became a more developed person, while paid work didn't require him to make the effort. In doing so, he became known in the neighbourhood and was recognised by the community.

The relationship that is established between the trader and his territory is certainly one of the main characteristics of the shopping streets in peripheral neighbourhoods, where most consumers also live, something that Hoggart (2009) observed. In these situations, the trader sees himself and is seen as someone belonging to the community, a worker of equal status within that space. When he keeps a business far from home, especially in a middle-class neighbourhood, he tends to internalise a relationship of servitude in relation to the customer, who is in a superior social situation. We often hear from traders in Vargem Grande that they don't have customers there, but rather 'friends'.

A few blocks from Delei's accessories shop, Lígia runs an optician's shop that stands out on the high street for its organisation and three uniformed employees. The stifling heat of the street combined with the dust contrasts with the shop's air-conditioning and its perfectly sanitised, albeit cramped, environment. She was an attendant at the shop until 2015, when she bought it from the previous owners. She says that since then she has been running the shop, she has been 'struggling hard'. Aged 46 and with a high school education, she started working at the age of 13. Her first job was as a seamstress, then she worked in an Arabic food franchise, in disc shops and as a market vendor in a fruit stall. She says she even started a university degree but gave it up and opted for a technical course as a necropsy assistant. Extremely attentive, she gave me tips about how to preserve glasses during the conversation, which she picked up in her 16 years in the business.

Lígia demonstrates a firm voice and conviction in what she does, as well as a solid work ethic. For her, who is an evangelical member of the Assembly of God, being an entrepreneur means "offering what we have to our customers, giving them all the attention, service, not just the 'before', but the 'after'. Helping our neighbours, running campaigns, so that's how I see it." The pandemic hasn't changed her routine much, which continues from Monday to Monday, with a day off for the two saleswomen and 'a *boy*' who she keeps on hand to take goods, documents, etc. Lígia minimises the economic crises of recent years as well as the impact of the pandemic since her establishment was considered 'essential' by municipal decree. "I can't complain, I haven't had any problems here financially, nothing, not even during the pandemic. During the pandemic we've worked normally, we've just had to take some breaks, but we've worked normally, I have nothing to complain about."

Like her colleague Delei, she has an emotional relationship with the neighbourhood. It is her second home, she says, as she lives in Grajaú, just a few kilometres away. Lígia is very proud of the relationship she has established. "We have a very good relationship with the population, people have known me for a long time, I have friendships with all the shopkeepers, with many residents who have become not only customers, but friends," she says, adding that she is always invited to baptisms and weddings. Her expectations for the future re-establish an ideal of the good life in the popular sense. "Today, I no longer have expectations, I think I'm at the level I wanted to be, I'm fine. So, I want to be able to retire and drink a lot of coconut water on the beach, without illness, in good health. That's what I want, to grow old in good health, that's all ... I think everyone wants that." Perhaps counterintuitively, in the popular world evangelicals, inspired by Protestant ethics, tend to attribute their success or stability much less to God than Catholics. For Lígia, recourse to the divine is not enough – hard work is needed to guarantee merit. It's not that popular Catholicism doesn't value effort, but what is often seen among Catholics is the attribution of their success to God's grace, legitimising the idea that working exhaustively won't bring guarantees, as success is not in one's hands.

The centre of Paraisópolis, around Rua Ernest Renan, is where most of the shops are concentrated, including the biggest ones. It's where the life of the *favela* really pulses. There, Carolina had only been running her clothes and make-up shop for three months and seemed satisfied with her choice, even though the inflation that hit the country in mid-2021 was already beginning to impact her. Aged 28 and with a high school degree, she quit her job at a Korean restaurant in Morumbi when she fell pregnant and managed to support herself by selling make-up from home. With the positive reception of her products, she and her husband decided to open a shop. Carolina represents a case of fluctuation between the formal and informal markets, between the permanent and the temporary. Her decision to leave her formal job for self-employment didn't have much to do with talent – it wasn't something she dreamed of or prepared for. It just happened, as the dynamics of life pushed her from one to the other. She doesn't complain about these changes, but isn't thrilled about them, either. At the age of fifteen she was already doing odd jobs to help out the family and avoid unnecessary expenses. Her father had a bar in his own house that provided a little income, and her mother went from being a housewife to a cleaner when the situation there worsened in the mid-2000s. "I used to look after children so that I could at least buy cream, shampoo, that sort of thing, you know? When you're a young woman you start to want to dress up. I used to earn 150 reais, that was good enough for me. Then I started selling things on the street, door to door. Then it was markets, restaurants, bakeries, whatever I could find I got into."

She seems generally satisfied. She likes her job because she can talk to the people and girls from the neighbourhood who frequent the shop. The small shop she runs is not a legal entity, and she indicated that she hadn't given this much thought. Her unemphatic opinions only change at two points in the conversation. When she talks about her last job in the wealthy neighbourhood nearby, her memories aren't the best. She stayed there for two periods of about a year, and says she had some embarrassing experiences, such as not liking the Korean way of eating ("they like soup there, and I don't like it very much"). Above all, what bothered her was the rigour of her bosses. At first, she tried to attribute the difficulty to communication, but ended up admitting that it was 'a bit bad' there, a small concession to the popular custom of avoiding complaining. Her second reason for excitement is the neighbourhood itself. 'I love it here,' he says with an undisguised smile on his face. "Ah, well, [I like] that it's busy here. It's not a quiet street, you know? Neighbours know each other, everyone knows each other here. I remember the time when I was younger, when we could play in the street, and I thought it was really cool". Today she feels that this is no longer possible, and her daughter stays with her grandmother during the day, until Carolina returns to take care of things around the house, which is nearby.

Many years before, Mari also found herself in business almost involuntarily. The experience of being in a registered job and, from one moment to the next, having to deal with suppliers, possibly employees, waking up at the crack of dawn to get to Brás, in the city centre, in search of goods, opening and closing the shop and paying the bills, are remarkably consistent characteristics of wageless life, which can become a reality without any planning. Something a little 'complicated' to define, as my interlocutors say – it's not exactly out of necessity, like someone who loses their job and has to make do with odd jobs, but the result of some confluence of factors that come together.

Mari has her shop in another large *favela* in the city, the Heliópolis neighbourhood. You could say that, given the opportunity, she succeeded. Today, at the age of 44, she has nine employees in her clothes shop, on the verge of ceasing to be a micro-entrepreneur and has moved to a middle-class neighbourhood in the Zona Sul. But her story begins a long way from there and is very different from her fate in São Paulo, where she arrived in 1992 when she was still running around in the streets of the periphery. Mari grew up in the backland of Paraíba and started working in the fields at the age of nine. She says she wasn't forced to work, but wanted to have a little money to buy clothes, shoes, etc. As soon as she arrived, she went to help her brother, who were already in town running a wine cellar, and opened a little shop next door. But he had to get rid of everything when he had to donate one of his kidneys to his sister – she was the only one of his eleven siblings who was a match. Back in the cellar/market, she freed up a corner for a friend in need to put her clothes on display. Eventually, the clothes took up more and more space and she decided to transform the place for good. Mari, who had also decided to go back to school to study medicine, let her practical side and the security of what she had in hand speak louder than this desire. "It wasn't like that at the time ... things aren't the way we want them to be," explain.

Even though she admits that she hadn't planned on becoming a salesperson, Mari has no complaints about the choices she made and is grateful for the stability she has achieved. However, she doesn't want her daughters to be as dependent on opportunity as she is. Having raised two girls (aged 13 and six) on her own, she insists that they take their studies seriously "because life is unpredictable", and they shouldn't expect anything to come easy. Once again, formal education appears to be a path that isn't exactly reliable, but promises to minimise the uncertainties that Mari knows all too well: "Building a better future doesn't just depend on me, it depends on them too".

Unpredictability as a perennial aspect of popular daily life implies that there are ways out that may not be welcome, but that in the interplay between formal and informal, legal and illegal, they end up being justified by their own normativity. Luís Alberto, born in São Paulo, is 50 years old and has owned a pet shop in Vargem Grande for over two decades. In his stuffy shop, bags of cat and dog food, bird cages and other supplies create a barrier between the door and the small table where he sits at the back, between calculators and calendars. He appreciates the neighbourhood and, like the others, considers his customers, all neighbours, to be his friends, which I observed during a visit from two boys who didn't know exactly what they wanted. They were looking for a specific product for farmed birds, for which the father of one of them had sent them and which Luís promptly identified, pointing to the container where the feed was to be found, not without first annoying them a little.

He usually runs the establishment with an employee, but at the time of the interview he was working alone: "I was with a boy here, but he was making me angry, so I sent him away. No, to get angry and spend the money, I'd rather be alone." The large 20 or 30 kilo sacks of animal feed on the shop floor look like burdens that are difficult to carry. Debauched, Luís made conversation wearing a mask with a slightly sinister and uncomfortable smile printed in it. As he was alone in the shop, he interrupted the interview several times to attend to customers and suppliers. Luís also has a bar on the same street, which operates clandestinely and which, presumably, hasn't closed or lost customers during the quarantine. "At the moment, I'm evading tax," he confesses without remorse.

The owner of the pet shop and irregular bar started working in an uncle's supermarket at the age of 12, studied until high school and never left the trade again. He works ten hours a day in the shop, seven days a week. Though obviously grueling, this routine is quite common in the region. However, in his case, it's a little more exhausting due to the volume of goods. Asked if he feels tired, he admits that he does, but resigns himself to it. He compares: "there's no point in a guy opening a bakery if he doesn't open at the time everyone else does. It's not even about the money, it's about the customer who arrives and he has to be open." Luís Alberto says that he even gave up his shop because he couldn't reconcile it with his marriage. Bored, he bought it back and infuriated his wife, pointing out that the shop is not just a source of income for him, but the main factor that organises his life. His wife made him choose between her and the pet shop. He chose the pet shop, and the marriage ended.

For Luís Alberto, an entrepreneur is above all someone who struggles, experiences setbacks, but knows how to reinvent himself. "I change something in this shop right away. I get different merchandise so it doesn't stay the same, otherwise I would have gone bankrupt. So that's entrepreneurship, you have a vision of what the market needs at that time", he points out. This perception is based on modest ambition and hard work, which involves personal refusals in order to simply make a living, maintain his family (who need to adapt to his work routine, not the other way round) and the loyalty of his customers, eventually resorting to petty crime such as running a clandestine bar. He works according to Candido's (1970) guiltless world, believing that his actions have little or no repercussions on society, moving between the always-tenuous boundaries separating the legal from the illegal.

2   Us and Them

According to the UMCP, there are more than 14,000 commercial establishments in Paraisópolis, which employ 21 per cent of its residents (Bernardo; Santos, 2021). One of them is 35-year-old Celso. Born in São Paulo to parents from Alagoas, he has lived in Paraisópolis all his life, where his four children and first granddaughter, who was only nine months old at the time of the interview, also grew up. In his small repair shop, washing machines, refrigerators, microwaves and whatever else he can fit into the space for the owner and one or two customers. In the spartan environment that characterises this type of popular business, there is no room for decoration. The only item allowed, which is essential, is the TV hanging on the white wall, which divides Celso's attention with the movement of the street. From there he watches life goes by, while José Luís Datena occupies the shop's sound space, with the well-known vehemence of police news programmes, denouncing the 'banditry'.[2]

With his high school completed, he works at the shop from Monday to Saturday from 10am to 5.30pm and takes Sunday off to spend time with his granddaughter. His leisure time starts with going to church in the morning and ends with a film on TV, something he couldn't do when he worked as a security

---

2 Datena is the best-known and longest-serving presenter of television police programmes in Brazil.

guard at the city zoo, also in the Zona Sul, because he worked all week with one day off a month for nine years. He has a CLT contract there but, when he left, he took into account that he hardly had any rest and needed some time for his children. His first job was at the age of twelve, facilitated by a brother-in-law who worked as a gardener. Celso did the sweeping and walked the dogs while his relative, who was also the driver, had to go out to drive the bosses. At the end of the month, he would get 'a little help', for which he is very grateful. "Thanks to God and him, I had this right path," he says.

Celso is a typical representative of popular commerce, with no great ambitions other than to have a decent working life in which exhaustion can be avoided, and in which he has time for his family, religion and some modest leisure. As we have seen with other interlocutors, he would like to have some holiday time, but is patiently waiting for sufficient prosperity. For the time being, he essentially believes in his family as his motivation. He attributes his decision to be self-employed to a certain affinity for fixing things, which he says he discovered at home with the family's household appliances. So, Celso went to a local college that offered electrician and machine maintenance courses. He took the small property he inherited from his father with his brothers and turned the garage into a repair shop.

Commenting on the pandemic, Celso recounts the initial fright and the difficulty of running the business with the isolation measures. But the health crisis reveals a discomfort that goes beyond the exceptional moment. He says that 'down here' (closer to Morumbi), people had been following the recommendations (wearing masks, hand sanitiser, etc.), but "up there in the middle … you go to places and people don't have masks, they're not taking care of themselves, they're chatting in circles. So, I think that up there it's a bit more – excuse the word – a bit more relaxed". He doesn't mean that as a compliment.

Obviously, narratives of crime and perseverance can coexist or create dissonance when reality imposes itself. For example, Paraisópolis is the scene of the Baile da Dz7, one of the city's biggest *flows* – spontaneously organised open air funk parties, with cars and huge loudspeakers vying for space in the *favela's* narrow alleys – attended by thousands of young people from all over the city, almost every night from Wednesday to Sunday. There are also plenty of street vendors, especially selling alcoholic drinks, cigarettes and illicit drugs, who don't mind the competition from the bars, which make their own *sertanejo*, *pagode* and *brega* playlists.[3] On Rua Ernest Renan, from where the *flow* begins to spread, there is practically no room to walk around after 2:00 am, and the

---

3 Apart from funk, these are the three most popular rhythms in Brazil.

view is constantly obscured by the profusion of LED lights advertising exotic combinations of energy drinks and coconut ice, marijuana smoke, shisha and burnt tyres from the motorbikes showing off a few streets away. Smells of urine and vomit waft through the alleyways, as there are no public toilets, and the bars charge to use their own. But the kids don't let up and the fun continues until it finally dies down the next morning, when the residents themselves start cleaning the doors of their homes and businesses. It is all self-managed.

The differential distribution of the state, as Veena Das (2004) puts it, can be seen in the occasional presence of the police, the only bearer of state intelligibility in that context. Their raids and 'framings' are relatively common, usually before the *flow* begins, precisely to prevent crowding, and have the backing of residents opposed to the parties. In the early hours of 1 December 2019, claiming to be in pursuit of motorbike muggers, the Military Police (PM) cornered around 5,000 partygoers. Nine of them, young people aged between 14 and 23, were trampled to death during the panic caused by the police operation, none of them were residents of Paraisópolis. According to Celso, the *flow* "it's good for these unemployed people, who manage to generate some money, but from my point of view, as I don't work with these things, it's bad for me, because there are many who come from outside and don't respect us residents." Despite acknowledging the fact that there are many residents of Paraisópolis who live off the income earned during the party, Celso, when asked about violence in the neighbourhood, immediately refers to the event.

Distinctions between different parts of the neighbourhoods are common, usually articulated in a derogatory tone towards neighbours who may only be a few streets away. This is the damaged side of the community, which Hoggart (2009) observed in the distinction between 'us' and 'them' in a context much less oppressive than that of a colossal Brazilian *favela* in the 21st century. In the English working class of the 1950s, the notion of 'us' still had a strong class character and opposed the rich, something that seems utopian in the face of the retreat of the individual in the contemporary world and the weakening of their collective identity. Expanding the scale, Celso shows less hostility to the upscale surroundings than to other neighbourhoods closer to Paraisópolis in socio-economic terms. "There are lots of people who come from Brasilândia [in the North of the city] to steal here. Then if it's in the newspaper, they say 'oh, he's from Paraisópolis', but he's not. Here, thank God, we're well respected. Like I told you, I'm 35 years old and I have nothing to complain about."

From the 1990s to the present day, while consumer standards and access to goods, credit, services and public policies improved, insecurity and uncertainty accompanied the undermining of the popular classes' way of life, surrounded and barricaded in their homes (Caldeira, 2000). In this context, Jurandir Freire

Costa anticipated the sedimentation of a country "where the experience of helplessness is taken to such a point that it makes the practice of social solidarity conflicting and extremely difficult". Faced with a sense of insecurity and uncertainty, the experience of the Brazilian working classes has been highlighted with a growing audience in police TV shows, extolling the defence of shopkeepers, workers and consumers. The discursive framework of crime brings the growing violence in the urban space into the hegemonic narrative.

There is a lot of controversy about the *flow*. Those who manage to make some money from it generally adapt their routines. In addition to the vendors, there are those who take advantage of it from car parks and even the slabs, which are transformed into boxes. The others, including the elderly and people with children, condemn the excessive noise and dirt almost every night of the week, without disguising the moral insult with the hypersexualised funk lyrics and the low average age of the regulars.[4] "It's all ages, we don't think so, but it's all ages, we see a lot of young people. *Novinho*, as they say. They're breaking up, really," says Celso. The death of the nine boys was a tragic end to a narrative created years before for São Paulo's second largest *favela*, as I analysed in the first chapter, but it hasn't changed its fate, saturated with daily struggles and new entrepreneurs.

But the ambiguity with which many shopkeepers observe Paraisópolis also appears among those who have businesses in the 'middle', suggesting that economic dynamism and moral decay evolve to the same extent for everyone, and that moralistic opinions are strengthened according to the family's social ascension. Otávio, 41, has a small market in the *favela* that he has run with his wife for around two years. He knows the business well, having started at the age of 14 working for the Grupo Pão de Açúcar (GPA) supermarket chain, formally, for two decades. He also spent time at Carrefour, another seven years at an *atacarejo* and in between he tried his first business, a pizzeria that didn't succeed. Recently, an opportunity came up to buy the business from an acquaintance; he took over the market but had to lay off three employees during the pandemic. The two who are left run the shop in the morning and the couple take over in the afternoon until 10:00 pm – with her at the till and him in the bakery and stocking products.

---

4   Two months after the tragedy, I was a guest at an event organised by the Rede Emancipa of popular courses at CEU Paraisópolis, which was attended by some community leaders and the family of one of the boys killed during the police ambush at the Baile da Dz7. Despite the general tone of solidarity with the families, and repudiation of the police action, some of those present vehemently criticised the holding of the parties, making their conflict over the issue explicit.

He seems moderately satisfied with his choice. "It's not that I earn twice as much. If I put it in perspective, I don't think I earn even 10 per cent of what I used to earn with a CLT contract, but nothing is missing at home." With the verve of a social scientist, Otávio sees three types of social classes in Paraisópolis. "There's the poor person, extremely poor, with very little income; there's the middle class who have a job and a fixed income, who manage to get by; and there are the people who have a lot of money, who already have money from other things they do, their husband works well, their wife works well, so they have a different condition." Apart from the former, this is a population that demands more expensive products and is generally associated with an entrepreneurial type that he greatly appreciates: hard-working, honest, who wakes up early "and who gets very upset when they can't pay off some debt".

Otávio and his wife were born and raised in Paraisópolis, but despite having their business in the neighbourhood, they no longer live there. Shortly before taking over the market, they moved with their two children to the neighbouring town of Taboão da Serra, where they live in a condominium. "Thank God I was able to raise my children elsewhere," he says without any remorse. His family has experienced remarkable social mobility in recent decades: his children studied as scholarship students at Colégio Porto Seguro, and the eldest is currently studying Business at the State University of Campinas (UNICAMP). The youngest was unable to renew his scholarship and continued his studies at a private Adventist school. Otávio himself studied Marketing at a private university on a GPA scholarship programme, under pressure from his manager who threatened him with dismissal if he didn't get a degree. He understood that, beyond a means of social mobility, having higher education is a matter of survival in the labour market. This is evident when he attributes all his family's success to his work, but intimately suspects that his children will need other credentials.

As the final chapter of Otávio's family project, his children's formal education is a condition for maintaining this upward mobility. That's apparently why they decided to leave Paraisópolis. As scholarship students, the partners of the Paraisópolis hamburger restaurant also studied at Porto Seguro, but they remain in the *favela*, seeing the rise of entrepreneurship happening there and becoming a vital part of it. So, the real reason Otávio took his children out of the *favela* is because of the influence that comes from others, from what is beyond his control, and which intensifies as they reach adolescence, imposing on him the need to shield them from everything he considers wrong with the *favela*. "I went to public school and the education was precarious, and today you have the chance to give your child a good education, to study at one of the best universities in the country, that motivates you to leave, you know? Not that it's bad, but if you're in a place where there's less crime, less drugs or anything like that, who doesn't want that?", he says.

Otávio seems to know that his own statements about the 'three social classes' of Paraisópolis are a bit of a self-deception, as they only cover part of what is real. There is a fourth profile in the discourse that remains hidden, but which manifests itself at other points in the conversation and points directly to the world of crime. Otávio longed to give his children what he thought they didn't have. "When I think back to my childhood, a very painful childhood, very poor, without many resources, having to leave home to work very early, at the age of 11. ... Today, as we have a little bit of means, we want to provide for our children." If from a purely material point of view, there seems to be no justification for moving to another neighbourhood since there is the possibility of mobility there, according to several interlocutors. So, he settles on morality. "I don't mean crime, but easy access: easy access to drugs, drink, dancing, early sex, all kinds of things ... it's everywhere, a bit more masked, sometimes not, but it's there." Otávio identifies the first years of Lula's mandate as the time when household bills improved, and better-quality products and services became accessible. Even so, he points out that "they experience the taste of power" under the PT government. In the case of Bolsonaro, he also sees him in two halves: one that "ended corruption in the country"; the other that "isn't effective, it gets bickering". At the time of the interview, it was the disagreement over the COVID-19 vaccine that was making the news. This indicates that his scepticism about politics corresponds to his popular *ethos* that includes, on the one hand, efficient management and ethical codes and, on the other, the moral foundations that are so important for a successful family.

In Otávio's life, the solutions have always been private, and problems arose from the public. At least that's how he sees it. As a businessman, he perceives bureaucracy as an obstacle and resents taxes, which he considers 'unfair'. He finds himself helpless and constantly provoked to resort to illegal behaviour. "Everything is done to make you evade, to make you do things wrong, you know? There is no support from either a bank or an NGO", two institutions that are just as dubious in the daily life of Paraisópolis. "After I started this way, as a little boy, I realised what a pain it is to pay tax. I pay the same tax that a big company pays, I pay the same tax that someone who has ten times as much as me pays." He complains that public policies to help micro and small entrepreneurs are created to deceive, because it's the private banks that determine 'who fits in' and therefore gets the loan. As is often the case among the interlocutors in this research, there is an awareness of inequality and the privileges of those 'at the top', as Florestan Fernandes would say. But it's a dammed-up feeling that doesn't find an adequate outlet in a world of individualism and scepticism.

Finally, the Paraisópolis of inclusion through consumption is for Otávio a good place to keep a business, but not what he perceives as ideal for a family that has reached a certain standard. This standard is not merely economic but anchored in moral values. While he tries to follow the rules and live honestly according to his strict work ethic, it was his distrust of his former neighbours that determined that this was no longer a decent place for his family. Along with the pride he feels in his university-educated children and the social mobility he has achieved, there is also the distinction between him and his competitors, explicit in what 'they' do that 'he' doesn't – evading taxes, buying stolen goods, etc. "How can you buy something that could be stained with blood? How many fathers of families have lost their lives for this to reach me?" Otávio outrages, summarising the moral code of the popular subject.

3   Mistrust

I had frequented the intricacies of Largo Treze before, as it was there that I carried out half of the fieldwork for my master's research between 2013 and 2015, focussing on a local private university. The context has changed since then, but even then, I could see a growing mistrust, partly due to the unfulfilled promises of *Lulismo*, among Prouni scholarship students (Costa, 2018). Now, the deepening of this process seems to finally prevail, and entrepreneurship emerges as both a consequence and a solution to the cynicism in territories such as this.

Luciano is 48 years old, and for the last three years he has been running an accessories shop on Rua Barão de Duprat, where he works alone amidst goods organised in a somewhat careless manner – this is a large shop with more variety than Delei's, for example. When Luciano came from Ceará in 1985, he first settled in the Zona Leste, where he stayed until 2000. Today he lives in Jardim Aracati, a neighbourhood on the banks of the Guarapiranga reservoir, more than 12 kilometres south of Santo Amaro. He had just sacked his wife, who was his only employee and who started working without a CLT contract. He himself only had a formal contract until 1995 and has been self-employed ever since. Luciano would like to define himself as a businessman, but he doesn't because, as he says, "I've been unregulated and I'm trying to regularise [the shop], there's not much left for me to be considered a businessman". Highlighting the difficulties he has had in his occupation, he believes that despite this, the economic situation has improved under the Michel Temer and Bolsonaro governments, which would have been interrupted by the pandemic that brought more unemployment and, therefore, a drop in the shop's sales. "Another major difficulty that has been going on for many years – and I don't know if it will change with some reforms – is the tax on national products. That's why I even work with some imported things 'made in China' like you're seeing."

Popular culture is undergoing a transformation, in which expressions of entrepreneurship are appearing in the speeches of traders and the self-employed. While scepticism about the state and its institutions persists, this change also reveals a great deal of insecurity about the steps to be taken. This has a direct impact on subjectivity, because it's one thing to be a *virador*, living from odd jobs and exchanging lunch for dinner. It's quite another to be an entrepreneur who aspires to a new identity and a material condition that corresponds to this status.

One example is Luciano's opinion on the emergency aid for the pandemic distributed by the government, which he himself was a beneficiary of. "Keeping it, everyone will say that they think it has to be kept, but let's see how the country turns out, how it's going to pay this bill," says Luciano, the businessman who at the time was receiving the emergency aid of 600 reais and who went so far as to say that, in the face of the crisis, "we're saving as much as possible, clinging to any branch so that we don't die". Even though he values the professionals from the Unified Health System (SUS) who have been on the front line fighting COVID-19, he wishes he didn't need them because it would be better to have a private health insurance. Embodying a recurring behaviour among aspiring entrepreneurs, Luciano, however, comes full circle and ends the conversation optimistically: "[now it's] waiting for it to get better, for a vaccine to come along and for us to expand the business."

A few metres away, Elisa and her husband run a shop selling paintings and picture frames. They came from Paraná about twenty years ago and now live in Rio Bonito, more than eight kilometres south of Santo Amaro. She is 40 years old and has seen the pandemic change her life. In mid-2020, I entered the gloomy atmosphere of the shop, observed only by reproductions of famous paintings by Monet and Romero Britto and framed photos of generic people who populate image banks. That's because, with the closure of 'non-essential' businesses by the state government, her shop had to lay off its six employees, so she had to leave her job at a law firm to help her husband with the shop. She is left alone at the front of the shop while he makes the paintings and frames, a family business that started with her father-in-law.

Elisa, however, was never directly involved in it. Studying law at a private university, she was on a stable career path, registered and with her labour rights guaranteed. When she finished her degree, she intended to continue practising law. She admits that she misses her formal contract and the benefits that the CLT provides. Being the boss doesn't give her any advantages, and despite following the shop's routine over the years, the responsibility suddenly fell to her, and she hadn't prepared for it. "I think that when you're the owner, many things have to be dealt with at that moment, there's no one above you that you can turn to, it's you and that's it," she states with frustration.

What exacerbates a sense of living adrift in that world of thwarted traders is the lack of community relations that abounds in the dirt tracks of Vargem Grande, for example. Luciano and Elisa's difficulties are different, and they face them from their own subjectivities, but the feeling that they are one step away from success or failure, balancing on quicksand, has similarities in the insecurity they show in the face of the uncertain. Even when there are crises and doubts, recognition in the community works like an anchor in rough seas and justifies their choice to live a wageless life. In the case of their colleagues in Santo Amaro, nothing gives them security, and even the little they do have is viewed with suspicion, a feeling that the COVID-19 pandemic has accentuated.

4 Prosperity

"Good evening, winners!" was the first phrase heard over the loudspeaker in the immense hall with beige walls and coloured stained-glass windows, decorated with a disturbing cross-shaped lamp. A message in gigantic proportions was placed on the altar and illuminated in blue and gold, looming above: 'Jesus Christ is the Lord'. Seen from Avenida João Dias, the imposing staircase surprises as much as the façade adorned with imperial pine trees, leading two boys with rucksacks to climb it to peek inside the building, "just to see what it's like" (said one to the other, reluctantly). The gloomy night in Santo Amaro couldn't obscure the second largest temple of the Universal Church of the Kingdom of God (UCKG) in São Paulo, with its 30,000 square metres and seating capacity for 6,000 people. About ¼ of the space was occupied on that Monday in November 2021, when I was at the temple for a participant observation. It was the day of the Congress for Success at the Templo da Fé.[5]

The greeting kicked off Pastor Marcelo's talk, who is responsible for the Monday service, which also takes place across other denominations in the Pentecostal world. Even though it goes by different names (prosperity service, service for businesspeople, etc.), the first working day of the week is used for

---

5 According to the 2010 Census, the UCKG had around 1.8 million believers throughout the country.

financial counselling. The purpose of these sessions is to offer words of self-help and examples of overcoming difficulties, in which financial success is attributed to devotion to Jesus, realised through the contribution to the church (the tithe). In the case of the UCKG, this is combined with the main characteristic, identified by Ronaldo Almeida (2009), as 'transit churches', i.e. built in places of intense commercial activity or close to bus, underground and train terminals, implying a sociability almost completely devoid of intimacy. In the impersonality that reigns in their services, everyone, except for the pastor (after all, with his social media up to date; his Instagram had more than 20,000 followers that month) are illustrious strangers, which helps with the strategy adopted: not always very convincing, the testimonies given there are unlikely to be scrutinised by a close acquaintance.

In the context of the UCKG, founded in 1977 in Rio de Janeiro by Edir Macedo and the main denomination of the neo-Pentecostal strand, the Congresses for Success have a specificity compared to the more traditional services run throughout the week, with their performances to expel evil spirits. Although financial health is an essential aspect for the discursive matrix of the church and Teologia da Prosperidade as a whole, and despite the numerous mentions of the devil that appear here (expelling him is a condition for prosperity), this is a more 'sober' session, and the audience is far from the 'poor and alienated crowd' of the unloading sessions that usually prompt derogatory descriptions in the media and academia. As Jacqueline Moraes Teixeira (2016) observed, many of these platitudes are the opposite of a well-articulated 'pedagogy of prosperity' in which money is not the only ritual mediator of prosperity, which works alongside other areas of life, especially the family.

In the service, a script is determined, in which prayers are interspersed with success stories, audience participation and donations. At one point, the pastor made a new exhortation that I didn't immediately understand. The next thing I knew, the masses around me were raising their mobile phones, wallets, purses and backpacks to be blessed. Pastor Marcelo's charisma is undeniable, alternating moments of surrender to prayer, usually with his back to the audience, when he increases the pitch of his voice until it becomes incomprehensible, with situations of relaxed exaltation, giving the floor to the faithful and interacting with them. The pastor's skits are essential in translating abstract issues of Christian theology (Mafra, 2002; Mafra et al., 2012). However, his performance was still powerful, especially when the three screens positioned for the audience focussed on him against a background that reddened, resembling fire.

There is no doubt, as Almeida (2009) argues, that even in this case the basic dichotomy between 'liberated' and 'non-liberated' people is in place, but the emphasis is on the former, those who have overcome debts and creditors and use their religious dedication to see their businesses achieve grace. What was most striking about the large audience at the 8:00 pm service, the fifth of the day, was the diversity within the uniformity, similar to that of a shopping centre: a notable middle and lower-middle class portion of many couples in apparent communion, many accompanied by their children, but also people on their own.[6] As Antônio Flávio Pierucci (1988: s/p) analysed the profile of the lower-middle class in the 1980s and which seems to apply here, these are "intermediate sectors in more than one sense: (1) they are intermediate strata between the bottom and the top of society, (2) who live in intermediate neighbourhoods between the centre and the periphery, (3) often exercising their economic activities in intermediary sectors (small commerce and services)". For these individuals, socio-economic and cultural-geographical factors 'push down and back' their social position.[7] This is a public that would also fit Norbert Elias' definition of outsiders (2000).

Black people, brown people and white people are present in comparable proportions. There are young people in their twenties and old people in their seventies, and a couple of middle-aged men a few rows in front of me, who exchanged discreet pleasantries. There are tattooed people, men with earrings and long hair, women in knee-length skirts and eye-catching glasses, football team and rock band shirts, and *cangaceiro* hats. Four women, probably straight from work, crossed the main corridor in uniform, and white writing on their black T-shirts revealed where they worked: *Sensualiza* Intimate Fashion, it said. All raised their bibles and sachets above their heads simultaneously when prompted by the pastor.[8] Some were exalted, but most showed moderate devotion. I myself was afraid of being easily noticed, when the comment of one of my interlocutors, who preferred to attend that gigantic temple precisely so as not to be disturbed by acquaintances, made sense. I wasn't approached at any point, no matter how suspicious I was of the *obreiros* (labourers) circulating. At first, I ignorantly thought they were security guards. In fact, one of the characteristics of the UCKG is that it doesn't turn away sporadic participants, which

---

6 Fundamental to UCKG's family planning principle, this aspect is emphasised in Love Therapy on Saturdays and Family Therapy on Sundays (Teixeira, 2016).
7 Pierucci had as a reference the electoral bases of Jânio Quadros in the 1985 mayoral election and Paulo Maluf for governor in 1986, which, with some differences, at the time were restricted to the more central areas of the North and East zones.
8 Among the Pentecostal denominations, UCKG is the most liberal. In addition to preaching Teologia da Prosperidade, according to which God reserves financial success, health and fulfilment for true Christians in life, it relaxes some customs that are severely observed by the Pentecostal faithful, such as the use of fashionable clothes, cosmetics, etc (Mariano, 2004).

expands the sacrificial economy to an even larger audience (Mafra et al., 2012). This diversity, far from being exotic, constitutes for Raquel Sant'ana (2017: 25) an 'imagined collectivity', in which "more fluid bonds of identification are possible, capable of giving vent to heterogeneities".

But despite the impersonality, people are there to pray, and their participation is fundamental in creating an atmosphere of optimism when sharing experiences. At the Congress for Success there are three categories that can be mapped out: The call to couples, followed by other groups considered secondary (single people, separated by sex), who cross the aisle in a queue that stretches for many minutes; those who are urged to quickly tell the size of the debt they have paid off; and couples who are invited beforehand to tell their success stories and who have plenty of time to tell them. The previously indebted queue is where there is room for some spontaneity. The bills paid are always in the tens of thousands, but there are moments when expectations are broken, such as a gentleman who replied in a defiant tone "I paid 180", drawing laughter from the pastor, and a young man who claimed to have paid off a debt of 18 million reais, which generated a few seconds of general disbelief.

Successful couples, on the other hand, follow a more standardised script: they walk up the aisle dressed in character, with their appearances aligned, unwavering smiles on their faces and very similar stories of success. There is the man who was addicted to drink and drugs and discovered the church; the woman who married the 'wrong' man, separated, 'fell into the club' and, in the church, solved her sentimental life. These cases reproduce, as Patrícia Birman (2019: 113) observed, religious narratives for testimonies of suffering, "in which the life lived in suffering stands out, in an existence without support, reduced to minimal sociability, since it would also have lost the most naturalised ways of inhabiting its own body", but finally sees entrepreneurial success. It's curious when the subject says that everything worked out for them when "*lacramos* (we sealed the deal) with God".

But conversion is not enough to resolve financial life, and in this case, sacrifice is necessary, which at the beginning could be, for example, the whole of a month's salary. "In the vernacular of the church, the *iurdiano* must insistently seek 'active faith', in other words, he must propose objectives for changing his life, ask God for the change, and sacrifice himself" (Mafra et al., 2012: 85).[9] The implicit message is that it's all for God, and He'll give back twice as much: as they speak, the screens play photos of the blessings the couple have

---

9   The gentilic *iurdiano* comes from the acronym IURD (Igreja Universal do Reino de Deus, UCKG in Portuguese).

received – the façade of the successful company, the house with a swimming pool and new cars in the garage. In another of the testimonies I followed, the husband recounts with a certain calculated shyness that his first tithe was 50 cents (counted in several coins); he then takes an envelope out of the pocket of his sand-coloured blazer and asks the pastor if it wouldn't be inappropriate to reveal the amount of the cheque it contained. He doesn't say, but he's happy to provide a hint: that sacrifice was in the 'six figures'.

It's interesting that messages of prudence are combined with ostentatious displays of wealth, but the pastor's insistence on the intention to make money tries to justify one by the other. In other words, a comfortable life requires rationality, above all the purging oneself of debt, because someone who owes nothing has the right to spend for his own benefit and obviously has more resources for tithing, while a person in debt, on top of everything else, is not a good promoter of religion. Right at the entrance, *obreiros* were handing out flyers for a special session of the Congress for Success, the 'Clamour for the Indebted', an invitation reiterated more than once by Pastor Marcelo. It's the cue for him to introduce the basic rules for the evangelical entrepreneur, which can be learned in chapter 4, verse 3 of the Epistle of James, "You ask and do not receive, because you ask amiss, that you may spend it for your own pleasure".

In one of the photos shown during the testimony, from the posh room of the believer's 'technological solutions' company, a phrase painted on the wall just behind his desk stands out: "I am number 2, because God comes first". Several implicit messages like this occur during the service, one of which is that, on the earthly plane, you come first. There's no question in that space as to what is considered 'success', and a salaried job certainly isn't it. If there's someone between you and God, it's probably your fault, as becomes clear when the pastor discourages the worker from claiming his rights in court, because "you didn't do your part, you didn't help the company grow". At one point, he exhorts the follower, sublimated in the totalising figure of the believing imaginary, to remember "when you had nothing, feet in the mud, riding the bus", because if the subject is living in a comfortable situation at the moment, he shouldn't cling to and settle for what he has, he should continue to seek success, but dedicate it to God.[10] And so the image of public transport emerges as a symbol of humiliation and failure. In his final speech, Pastor Marcelo asked the audience

---

10   Similar situations arise in the context of therapeutic communities, which, although not necessarily Pentecostal, understand their "residents" solely as people "willing to recover". This makes markers such as class, race and gender irrelevant. One resident, Taniele Rui (2010), told me that she didn't need to hide her real name because "our stories are all the same". There, too, the link between addiction and the figure of 'rock bottom' is frequent.

for a credit card. With a believer's magnetic strip in hand, he explained that "as I often say, life is like a credit card". Someone in the audience anticipated his answer, and he laughed, "If you don't use it well, the bill will come", finally completing with the blessing of the *maquininhas* (card machines) that the *obreiros* always carry with them.

With that, "do you want to be equal, or do you want to be different?" – rang out over the loudspeakers, while the screens lit up with the mathematical symbols for 'equal' and 'different'. The pastor, like a self-help speaker, pointed to the latter and repeated the exhortation for the evangelical entrepreneur to succeed. At the end of the Congress for Success, which lasted about an hour and a half, the temple switched off its lights, leaving the surroundings in darkness, and the bus stop on Avenida João Dias was filled with believers with a purpose in their hearts.

5 Family Ties

A few days after my first visit to the Templo da Fé, I returned to the Congress for Success to follow an afternoon session, given by the same pastor Marcelo, but attended by a noticeably different audience, in much smaller numbers. Justifiable, after all, it was the 3:00 pm prosperity service. As soon as I entered, I saw a white tent positioned between the gate and the pavement, where some workers stood and approached pedestrians. I received a copy of *Folha Universal* and went inside, analysing the church's newspaper, circulated in 1.6 million issues, and the cover story about how a young woman had overcome suicide attempts, obviously through faith and the church's counselling. With the auditorium emptier, I was able to position myself closer to the golden pulpit from where the pastor was modulating his speech compared to the lecture a few nights ago, not by chance. In front of a membership that is visibly poorer, blacker and older than the one that attends at 8:00 pm, there is an effort to ensure that the audience doesn't get lost in the script of the service, notable in the countless occasions when Pastor Marcelo repeats the phrase "who understands me, guys?" and variations accompanied by requests for those who were understanding to raise their hands. This ritual would have seemed like a mere tic if it hadn't been for my previous visit to the evening service. On this occasion it was also possible to observe the cameraman following him around the stage, filming him almost always from the bottom up, a remarkable display of professionalism and spectacularisation of faith.

The message about making a difference was present, but with less emphasis. The theme of suicide would come up again for me in the story of a military policeman who had taken his own life, which the pastor referenced several times. The darker tone came with a sense of warning. Unlike the evening service, there was no queue of ex-addicts and only one person made his way to the altar. The unaccompanied man had given up commitments at his company in the city of Bauru to attend the service, where he presented a story very similar to the ones that I saw on my first visit: the young man with the comfortable but unruly lifestyle who, lost in 'nightlife', mistresses and cocaine, reached rock bottom, which in his case culminated in the loss of sight in one eye after a car accident. "Twenty years deceived by the devil," he reflected. Now transformed, he rediscovered his love for his wife and became a successful and faithful businessman, who in a conversation with God decided not to buy the jet-ski he coveted, but instead to buy a bigger car "to take more souls to church". There was one more detail to his story, however. His son, who seemed to be following the same erratic path as his father. "Even though he has the Holy Spirit inside him, he's fighting a war for his son!" the pastor shouted. The message was clear: we're all living through various wars, and we mustn't lose heart, because the devil is lurking and will take advantage of any slight hesitation.

In the theology of spiritual battle, the figure of the devil is responsible for any misfortune, whether public or private, and there is no separation between spiritual or material evils. According to Cecília Mariz (1997), the devil's actions explain individual illnesses and misfortunes, as well as the corruption and misery that affect society as a whole. As there is no such separation, the market is diluted by the same principle. When the man left the stage, the pastor said that he knew him from when he preached in the interior of São Paulo State and had followed his career. "He wasn't a great *obreiro* because he had a lot of money, but because he was a servant," he praised, winning the audience's approval.

It's likely that many unemployed people were at the service at that time. A few seats to my right, a very young couple were praying, the boy with the bleached fringe even more intent. Aware of the poorer audience, Pastor Marcelo was modest in his request for donations, and few went up to the altar to make their contribution (not to be confused with a tithe). "Donate your best," he repeated, and almost at the end he asked for donations of *panettone* for the church's social work with homeless people at Christmas. But that week, lawyer and Presbyterian pastor André Mendonça was approved by the Senado Federal for a position on the Supremo Tribunal Federal, after an intense campaign sponsored by the evangelical caucus. In this context, the pastor couldn't help but bless two of the leaders directly linked to his denomination, pastors Milton Vieira and Wellington Moura, respectively federal and state deputies for the Republicanos, the party of the UCKG.

As can be seen in all the UCKG's visual communication, 'Stop Suffering' is the slogan that informs its manifest purpose, and it was this sentiment that led Aparecida to conversion almost twenty years ago. This thoughtful 58-year-old works most of the time as a domestic worker, but she won't give up on her project to sell homemade chocolate truffles, a business that has given her both joy and anguish and that blends in with her busy family life. From working in the fields in the Northeastern state of Pernambuco to moving between her cramped and crowded house in Interlagos and the upper-middle class condominiums where she works, Aparecida has been moulded by the suffocating routine of looking after her daughters and grandchildren, resolving her husband's confusions, who systematically let her down, and putting money into the house. All of this made Aparecida a bitter person who thought about taking her own life more than once, but who found in the evangelical faith a way out of her suffering, as the slogan promises. The self-help offered by the UCKG has helped to pacify her spirit, but it hasn't entirely eliminated the challenging tone that permeates some moments of her speech, the way she has found to deal with a world that does everything it can to keep her cornered.

"Do you understand?" Aparecida asked several times before I could switch on the recorder for the interview. She wanted to make sure I was really interested and didn't want to make fun of her explanations. As well as echoing the pastor's catchphrase, the sentence was laden with anxiety, conveying the clear feeling that she had already tried to make people like me not see her with prejudice. Understandable, since in the house where she worked, she could hardly get along with her boss, a university professor and ardent defender of science. For her, it's not just a matter of getting her interlocutor to accept her religiosity, but of making him understand the reasons why she chose the church. Aparecida is not a fanatic and doesn't like to be seen that way, but it's not easy to understand her logic, not so much because of the renunciations she makes in her personal life in favour of compliance with the tithe, but precisely because one of the pillars of Teologia da Prosperidade is a heavy anchor for her, her family.

Our first conversation started with an unusual visual component, which first generated laughter, but which served to make Aparecida severely rethink her characterisation of the UCKG: she was wearing a worn-out T-shirt (since she was coming from work) from a competitor church, Bola de Neve. I found this curious and asked her about it, receiving back a reaction that was first gracious and then restrained: "It's not like that at Universal, no!". In other words, her church welcomes everyone "without prejudice" and doesn't impose specific dress code rules, as happens in other Pentecostal denominations. "Even Bishop Macedo said he drinks beer. It's exaggeration that's bad," she warns. In fact, she confirms what specialised literature observes about the flexibilization of customs among the faithful, as we saw earlier. For Aparecida, the church is like a college, "because it talks about everything, like that, about people's lives, from spiritual, financial, life after death, everything". She even attended other churches, but only at the UCKG did she receive retribution, which in this case cost her a Christmas dinner at the Holy Bonfire sacrifice.[11] "But people think it's all about the money," says Aparecida. Her argument indicates that it is precisely the detachment from money that would justify such a sacrifice, which becomes the church's welfare work and which, for her, is what keeps the UCKG growing. "The work is very much in this pandemic, the basic food basket ... they help people a lot, it's just that nobody sees it."

Aparecida was born in Jurema, a municipality with around 20,000 inhabitants in the *sertão* of Pernambuco, into a family of thirteen siblings, and migrated alone to São Paulo at the age of 23. Although she did so to escape poverty, her first feeling in the São Paulo capital was one of regret. In the first house she worked in, in the upper-middle class neighbourhood of Moema, she had to look after three children and her adaptation was difficult, especially to the family's eating habits. Aparecida says she cried a lot and lost weight "until she was a stick", because she hardly ate. She started to get used to it but was still too scared of the big city and going out at night, the only time she had to study. She kept putting it off and only finished secondary school in 2015. "People thinks it's easy, but it's not," he says. Except for a period cleaning a print shop, she has worked as a domestic worker for most of her adult life. She was recently sacked from her teacher's house, where she had been employed for the last seven years, but she made a deal with them and continues to clean there as a *diarista* three times a week. The long relationship with her bosses makes Aparecida look back on her history with regret, analysing above all the different choices they made. On the farm, she says she was always a 'hard worker' and earned her money, but she couldn't accept the situation any longer. "I wanted to change, but only when I got here, I think I stood still for a while, I didn't really go after university." Today, she reflects that she would have done things differently.

A few years after arriving in São Paulo, Aparecida got married. Her goal of studying grew more and more distant as the gale of family events thwarted her plans. In the small house where she lives in Interlagos, her husband, their

---

11   Israel's Holy Bonfire takes place twice a year with an intense call to the faithful to write their requests for blessings on papers that are then supposedly taken to Israel by pastors from the UCKG. There they build a bonfire with these requests. The justification for the campaign is the symbolic exchange of material goods for the blessing of the bonfire.

two daughters (aged 26 and 28) and four grandchildren, whom she looks after when she's not working, share the space. Her eldest daughter became pregnant at an early age, her ex-husband had drug problems and beat her often; some time ago she got a job as a manicurist in a well-known chain of beauty salons, "but she's not good spiritually". Aparecida tried to get her to join the church when things were worse – before her current job, she went through a series of difficulties – and she accepted for a while, before she started working in a friend's father's cafeteria.

"Boy, when the devil rules, he rules, right?" The girl started dating her friend's brother, who was in prison for murder (trying to be discreet, Aparecida lowers her voice and makes a gun sign with her hand) and became pregnant again during an intimate visit. The four-year-old boy particularly irritates Aparecida. "The boy is annoying, he's whiny, gee, he's even sick … he doesn't eat properly." Regarding her daughter, she also expresses her discontent, amplified by the fact that she has left the church. She says she has high blood pressure. "She's just nervous, has no patience with the kids", doesn't help out around the house and has gained weight. For Aparecida, this is the result of envy at her good professional fortune. "It's a shame, isn't it? But what can I do? She was following, she left [the church], she went off to make a life for herself".

These are feelings that Aparecida tries to stifle, along with her dissatisfaction with the whole arrangement of the house, justified by the autonomy of her daughter who, after all, "fell into temptation" and chose the wrong path. But if the path is chosen, shouldn't Aparecida also bear the consequences of her own? She was on the verge of exploding long before her daughter's episode, when she became depressed and considered very drastic solutions. The fact is that her most important choice to date continues to mould her present and introduces mistrust into her private life, namely, that of marrying (and, above all, staying married) "to someone who cheated on me from the start. He's still a liar. I don't even know why I'm still with him, he's been in the church since I went, but he won't convert, he's someone you can't trust." Aparecida says she became bitter, sad and angry. Diagnosed with depression, she took anxiolytics on medical advice, which aggravated her instability. "My God, how can I take this? I took this medicine and I'm already like this! Then I wanted a place that would take that away, that I could feel peace and joy. I felt it at Universal, you know?". So, despite listing a series of magical rewards for his participation in the Holy Bonfire, such as the disappearance of debts, the conversion's main contribution to his life was to pacify relationships at home, in other words, to keep them at a level that was sufficiently manageable at the limit of eruption, in favour of family unity, which is essential for the church's discourse.

It was in her post-conversion life that Aparecida idealised what could have been her way out of poverty – the homemade chocolate truffle business. She doesn't have the required university education, and in São Paulo "if you don't have an education, a university degree, you can't do well here. You can't win because how are you going to win earning a salary, working in a family home?" Aparecida saw a completely different life in her own business, encouraged also by her second daughter, who has a talent for sweets and for whom "your success is in the truffles, but you want to stay working for others". She proudly tells of the quality of her sweets, which were much appreciated even by the wealthy families she worked for. Her husband also had a chance to prosper by cooking for others – he had experience in the kitchen having worked in a snack bar – but, in Aparecida's words, he received guidance from God and didn't know how to seize the moment: "You didn't know how to do anything," she says referring to her husband. "It was from 'there' that God opened the doors and gave you a direction and when you're growing up, you see the money, you set your heart on the money and you forget that it was God who opened the doors for you, and you move away from there; that's what happened to my husband."

Her best phase, she says, was when she did evangelisation in the *favelas*, "because when you do something for God, you feel peace", but again her husband, jealous, made her leave the activity. This fear appears at every moment in her speech and conditions her own faith, because "envy is something spiritual" and can turn into 'witchcraft' and *'macumba'*. Afraid of gossip, she left the smaller churches closer to her home to attend the temple on João Dias, where she feels anonymous. "Not everyone is a child, but we're all God's creatures, right? And everyone has a talent and there you discover what your talent is." Aparecida believes that through obedience to God it's possible to get rid of curses, and in the case of the prosperity that didn't come, the Congress for Success helped her transform the anger she had against her family into an entrepreneurial mindset, and redirect this feeling towards the world of work. "The first thing the pastor said to me was 'God doesn't want you to be an employee, God wants you to be an entrepreneur, God wants you to be the head and not the tail'." In fact, this is the revolutionary step of neo-Pentecostalism, as observed by Mafra et al. (2012), which incidentally feeds back into the UCKG's own discourse of persecution and reaction to the injustices committed against the church and its leader Edir Macedo, and which is also evident in Aparecida's testimony.[12]

---

12 Mafra et al. (2012) analyse Edir Macedo's own trajectory as the result of traumatic events, which prompted in him a reaction against what he saw as injustice. With this foundation of nonconformity, he developed his pastoral project.

When I met Aparecida again, she kept her promise to bring me a book that would answer aspects of theology that she thought she hadn't been able to clarify for me. The book, which had a black cover with gold lettering, followed the same pattern as the self-help books you see in bookshops, and had the suggestive title *50 Shades of Success: Advice for a Prosperous Life*. Its author, Bishop Jadson Edington, is an entrepreneur, speaker and 'prosperity expert', and was the creator of the Congress for Success. Leafing through the book, I noticed several quotes attributed to Macedo and the Old Testament, as well as the preface signed by Bishop Clodomir Santos, presenter of a television programme on Rede Record, the TV channel owned by the UCKG. In one of the '50 tones' that make up the book, Edington refers to the "power of conscious revolt", in which he encourages non-conformity in the face of injustice. "Revolt is not a primary cause, it is a consequence. It arises from a person's vision of God's greatness. You know that He is very great, so you understand that you can't conform to anything that isn't compatible with Him" (2015, p. 87). Therefore, "it makes no sense", says the bishop, to accept a life of subordination.

"How can I be passive in the face of a humiliating life?" asks Edington in the book. Symptomatically, the main function Aparecida sees in wage labour is to keep her subordinate, stunting true individual talent and chaining the poor worker to this condition.[13] "Working for others you can't win, can you? And God showed me that," says Aparecida. This is an aspect emphasised by the UCKG, which harks back to the lessons of the Old Testament (Côrtes, 2017). Aparecida finds her potential diminished and feels attacked by the envy of others, which erodes any confidence in those around her. This, counterintuitively, traps her in a situation of mere survival management, because she can't give up her family either, which is both a source of suffering and her only strength. The evangelical discourse of prosperity stimulates her rebellion, but she doesn't know who she should rebel against, because class conflict exists outside of her symbolic universe, which is rejected by the church. She makes an effort to spare her employers, who didn't sacrifice themselves at the Holy Bonfire, but live comfortably, nonetheless. For Aparecida, they prepared themselves, they invested in 'study', revealing that a certain form of submission present in popular culture, a divide between those who own the competent discourse and those who don't, is still present to maintain the structures of class society.

There is, however, a little mischief that she allows herself, and that deep down reveals not only a social reality, but also a project disseminated in

---

13   As Lima (2007: 147) observes, "in opposition not only to unemployment, but also to employment, which is unanimously assessed there as something that 'has had enough', because it is a source of 'little life, misery, humiliation' and 'living cramped in transport'".

homeopathic doses by the theology she follows, that of a slow and implacable penetration through the pores of society. Commenting again on the house where she works, Aparecida notes that all the cleaners and nannies who have worked there have been evangelicals. "Sometimes the bosses don't like [talking about religion]. They're unbelievers. But only people from the church come here, right? It is what it is".

6 God Willing

Certain terms that permeate the daily lives of the working classes sometimes seem exaggerated to those who are unfamiliar with their misfortunes. Seeing social reproduction there as a struggle, in which some people survive and others don't, can sound violent and ideological. This is the fruit of a society that is above all alienated from civilising assumptions, manipulated by the culture industry, the interests of the ruling classes and the opportunism of politicians, and interested in maintaining a population who is frightened and subservient to those above and demobilised in their class consciousness. All of this can be seen when we switch on the TV, radio or some social network and follow the infamies that thicken contemporary entertainment. But that only tells part of the story. In reality, it is in a certain brutality present in social relations that are born out of and perpetuated by inequalities, that the insecurity, suffering and resentment overflows. It is in the world of work that this bitterness is revealed, where popular experience also takes root, as in Carolina Maria de Jesus' (2014) account of her life in the *favela*, surrounded by jealous neighbours, domestic violence, broken homes and little hope of escape.

In his dialectic of order and disorder, it escaped Antonio Candido (1970) that, when read through a materialist lens, the peaceful coexistence that seems to characterise that utopia of the guiltless society he illustrates in the classic of Brazilian literature *Memórias de um sargento de milícias*, actually depends on an 'attenuation of the empire of actuality', in which the limits of a perception of (Brazilian popular) culture as opposed to – or overcoming – capitalism, are shown (Schwarz, 2002: 151). In this section, order and disorder are shuffled not as the utopian contribution of a peripheral nation to the post-capitalist world, but as different moments of oppression, in which entrepreneurship appears as an alternative to subjugation.

Another word that has become fashionable in self-help literature and on social media loses its euphemistic and advertising character when we follow the trajectory of people like Estela. In physics, 'resilience' means 'elasticity'. In its figurative sense, it refers to the ability to bounce back easily or adapt to bad luck or change. When someone comes across the easy smile of this 61-year-old lady from Pernambuco, they can hardly imagine the mountain of suffering she has been through and how she continues to have faith in a better life despite it. In her story, people, events and places are mixed together, tragedies are narrated as if they were commonplace or the result of mere bad luck. To revisit her interview is agonising: when you barely recovered from the last stab, a new one hits, and so it goes for more than two hours. It's tempting to attribute her misfortunes to chance, to mysterious designs that, after all, she herself seems to believe in as a convinced evangelical. But the truth that overflows from her words have much more to do with real people than with deities.

Estela started working in Recife when she was just eight years old, in a job whose terrible conditions would lead her early into the heart of darkness. Her father worked at the National Institute for Colonisation and Agrarian Reform (INCRA). There, he met the family of a foreman who a few months earlier had gained a daughter and needed someone to help with the housework. Hiding this from her mother, her father took Estela out of the house and sold her to the couple. For her, this was the beginning of an agony that would last six months. Estela spent this time in private prison, she was fed precariously, surviving only on bean soup and stale bread, no meat or milk, and she could barely bathe. "I couldn't shout because they would hit me with a whip, like it was during the dictatorship, you know? In the time of slavery, really." She was beaten and fought hard to avoid being abused by the man. She cleverly sent her mother a letter telling her what had happened to her, and that's how she managed to be freed. "My father sold me for a litre of *cachaça*," she concludes, with a look that lost its innocence a long time ago.

It was indeed the time of the dictatorship. When she was 16, Estela moved to São Paulo, settled in Jardim Ângela and has been back and forth ever since. She also lived in Rio de Janeiro for 11 years, working in the home of a Polish couple. As soon as she returned to São Paulo, she went to work in the house of a 'Japanese lady' and stayed there for a year. "But it was suffering, as they say … because she put me under a lot of pressure, I worked too much, and it didn't pay off". During this time, she returned to Recife and spent a season working for an elderly couple in São José dos Campos, in the countryside. She went back to São Paulo for the third time and did nails and hair at home until she started working for a middle-class household in Pinheiros as a domestic worker.

Estela is also a manicurist and hairdresser. Side-lined during the COVID-19 pandemic, she received emergency aid and returned to the same house as a *diarista* when the health crisis subsided, but she had only 50 reais left over to pay the household bills. One day she baked a cake for a friend from church, who since then has been ordering cakes from her, and this spread among the other

Assembly of God 'brothers'. At the time of the interview, Estela was trying to get her cake-making back on track, with the help of WhatsApp and Instagram that a grandson managed for her, after a period of only cooking lunchboxes for the employees of a firm near her home in Parque Ipê.

Nearby there is a church that she attends four times a week. The largest Pentecostal denomination in the country with over 12 million followers, the Assembly of God (AD) has become synonymous with popular religiosity.[14] According to Almeida (2004), it is a characteristic of the AD to be based in areas of great social vulnerability and to be close to the homes of the faithful. This implies a much closer relationship of sociability between them and the constitution of a certain network of protection from which Estela benefits, which is very different from the UCKG model we saw earlier. Until she converted, she was Catholic and, although she enjoyed the *forró* parties, she decided that she needed the therapeutic order promoted by the Protestant religion. "It's the word and the teaching that it has, it's completely different from Catholic things. In the Catholic religion we can drink, we can smoke, we can party and in the evangelical religion we can't, in the evangelical religion you don't drink, you don't smoke, you don't go to parties, you don't listen to music like that". But this need for discipline in her personal life didn't come about by chance.

Her story of countless ups and downs could seem trivial, one more story of daily struggles with husbands, children and grandchildren, sometimes worse, sometimes better, but contained within certain class limits that hold her in a manageable poverty that never lets her rise up the social ladder. The point is that, in her case, the story is always interspersed with picturesque episodes, which further emphasise her resilience. As a domestic worker in Pernambuco, Estela was registered, but when she tried to retire she discovered that her employers there hadn't collected her pension fund and had already died, so she would still have to work for another eight years. "I've worked so hard that I've been cheated, you see?". She spent some time in Olinda, after leaving Rio

---

14   The Assembly of God (AD) was the second Pentecostal church to emerge in Portugal, after the Christian Congregation, both founded in the 1910s. Its initial followers were lay-people who were marginalised, resistant to theological scholarship and with modest social aspirations. Over time, the AD became institutionalised and created divisions, the first of which was between the original preachers from Sweden and the rise of 'presiding pastors' and 'headquarters churches', independent of the others. It received a lot of North American influence, including resources for the creation of the Publishing House of the Assembly of God (CPAD), AD's publishing house, in the 1940s. From 1988 onwards, the power struggles between the groups grew, which in turn stimulated the expansion of the denomination and made it more like the population in which it was introduced (Alencar, 2010).

de Janeiro to look after her mother with leukaemia, opened a restaurant in her own home and was mugged. She stopped; she didn't want to live in the Northeastern state that brought back so many bad memories. But the main tragedy she experienced in those corners would appear in her account almost by chance, related to a son who doesn't work because he 'suffered an accident there' and retired early.

The 'accident' was actually a crime that was motivated, according to Estela, by envy. Her young son had a *brega* band and dreamed of becoming a footballer. He and two of his band mates took part in a trial together at the Náutico club, one of the main football clubs in Pernambuco; he succeeded, but one of them failed, and his reaction was to try to end the life of Estela's son. At Estela's request, her boss at the time dismissed her. "She came and let me go, gave me my bills, then I stayed at home to look after him because I couldn't afford it and he needed a lot of attention". The boy was hospitalised for six months, his trachea atrophied and since then he has lived from bed to wheelchair.

It's a well-known story in the peripheries – that of the dedicated son who dreams of succeeding in life in order to repay the struggles of the mother who took care of her offspring on her own. This story holds many parallels to that of João Vicente, for example, which we'll see in the third chapter. Estela and her son would perhaps have written a different tale of a mother and son who hold on tightly to each other and, together, create extraordinary solutions that leverage the trajectory of both. At the age of 17, the boy had only taken the first step, crossed the first barrier to become a professional footballer, one of the few chances of true social ascension in Brazil.[15] But success and failure coexist tragically, and the violence that surrounds the success of some and the failure of others sometimes finds perverse syntheses. He wasn't drafted into a war, nor did he, in fact, suffer an 'accident' as Estela suggests: The very realisation of his dream was the trigger for his trauma, seen by others as extravagance and injustice and making him the victim of a context of extreme suffering and narcissism.

In the Northeast, Estela also worked as a street vendor for a while in Porto de Galinhas, where she sold hot dogs, chips, popcorn, peanuts, ice water, soft drinks, coconut water and cigarettes. She took some courses while she was in Pernambuco, in cooking and even one in accounting "to occupy the mind, but it didn't do any good". But what she learned she only keeps in her memory, because she lost her certificates and handouts in a flood. "I was left with

---

15   An admirable representation of the cruelty and popular utopia that coexist in the fascination with a football career can be seen in the feature film "Linha de Passe", directed by Daniela Thomas and Walter Salles in 2008.

nothing, we even lost our clothes, because it was so sudden, you know? It was a hurricane, it took everything, I lost everything, even the ladybirds that my children were raising." So she decided to move back to São Paulo. Her first husband died, and she remarried, "a guy who just wanted to suck me dry", but unlike Aparecida, she sent him away. Without a bank account, she was robbed again by her own colleague who lived with her. Finally, tired of struggling, she decided to convert to Pentecostalism and started making cakes around the same time. She says she lost a lot of products in the beginning, as the business itself was quite amateurish. "I'm not going to lie to you, I lost a lot, a lot because people asked for them and didn't go and get them, you know? That's when the cakes stayed at home". The pastor encouraged her not to give up and she doesn't lose her good humour when she says that she gained weight eating the leftover cakes.

Estela also has a daughter at home who "doesn't know how to make anything, not even coffee". Her other daughter works in a bakery, and as if working were a punishment, she was the victim of a mugging when she was on her way to work in the morning, a 'dirty little pothead' who cornered her, and physically and verbally assaulted her. The psychological trauma left by what happened has never dissipated and hangs over the family like a ghost, encouraging a new escape from the reality suffered. With all the experience of someone who has been through almost everything, Estela sees no simple solution and realises that moving house again would only make them start from scratch, perhaps in a worse situation. Family arrangements are then necessary to avoid new forms of violence, which end up becoming security practices and discourses. The husband started taking the girl to and from the bakery every day.

In Estela's confusing timeline, the same events seem to come and go, and a certain effort is required to integrate them into her story. For example, her accounts of robberies are very common, and the content develops in a similar way: she starts a business, it does well for a while, further fuelling her entrepreneurial ambition; then there's a robbery in which she loses everything and has to start again. It's this cyclical nature of the lives of the poor that we see here, but with each turn a new layer of scepticism and the desire to close the doors to the rest of the world, to live only for herself and her family. Another round of discouragement was to follow: before returning to her current occupation as a *diarista*, Estela set up a breakfast stall near a police station, which didn't prevent her from being robbed again, this time at gunpoint. No one helped her at the time, and she racked up another loss of 2300 reais, all her earnings and those of her niece with whom she shared the stall and to whom she owed as much, without the interest.

"As I told you, I need the table to put it on, to sell on the street. There's no problem, shame is taking what isn't yours, you're mixing with the wrong crowd and getting slapped in the face, I think that's what's shameful, you know?" justifies Estela, adding a layer of distinction to her narrative. "But if you set up a table in the street, put up a white tablecloth and put things out there to sell, I go to work happy because I know I'm selling something that people will like." Since the last robbery, the church gives her a basic food basket every month and rewards her for cleaning the place.

The delirious sequence of falls and new beginnings contained in Estela's story cannot be minimised, but it begins to take on the tones of deep anguish as her age starts to weigh on her and cloud her future. Her plans to 'start a business' are contaminated by the uncertainty of someone who may be reaching her limit. She says she has wanted to take an entrepreneurship course but felt held back by her age. "I've thought about it, you know? I think a lot about my life from now on, but there are times when I'm so anxious … I mean, I'm already 61, where am I going to go from here? What am I going to achieve? There was another fact she hadn't mentioned: Estela has a tumour in her head, which required 28 weeks of radiotherapy and deprived her of the sight in her right eye. She also has diabetes and for a while she had to pay for her own medication and that of her daughter, who had to have one of her breasts removed, because former mayor João Dória had cut the drug distribution programme. His successor Bruno Covas resumed the programme and was viewed with sincere admiration by Estela: the then-mayor was at the time battling cancer of the digestive tract. "He's a winner just like us because he has this cancer, and I believe in Jesus that he will win," she cheered. Covas died in May 2021 at the age of 41.

Estela's trajectory accumulates events that, on their own, would be immensely traumatic for any individual, and she has withstood them all. Her is a lifetime of hard labour that has been rewarded with pain in all its dimensions. And now that there is no more justice for Estela, that her children can barely walk on their own feet, she is finally beginning to fade, to show signs of exhaustion, her hope is beginning to fail. She insists to her reluctant son-in-law that they open a restaurant together, and the pastor tells her not to give up. At this point, she only has one goal.

"That's it, that's my life," Estela concludes. "I don't have a father, I don't have a mother, my sisters all live far away, I only have one who lives here in Jundiaí, the other lives in Rio de Janeiro, the other is an entrepreneur – she has a beauty salon in Porto de Galinhas – and I'm going to set up my restaurant. God will help me, I will do it, I can do it, before I die I can do it."

7 Uncertainty

Fear permeated my visit to Parelheiros in mid-2021. I arrived in the neighbourhood in the morning, a few months after my first visits, and got off the bus at the entrance to Vargem Grande, a short distance away from the commercial hubbub, but still with its establishments: a building materials shop, one or two bars, a pizzeria, mechanics' workshops and a wide variety of evangelical churches. I went to a tiny snack bar tucked away in the garage of the nice couple who worked there, helping myself to sweetened coffee, the only kind available, and bread with butter while I waited for my appointment with Ronaldo, a security guard and app driver who had been recommended to me by Renato. I was reluctant to go to his house, as the property was not numbered and in fact looked like several. In the unfinished, autoconstructed house, the corridor on the second floor seemed to lead to other dwellings, so I went out to ask for him, only to be greeted by an unfriendly dog standing at the door, who got annoyed when I clapped my hands calling for his owner. It turned out to be the right house, and Ronaldo came out to answer me and chase away the animal, which belonged to the neighbour.

But as soon as I took my first step inside, still not familiar with the place and watching the neighbour's dog retreat, another decorative detail caught my attention. On the small bookshelf facing the door, suspiciously positioned with the cover forward to cover the books behind it, a half-crumpled edition of *Esquerda Caviar*, an anti-PT bestseller by right-wing journalist Rodrigo Constantino, was on display welcoming me. Purposefully positioned that way or not, the book would accompany me throughout the conversation. Completing the scene in the cramped room were dozens of picture frames and the interlocutor showing a certain anxiety with his leg swinging and his hand lightly tapping the table as he spoke.

Ronaldo speaks very little, hardly smiles and stares at his interlocutor, creating a certain discomfort. He is 36, married, has a stepson and two daughters from another relationship. Born in São Paulo, he moved to Vargem Grande ten years ago, just when he met his current wife. He says he appreciates the neighbourhood's country atmosphere, surrounded by the Atlantic Forest. "There's a bus that you get on at the Varginha terminal, you go on a trip like that at the weekend, it's cool, it's ecotourism, right? I've never been, but I also follow it on social media, it's cool." He says there are waterfalls in the forest, but he hasn't been there either. Having only completed primary school, Ronaldo signed up for the National Exam for the Certification of Competences of Young People and Adults (ENCCEJA) a few years ago, but although he found the exam 'very interesting' he didn't pass, according to him, because he was overworked.

He earns below two minimum wages in his job as a security guard and, unable to make ends meet, he started driving for the ridesharing apps Uber and 99 a few months ago, but couldn't say how much he made from it, "because I haven't found myself on the street yet". He had been with the security company for around four years. Before that, he was a bus collector for around seven years, but at the co-operative he wasn't registered and earned a daily wage of 50 reais, from Sunday to Sunday. "It was a bit stressful, man, a bit stressful. During the week it was a lot, five, six journeys every day," he says.

For the last eleven years he has worked between one little company and another, with his first job in security for a pharmacy. After taking a professional training course to become a security guard, Ronaldo remains in a job he apparently doesn't like, and is looking for ways out. One way out is to work as a driver, and another, which is still hypothetical, is to take a course as a veterinary assistant. According to him, surveillance is an area that is 'dying out', with most of the staff being replaced by electronic gatekeepers and access controllers. His dissatisfaction comes from the horizon of unemployment that he seems to be moving towards, and which he blamed at the time, to Constantino's disappointment, on then-president Bolsonaro.

During Lula's first administration, Ronaldo worked for two companies at the same time. "In the security area you could work in three companies, two companies at night, 12 hours, and during the day as a lunch boy," he says, wistfully remembering the possibility of working endless hours. His way of explaining the problem of the 'extinction' of the property surveillance area is confusing: it has to do firstly with the evolution of technologies, then with the economic crisis and, eventually, with the COVID-19 pandemic. When asked, he admits that the multitude of commercial and industrial establishments that closed down because of health measures may have had an impact on the area, but he isn't entirely convinced.

As he spoke, I looked for ways to uncover his signals. As our meeting was mediated by Renato, a well-known left-wing activist in the neighbourhood, this must have influenced the way Ronaldo behaved towards me. But Constantino was still there and at one point I asked him if he had a reading habit, at which point he seemed to look specifically at the book. "I'm very relaxed, but reading, reading, any kind of book to read ... I'm a bit short of time, I've got a lot of books, there are some books there, you know?" he replied, analysing my reactions just as I analysed his. One might consider that a higher demand for private security is not necessarily positive. In any case, although Ronaldo is unhappy with the country's economic situation and evaluates it ambiguously, there is a structuring feeling that is more explanatory and that also mirrors his personal difficulties, which is scepticism. With his entry into the world of platform capitalism (Abílio, 2020), other worries have arisen and have further highlighted his anxiety about how to deal with them, since neither his job as a security guard nor as an app driver alone would be enough to pay his bills.

His entry into the world of transport apps "came out of the blue", according to him, emphasising once again the uncertain fates to which these precarious workers are subject. Through Facebook, Ronaldo came into contact with an employee of a used car agency, who approached him and convinced him that his score was high enough to buy a car. But this was not the case: Ronaldo was unable to pay the instalments on time. In addition, the car had mechanical problems and while it was being repaired, Ronaldo couldn't work for the apps. His income from his job as a security guard was already compromised. "Then it got late, I've got this car under 'search and seizure', I'm going to see if I go for it, abusive interest, you know?" Ronaldo speculates about the possibility of resolving his debt in court.

Though his car is in need of repair, Ronaldo continues to drive and even offered me a lift. Situations of uncertainty lead to the individual's withdrawal in the face of the immense transformations brought about by the development of technology and managerial rationality, of which 'gig economy' is the latest case. Ronaldo's smartphone manipulates the boundaries between legal and illegal so that he can continue driving. When asked about the safety requirements of the apps, he summarised them as 'mask and alcohol gel'. The devaluation of practical experience in the generational break is compounded by the instability of the world of work in this century, in which insecurity has become a recurring feeling. His increasingly diluted subjectivity in these worlds of extreme individualism and uncertainty is the opposite of what is found among the neighbourhood's small traders, who are fully integrated into the community dynamic. For Ronaldo, it's down to a few services and a few leisure activities that take place there and that he barely mentions, even though he finds it all 'very interesting'.

But it's when he reconstructs his youth that Ronaldo reveals the conflicts he tries so hard to disguise. During his school days in the town of Diadema (where his family still lives), he says he was 'a bit of a daredevil', but his self-description ended up evolving into 'terrible' and 'a bit of a terrorist'. He used to get into trouble a lot, but he says he misses it because "I have my friends, my mates, it was really nice, right? There were parties at school, it was good, it was really nice. Nowadays you don't see any of that, nowadays it's all more," which leads the conversation directly to his children – a 15-year-old boy and a 13-year-old girl – and the relationship that gave birth to them and that made him, he claims, leave school to work – a minor problem compared to their mother, who was only 14 when the first was born. Ronaldo says they need to be watched because 'everything is free there' on social media, but pornography is what particularly worries him. His reasoning strongly suggests something that recurs among my interlocutors in this age group, a feeling of nostalgia. The presence of teenage children thus becomes a trigger for more reactionary opinions, and typically contemporary phenomena that didn't exist in their youth, such as social networks, are perceived as uncontrollable devices of perversion.

However, the conversation still held novelties. Ronaldo's youth was somewhat more complicated, his nostalgia is hardly justified and the reason for his vigilance when it comes to his offspring is his own past choices, always more difficult to self-evaluate. Around 2013, Ronaldo was working seven days a week in transport and his children were born. Now out of his teens, he experienced moments of tension that he could only resolve by abusing drugs and alcohol. His wife finally left him, and he fell into depression, worsening his addiction. He went through rehabilitation clinics "that just doped us up and left us there". In the last one, he spent 45 days, met his current wife and his life took another turn: he gave up his addictions and "came out focussed on what is right". In the end, his story makes him re-evaluate his friendships at the time. "I learned a lot, man. I left there, where are my club friends? Where are my drug friends? None of them came to the house to ask 'Does your son need a nappy? Milk?' No-one came".

Ronaldo had also been attending the Apostolic Church of Faith in Guarulhos, more than 70 kilometres north from Vargem Grande. For him, "everything in the Bible is here, what's happening in the world," he explains. He reproduces what Taniele Rui (2010: 57) identified in another context as "a discursive link between 'drugs', criminality, lack of control and self-destruction". Ronaldo says that he tries to talk to his children, give them instructions and encourage them to play with real things. It is remarkable, however, how he endeavours to make it believable. The kids live with their mum a long way away and his work routine is impressive: he's on surveillance from 7pm until 7am the next day, leaves with the apps switched on to drive until late afternoon, when he 'collects the car'. Too many uncertainties surround his life, from the car being searched and seized, to a possible relapse into drugs, unemployment due to the crisis in the private surveillance sector, and his children, for whom he would like to be a good example. At least in this case, he's already spoken to their mother and the boy will soon get his work card.

8   Know-How

Almost a year after my first participant observation on the Projeto Rede pitch, the whole world was shaken by the COVID-19 pandemic. In February 2020, sparse news about the virus that had emerged in the Chinese city of Wuhan appeared here and there, but everyday life in São Paulo was business as usual just over a month before the first cases appeared in the city. The would-be entrepreneurs I met at the time saw the opportunity with great enthusiasm and projected hope for the future, though these plans didn't materialise as imagined. Fast-forward to 2021, and I'm back in touch with some of them while the pandemic is still raging, but with the isolation measures no longer effective in the popular territories – a large part of the population, with more or less precaution, had returned to their normal routine. The situation among the project participants was more complicated, as their businesses were still poorly structured, and absorbing the lessons of the course was no simpler than baking cakes, pies and *acarajés*, which, by the way, they already knew how to do very well.

Within certain limits of class and geographical origin, there was a range of experiences in the food business that were curiously homogenised in that space, so that individuals could differentiate themselves within the terms proposed by the Rede instructors. This was a place for people who really wanted a gateway to entrepreneurship, and the course promised them the intellectual tools to do so. The would-be entrepreneurs had to go through a selection process, which is done by lottery as the demand is quite high, and there is also a participation fee. When they get there, they are introduced to the terminology of innovation, learn how to use basic administration and accounting tools and how to carry out the SWOT (Strengths, Weaknesses, Opportunities and Threats) analysis of business planning. Finally, the last step is to define and present the product, which of course must be innovative. This is where the ideology comes in, subjugating popular knowledge, combining random terms like 'guerrilla' and 'affection' and mixing homemade cuisine with vegan versions of popular dishes.

It was only with his second attempt that Geraldo managed to get accepted. When I was invited to evaluate his prototype he had prepared for his *acarajé* business, a ball of bean batter fried in palm oil, I was struck by the charisma of this 61-year-old from Bahia, who has lived in São Paulo since 1976. His smile framed by his grey beard could only compete with the equally friendly face of his wife Soraia, who accompanied him throughout his journey through the entrepreneurship course and acted as Geraldo's pitch hostess.

After the presentations, we were offered lunch in the Rede cafeteria, where I was able to sit down with the couple. The meal was simple and honest, the same as that offered to the children and teenagers who attend the school, which operates under an agreement with the town hall. Geraldo told me about how he prepared his *acarajé* and Soraia showed me on her smartphone her work as a presenter on an auditorium programme for a community TV channel. She had used this experience to line up the pitch. In fact, not only did I maintain a vivid memory from that day, but when I contacted them a year later, I received their warm agreement to chat.

Geraldo's life was almost entirely unpaid; he started working in the street markets at the age of 12 in the interior of Bahia. Between jokes and melancholy, he recounts his days at the market, first setting up the stalls while it was still dark and then selling water, "but it wasn't bottled water like it is here. We used to put the bottles to freeze in the neighbours' houses, because the heat in Bahia is hellish, it's really hot there!". He would also carry people's shopping for extra cash, depending on the distance. And that's how Geraldo already had what he calls 'a certain independence', a notable characteristic of the passage from childhood to youth in the popular world, in which parents sweat to guarantee the basics and the young person, in his process of individuation, looks for alternatives to have an income of his own with which he can buy a pair of trainers or a cap. It's a typical trajectory that endures, even if it is challenged by other forms of quick access to the world of consumption.

It was curious and a little exasperating to follow his story with Soraia by his side, scolding him when he seemed to go on too long. His wife, who is from the neighbouring town of Osasco, was especially attentive when he talked about Bahia and how much he missed his homeland, where his mother, who is about to turn 90, still lives. But Geraldo is a realist and understands a life built up in São Paulo is not easy to change, especially for himself, who can't count on a quiet retirement, so entrepreneurship seems like a predictable way out. His 33-year-old son works with him in construction and has given him a granddaughter, aged two and a half at the time, who he helps financially. More than four decades after his arrival, he still sees opportunities in the São Paulo capital that he wouldn't have had in the Northeastern state: "I often say that whatever you earn here, you earn more than in Bahia, because if you go out in the street to collect cans, you can get there at the end of the day and buy a can of oil, a kilo of rice, a small piece of sausage or something along those lines".

As soon as he arrived in São Paulo, he went to work as a bus collector, and did so for a year and seven months. At the same time, he learned to make *acarajé* and other typical African-inspired foods with his *família-de-santo* with whom he travelled to the Southeast. When the family's mother died, Geraldo went to live on his own: "He had to struggle along his way".[16] He settled in Taboão da Serra and, at the age of 17, began working as a bricklayer, his main occupation to this day, along with painting, texturing and flooring. "I work in construction, that's my income. In my spare time I run the kitchen like nobody else," he says with his usual broad smile. As a master builder, Geraldo works on temporary contract and despite the heavy workload, he doesn't complain about his livelihood. "Because this job pays off my debts, I can put food in my house and every now and then I can have fun somewhere, take my family, my wife, my son, so I like what I do."

Geraldo's modest ambitions seem to contrast with his belated initiative to find a new occupation. His trajectory is typical and at the same time particular, combining immigration from the Northeast to São Paulo with religiosity. In other words, his displacement wasn't just about looking for work. He learned how to cook with his *família-de-santo*, and around 1999 he decided to sell his *acarajé*, only in the vicinity of his home and in a non-professional way. To realise his goal of starting a business in the kitchen, Geraldo relied on his in-depth knowledge of African cuisine, which he had accumulated since his youth, and the praise of those who had already tasted his talent. So, the decision to migrate would have unexpected consequences for him, and many decades later he would see in that same religious justification the core of a new chance to turn it into a source of income and a more peaceful old age.

Bahia is known for its religious syncretism, where over the centuries popular Catholicism has been intertwined by religions of African origin brought by the enslaved. In the capital Salvador, on December 4, there is a big event in honour of the figure of Iansã, an orisha revered by both Candomblé devotees and Catholics (who know her as Santa Barbara). In the tradition of the former, it is customary to make *acarajé* as an offering. The magical element gives Pai Geraldo's *acarajé* a special character, a title he assumes both in the *terreiro* and for commercial purposes. But it was only a few years ago that he decided to turn this practical knowledge into an enterprise, and this was also the result of family pressure to overcome what they saw as a limitation in him. That is, his supposed unwillingness to intellectually operate a business of his own. It is this gap that the Projeto Rede courses have filled. "I wanted to do this course to perfect what I already knew how to do. For example, I didn't know how much

---

16   According to Reginaldo Prandi (2004), it is common in religions of African origin, notably Candomblé and Umbanda, for *famílias-de-santo* (saint-families) to break up with the death of the father or mother-of-saint, usually because the civil heirs of the *terreiro* are not interested in its continuity or even because of succession disputes.

my *acarajé* cost, the cost-benefit ratio, I didn't know how much I was spending and how much profit I made. Today I know how much my *acarajé* costs".

Soraia, his partner for 35 years, was present at almost every weekly meeting, so that Geraldo wouldn't be put off by the intimidating world that was opening up to him. But she herself has a struggling life, which began with a forced retirement from her old job as a nursing assistant. Aged 57 at the time of the interview, Soraia oozes friendliness with a little malice, and her life story hardly seems to belong to the same person. For her to live in good health today, proudly showing off as a model and TV presenter (she prefers the title 'CEO'), she had to go through years of deep sadness and hopelessness. It was in the same Campo Limpo neighbourhood as the Rede that she suffered an accident in 1996 that would change her life forever. Inside the ambulance in which she worked as a rescue worker (a public service known as Samu), she fell and hit one of her knees; she returned a week later and realised that it was much more serious than she had imagined. "At first it was a fall, I hit my knee, I stayed at home for a week, when I came back to work, I couldn't step, my leg was too big … three months, and it was seven years and then I retired," she says with a choked voice. That was followed by four years without walking, during which she was looked after entirely by her son, who was only eight and became responsible for the house while Geraldo worked on the building sites. "I was kind of vegetating there; my space was from the bed to the sofa. I cried a lot, I cried a lot because nobody wants that life, I've always been very active and it took me three years of crying," which also cost her health: at 110 kilos, Soraia was diagnosed with morbid obesity.

Geraldo was always by her side when work allowed, and their complicity is corroborated by affectionate glances between the little teases of those who have known each other all their lives. "Every now and then I feel like slapping this black guy, but I wouldn't trade it for anything, he's my best mate," says Soraia. In 2013, her life changed again when she was called by the Hospital das Clínicas, a public institution linked to the University of São Paulo, to undergo the long-awaited bariatric surgery after more than four years in the queue. As if she needed to justify this to herself, Soraia emphasised that she didn't have the procedure for aesthetic reasons, but because "I wanted to own myself". The result is that, many years later, with her physical and mental health recovered, she would also become an autonomous person, just like Geraldo, from a seed planted long before. In this spirit, they decided to set their sights together on the sun that seemed to be shining for them, that of entrepreneurship. Geraldo almost dropped out of the course of Rede because he had so much difficulty with the computer. Soraia says he was 'mentally lazy', but she never stopped encouraging him. Geraldo thought the pitch was 'a big deal'.

Was it a dream or a necessity? It's not easy to identify in their narratives the situations where one ends and the other begins. In popular experience, there is usually little reflection on this simply because the fluidity between paid work and odd jobs means that they overlap, succeed each other and disappear. In the case of Soraia and Geraldo, there is a diagnosis, tasks to complete and a goal: to see the vegan version of their *acarajé* recognised for the quality they believe it to have. Under the guidance of teachers from the Projeto Rede, Geraldo was asked to innovate his product, carried out dozens of tests and came up with a formula that he claims has no competition, an opinion corroborated by those who have tasted his *acarajé* without prawns. But there is also the difficulty of getting their fritter to circulate beyond the typical consumers of vegan and vegetarian products, which in their case can be found at the entrepreneurship and gastronomy fairs they usually attend, such as the Percurso festival organised by Agência Solano Trindade in Campo Limpo, or in wealthy areas of the city. The pandemic would put a stop to these events. "As Geraldo said, he works, so do I, but we can't take time off, there's little to keep a shop going, because something will be missing and getting sponsorship these days is complicated," explains Soraia, referring to the 'angel investors' who appear on the pitches of accelerators, brokers and investment funds, some of them specifically aimed at social impact businesses.

Thus, popular entrepreneurship makes its triumphant entry when there is almost nothing left of the dystopian battle scene. Those who live there manage their own suffering and have learned from experience that only the basics can be expected from the state. 'I wanted to own myself!', said Soraia, after years of not even being able to walk around the house because of an accident at work and the negligence that followed.[17] It is the freedom of being able to dictate one's own course that informs the longing of those who have suffered an existence under the yoke of disrespect, people that the controversial Brazilian development has pushed to the margins. Soraia and Geraldo have overcome many battles, but they know that others still await them.

They are the very representation of popular entrepreneurship and its ambiguities. So much so that, even when faced with the same proposal to reinvent African cuisine, they each add their own layer of understanding about what

---

17   For Dejours (1999), managers and individuals in leadership positions who deliberately disregard or subvert legislation, inflicting suffering on workers, are also agents of evil. However, for Dejours, the resignation on the part of "good" people who don't associate the suffering imposed by precarious work, or simply ignore its sense of social injustice by attributing the misfortune of millions to economic rationality, is proof of collaboration with this world of suffering in which the majority live.

it means for an entrepreneur to have knowledge: he believes in practice, in knowing how to do things and in technique. 'It's knowing how to make *acarajé*,' he emphasises, with an attitude that conveys pride and confidence in what he does. She insists on continuous study and learning. But are they irreconcilable? Explaining her entrepreneurial *ethos* in her own terms, she states, 'you show the world what you can do'. When reflecting on how they honed this in the weekly classes at the Projeto Rede, Soraia elaborated that "we were already entrepreneurs, selling the products, but without having the knowledge of," Geraldo jumped in, as though they were following the same train of thought: 'technique'.

But she corrected him. 'Values, right.'

CHAPTER 3

Mirages: Utopias of Modernity in Social Entrepreneurship

> It's tough, you see. It's bone-chilling. I see situations that I think will never end. Because we talk, we debate, I see people, man, ready. Ready to shine and starving. And when I say these people, I mean the people who go to the soiree, who recite...
> ELISÂNGELA, 24, producer

∴

> Because I hate labelling. I don't like it; I can't do it. Today I feel like a facilitator, a person who facilitates encounters, who facilitates relationships, who facilitates access, I think that's it. So, I think it's difficult to put myself in a box because I always get out of it. But if I were to define myself in one word, by choice, I see myself in that place, producer and all. But much more than that, I think I encourage people to believe in their own dreams, to believe in themselves, because I think that from the moment you believe in yourself, you can be whatever you want. You'll be a facilitator, you'll be "I don't know what, I don't know what", so today I believe in myself. If I'm going to believe in myself, I don't think I'll need a label. This is very much the new era that brings me, that I'm very much in the future, looking at what the future wants to emerge. And the future doesn't want boxes.
> VITÓRIA, 27, producer

∴

In the first chapter, we looked in depth at some of the major transformations that have taken place on the peripheries of São Paulo over the last few decades, experienced by self-employed workers and shopkeepers who flourished in popular entrepreneurship and experienced social mobility as a result. They seek to reproduce an idealised past in the condominiums of the new peripheral middle class, without the criminality or perversions that they identify in mass culture, the result of which is a way of life that has been re-signified or adulterated. In this chapter, we follow those who may not have experienced the same mobility, but who are the guiding thread of cultural modernisation on the periphery.

These changes can be observed on a rainy morning in the basement of an autoconstructed building that stands out in the Jardim Maria Sampaio landscape for its three floors and unfinished brick, where a young man makes a living in his barbershop, with decor that resembles those in the wealthy Zona Oeste (which, in turn, imitate the American ones). Or in Campo Limpo, where an organic food store attracts the attention of the cool middle class for its potential 'social impact'. And around them, many others – app drivers and couriers, street vendors, crime workers – perpetuate the *viração*, now positivised according to the prescriptions of the entrepreneurship/employability set. There are thousands of examples, some more successful than others, that all share the need to generate income and the transformative ways of doing so (Simone, 2004).

Here, I'm looking at a younger group of residents from the periphery of the Zona Sul who are or have been involved in some kind of activism, and who have raised entrepreneurial values that not only cause a rupture with the space of popular experience, but also draw directly on globalisation in the form of philanthrocapitalism (Sklair; Glucksberg, 2021). Thus, the model that is currently expanding on the peripheries of São Paulo and captivating its new entrepreneurs are social impact businesses. According to SEBRAE, these are ventures whose "main activity should directly benefit people in the lower income brackets, the so-called C, D and E classes. ... Therefore, economic viability and social and environmental concerns are of equal importance and form part of the same business plan".[1]

In a global culture circulates at an ever-increasing speed, the same language applies to precarious individuals in many parts of the world. Whether it's disseminated by the World Bank, NGOs and social organisations through funding notices, or through narratives of suffering and success on social media or the internet, this language gives entrepreneurship a utopian character that bring it into contact with the anxieties of humiliated people with limited horizons, creating a global imaginary made up of micro-entrepreneurs in a classless society.

---

1 Available at: https://sebrae.com.br/sites/PortalSebrae/sebraeaz/o-que-sao-negocios-de-impacto-social,1f4d9e5d32055410VgnVCM1000003b74010aRCRD.

Not only did the World Bank contribute to a renewal of microcredit policies, but it also imposed the standardisation of a certain global discourse for access to its funding. In order to reach the impoverished population in every corner of the world for whom it was allocating a small part of its money, the bank began to demand a universal language, which carries not only technical terms, but also political norms of environmental sustainability, diversity, youth protagonism, empowerment, entrepreneurship, etc. In these development policies, therefore, there is a discursive metamorphosis that standardises not only the way in which subjects with certain social requirements should express themselves – in the terms of public and private calls for proposals to fund social projects – but goes further, as the subjects are also called upon to practise 'compulsory voluntary action' as a condition imposed by these funders (Escobar, 1995; Souza, 2008; Sposito; Corrochano, 2005).

These principles have landed in Brazil with great success. Specifically in the Zona Sul of São Paulo, an extremely active social entrepreneurship ecosystem has formed, bringing together social organisations and projects, business schools, universities, accelerators and foundations. It reproduces globalised principles and successfully disseminates them at the popular territories, especially among young people from the periphery looking for a place in the sun. More than an ideology implemented from the top down or an ethereal neoliberal logic, it is a structure of feelings that thrives on the ground of growing dissatisfaction with the labour market. Among younger people, it's not necessarily the conditions of employability that have worsened, but the perception of their precariousness: these are people who don't accept putting themselves in situations of subjection.

Between the 1990s and the 2010s, the periphery gained new prominence with the incorporation of an identity linked to the territory, intertwining experiences of work and the city (Telles, 2006). For Tiarajú D'Andrea (2013: 45), a turn towards the periphery took place from the 1990s onwards, when 'political making' fell into crisis in big cities due to the "reflux of social movements and the advance of neoliberalism", causing the term 'periphery' to take on a critical meaning, of "shared subjectivity and mutual recognition of a condition". Under the umbrella of peripheral culture, activists, artists and social entrepreneurs came together in the early 2000s to claim their belonging to the territory. At that time, "the term 'periphery' would come to designate not only 'poverty and violence' – as had previously been the case in official and academic discourse – but also 'culture and power'" (Oliveira, 2018: 21):

> The culture of the periphery would then be the combination of the way of life, collective behaviour, values, practices, language and clothing of

the members of the lower classes located in the neighbourhoods considered to be peripheral. It also includes specific artistic manifestations, such as hip-hop expressions (break, rap, graffiti) and marginal-periphery literature, which reproduce this culture on an artistic level not only because they portray its singularities, but also because they are the result of the manipulation of peripheral cultural codes (such as language with its own rules of verb agreement and use of the plural, specific slang, neologisms, etc.).

NASCIMENTO, 2010: 119

Entangled in this dilemma, sometimes begrudgingly, is the 'peripheral subject', who has become, based on D'Andrea's doctoral thesis (2013), an ideal type of young person from the periphery who participates in cultural movements, is politically engaged and circulates in soirees exalting their origin and belonging. According to him, the peripheral subject found his means of expression in hip hop, samba and marginal literature, but today other forms of interaction share aspects of this peripheral culture, and these political subjects find themselves in the almost inescapable context of social entrepreneurship. Former leading figures discuss the subject at their events, responding to the demands of the younger generations; others, closer to the traditional left and opposed to what they see as the legitimisation of precariousness, avoid the term, but the contradictions between discourse and practice are relentless.

Therefore, in the periphery, the biggest obstacle to this transition turns out to be family culture, which, according to one manager, 'is not yet entrepreneurial'. For a typical working class family, it's more than understandable that they would want their children to continue the family project of mobility with stability. After all, they don't have to live hand-to-mouth. On the other hand, in the contemporary structure of feelings, knowing how to get by is precisely their main defining characteristic, and this is how these young people come to see themselves. What's more, they internalize the sense that their parents are fundamentally wrong, outdated and even unworthy for having accepted such submission to the 'system'. In the absence or rejection of references and examples of life in the family, the new peripheral subjects take refuge in therapeutic narratives, which are interwoven with their short trajectories, filling the empty space of realisations. As their professional lives are pushed forward, the entrepreneurial culture is legitimised by promoting aspirations for self-realisation, welcoming environments and the recovery of self-esteem.

The expression *nóis por nóis* (us for us), with the intonation of the São Paulo periphery, tries to translate the spirit of these individuals and their discourse of cooperativism inspired by the solidarity economy, but it also reveals a characteristic scepticism.[2] Although they often take a stance against conservative governments and politicians, it is not the political situation that guides the actions of these entrepreneurs, who are much more concerned with creating survival/emancipation strategies regardless of the ruler on duty and the economic crisis, which makes the money circulating in the periphery scarce, but disappears in their committed discourses. On the one hand, young people from the periphery position themselves as vanguards of social entrepreneurship, who have carried out a deliberate project of breaking with the space of popular experience. On the other hand, they embody a desire to decommodify relationships and nonconformity with the abuses and exploitations of the world of work, thus fulfilling their own utopia of freedom.

The word 'individuality', by the way, is not usually mentioned by them, perhaps because it doesn't fit well with the personal narratives inspired by famous pedagogue Paulo Freire and cultivated in parishes, soirees, culture collectives and laboratories of social organisations. But this is also an important force. After all, this youth protagonism is directly linked to personal achievements. As one speaker put it, "my victory is already an impact, because they don't want me to win".

1 Anti-capitalist

I met Elisângela one evening at SESC Campo Limpo, a relatively new unit of this important network of cultural centres, where the basketball and futsal courts and the colourful containers stand out, very different from the better-known units designed by famous Brazilian architects. Since my first visit, back in 2018, I've seen many young people taking ownership of the place, practising sports and taking dance classes. In one of these containers, which served as both a study room and a meeting room, we talked about the path that led her to entrepreneurship from an early age. Whether by vocation or affinity, Elis, 24, an indigenous woman from São Paulo, has developed a remarkable ability

---

2 Robert Castel's (2015: 538) diagnosis in this regard can be useful here: "if certain groups, or certain regions, are the object of extra attention and care, it is because it is noted that they have less and are less, it is because they are in a deficit situation. In fact, they suffer from a *deficit of integration*, such as the inhabitants of underprivileged neighbourhoods, pupils who have failed at school, poorly socialised families, young people who are underemployed or unemployable, those who have been unemployed for a long time … Integration policies can be understood as a set of rebalancing endeavours to make up the distance from complete integration (a decent standard of living, 'normal' schooling, a stable job, etc.)".

for management, which is evident in her business-speak, but also in her keen awareness of the reality of the periphery and her strategies for reaching its residents. What is striking is precisely her down-to-earth attitude: her steps are not measured by dreams, and she has a surprising willingness to wait for the right moment to take bigger leaps. Her ambition is palpable, because Elis knows her limitations and what she'll need to overcome them. The main one is precisely the one most common in the *quebrada*: insufficient capital to accelerate the business.

Elis has a steady job at a philanthropic institution in Capão Redondo, where she works with private fundraising and agreements with the city council. It is precisely her lack of capital that is forcing her to take up a job with a CLT contract. "Man, I don't like fixed hours, I just want to be an entrepreneur ..., but I like fixed money. I can't live without certainty now," she says, aware of the insecurities that come with choosing entrepreneurship. However, there are other reasons, and they are not based on the security of a formal job, but on an identity that seems to have been moulded for her: "So, having a steady job today guarantees that I can be an entrepreneur".

A resident of Jardim São Luís, Elis runs an audiovisual production company with a partner, and the two also run a sustainable fashion thrift store. They bought the equipment for the production company when they won a call for tenders from the state government for the creation of a community TV, and after the projected they were able to keep the equipment.[3] From then on, they began to make small local productions and do photo shoots exalting a peripheral aesthetic. The idea for the thrift store was born out of the need to raise more funds, since the collectives they worked with were struggling financially. In its second year, the company was still operating essentially based on bartering with local businesses. "We still go to the cultural spaces and sporting events in the community, but we've tried to be in other places where the periphery meets," she explains. As an example, she mentions an entrepreneur friend who is investing in marketing video lessons, which they produce.

Elis hopes that money will come with the professionalisation of the business, and it is this aspect that she wants to emphasise in her peripheral identity. "Dude, if the *boys* can do it, we can do it too, but with our own face, with our own identity," she says, referring to her middle-class contemporaries.[4] She

---

3 VAI TEC is a business acceleration programme promoted by the São Paulo Development Agency (ADE Sampa) in collaboration with the Municipal Secretariat for Economic Development and Labour.
4 In the lower classes, the slang *boy* is often used pejoratively to refer to upper-class young people.

gives as an example the fashion produced at São Paulo Fashion Week: "We're studying their world, which is a world that is actually for us, because they dictate fashion at Fashion Week so that Brás can sell massively". Brás is a central neighbourhood known for its popular clothing and fabric trade that attracts buyers from all over the country, and which today employs a notable number of immigrants, especially from Bolivia, which does not go unnoticed by Elis. "Fashion Week launches, the Bolivians sew, Brás sells, and we consume", she summarizes.

Elis' story is emblematic of the transformations in the lives of young people from the periphery over the last decade, which go beyond urbanisation and access to goods and services: a group formed to practice social entrepreneurship (Catini, 2020). She attended a social organisation (OS) in Jardim São Luís as a teenager and received a scholarship for a pre-university course, where she had her first networking experience. At the age of 15, she took an entrepreneurship course at another social organisation, where she learnt about the national register of legal entities (CNPJ), municipal registration and tax exemption. At 18, she started a degree in Public Relations at a private university, paid for by the company she was working for at the time. "But I never really got on with hierarchy, and at the same time [I started to] think about the value of capital. So, when you understand the value of your time and the money that doesn't come to you, you start [to think]: "I'm going to give all this time to myself"". So, she completed just four months of university and dropped out.

Back in the neighbourhood, she started working as a socio-educator at the Centre for Children and Adolescents (CCA) and became a member of an 'anti-capitalist' PSOL collective, experiences that encouraged her to become an entrepreneur. This is a statement that to most readers will sound nonsensical, but let's see how this process developed for Elis. During her time as a far-left activist, she says she "started thinking about organisational strategies" and "understanding how you can manage people, because I think entrepreneurship and business management are related to people and how they organise themselves to make their interests work". Bringing several of these experiences together, Elis began to specialise in fundraising; her first initiative was with a social project called Rede Jardim São Luís, which encouraged collectives to think about entrepreneurship in the periphery, with the support of Casas Bahia. The convenience was that she began to pay attention to money and how it could be used for real actions. "In the collective, at the time, that was the focus," she says, but "it was a lot of effort for little return".

Elis says she had a revelation when she heard popular educator Tião Rocha tell the story of a town in the interior of Minas Gerais where young people left school at 17 to work cutting sugar cane. She then began to compare this fate with that of her own friends and thought: "Well, it's real, I see a lot of people who were with us, building soirees, building various cultural and political processes. They're not doing it anymore because they've had to go to work. Working for other people, working in insecure jobs." The truth is that, for Elis, it doesn't matter whether a job has a CLT contract or not if it's precarious work, and for young people from the periphery, it probably is. "The guy who makes the hamburger for McDonald's, he knows how to make the hamburger, but he makes the hamburger for McDonald's. So how can we think of ways to encourage people to start their own businesses?" she asks. So, she interprets entrepreneurship through the power wasted on occupations that pay barely enough to make a living.

This utopian function, which saturates the structure of feelings of thousands of young people like Elis, is what escapes many analyses that remain restricted to the critique of ideology. In fact, she went through a series of 'ideological apparatuses' throughout her short career, which certainly had some influence on her subjectivity, but it was real life, living in the *favelas* with people "ready to shine and starving", with friends who abandoned their cultural or militant collectives to make hamburgers in a fast-food outlet, that prompted her action. Militancy, by the way, brought her many lessons, as well as many frustrations, and this experience also helped shape her way of seeing the world of work. According to Elis, her collective was made up mostly of middle class university students, so they didn't understand the basic needs of those from the periphery. She draws attention to behaviours that, she suggests, were not part of her peripheral culture and that caused her some opposition, such as the 'liberal consumption of drugs'. When she pointed out the contradiction, she was called a 'prohibitionist'. She also perceived inconsistencies in the so-called radical party which, after many years of left-wing opposition to the PT, suddenly changed its position with the arrest of Lula by corruption charges. With Bolsonaro's victory in 2018, Elis decided to give up. "Man, is it worth it for me to spend my energy ridiculing the jokes he makes, or is it better for me, in the particular universe in which I live, and in which I can have an impact, to do something that makes a change?" she asks, without having much doubt about the answer.

As we'll see many times in this chapter, the relationship with the *boys* is always ambiguous, alternating disdain and rejection with a kind of compulsory networking so that higher-value ventures can be established, such as Elis' audiovisual production company, which, in order to start generating capital, has to be hired by agencies based in wealthy neighbourhoods. In this ambiguity lies both irony and resentment. Elis believed in the proposal of her anti-capitalist collective and was committed to it, but she also recognised the inconsistencies that at a certain point became untenable. Her only moment of empathy with her former colleagues she dedicates, not for nothing, to a neighbour from the periphery who was hospitalised for mental health reasons. "He's white, he has a better condition in the *favela*, he studied at USP, Philosophy, he graduated ... but he was that person who got on with things, he believed in the Revolution, so I think Bolsonaro messed him up." she laments.

With these experiences, combined with her knowledge of management, Elis positions herself between activism and business, thinking up strategies that are true to her concerns about sustainability, but which also have the potential to create a market. So, for her, the connection between ensuring the equal representation of gender, race, sexual orientation and place of residence in her productions is not only a way of exalting principles of social justice, but an asset, a guarantee of authenticity that gives a progressive stamp to her enterprise.

A remarkable sense of timing also has its pragmatic side, as when Elis agreed to do a job for a pastry shop, and the relationship with the owner of the establishment was one of her worst. But for the time being, she's willing to do the job even when it doesn't meet her political criteria. The main reason is that Elis' partner doesn't have a steady job and earns all her income from the audiovisual company. "Handling her money is very complicated, and it's this very peripheral context that needs money for subsistence, so not accepting the job means not having money for her," reflects Elis, who nevertheless blames herself for 'bad management', revealing that this is also a job of care.

These are contradictions that cause her some discomfort. The scars of her activist past are still sensitive for Elis, who ended up turning mainly to the 'business crowd', with whom she has no personal issues to discuss, "and I'm more concerned with the result of the product, how many people are being impacted, what kind of income is being generated." Elis considers her lifestyle to be sustainable, which allows her to support the causes that are dear to her, but she manages to remove from herself the responsibilities imposed by others, such as activist and cultural collectives. In the same way, she would like to eliminate the tutelage of wage labour: "What if people did not work? This idea of work, of profit, of remuneration. What if there was another way of life?". In this way, she defines her situation today, and how she sees society in general, in which entrepreneurship is an exercise in the utopian affirmation of freedom, which includes collective values, but which is realised above all in the sphere of individual agency. For example, when she sees 'potential being wasted' Elis is indignant, but her impulse is not to help those who have nothing to eat, but to reflect on "how do I help this person provide food in their home?".

She applies the same criteria to herself and to unpaid labourers. Elis is extremely sceptical about welfare policies and has a liberal interpretation of them, "the switch that the parties don't understand". At the same time, she sees everything that isn't entrepreneurship as a 'mega-billing of life', of which she refuses to be a part – the institutions of democracy, the labour market, etc. "You invoice everything, the grass becomes invoiced, so I can't be invoiced, I'm not in it," she says. Her utopia involves the realisation of individual potential, a key turning point in the Brazilian peripheries. But Elis still can't escape all the pressures of society. Hers is a structure of feelings that operates from the beginning to the end of her narrative, in which entrepreneurship is at the centre of a project of autonomy, but which is often contained in therapeutic discourse.

2   Social Impact

Known for some years as the most violent neighbourhood in the world, according to a ranking produced by the United Nations,[5] Jardim Ângela hosted the 2nd Periphery Impact Business Forum (NIP) in August 2019. Organised by local cultural producer A Banca and accelerator Artemísia, the event was supported by the Centre for Entrepreneurship and New Business of the Getúlio Vargas Foundation (FGV), the British Council and the Lemann Foundation, among others. Held at the parish of Santos Mártires, a well-known progressive Catholic centre in the South of the city, the meeting included panel discussions, performances by artists, a sustainable lunch and coffee break, engaging speeches and corporate-style dynamics, all watched over by pictures of Pope Francis, Marielle Franco and Che Guevara.[6] The mix of symbols might seem odd at first glance, but only to someone still nostalgic for the old popular struggles. Within that space, the discussions didn't pass by those icons – they didn't ignore or exalt them, but rather tried to reconcile engagement and entrepreneurship.

The large auditorium of the parish led by Irish priest Jaime Crowe was still empty when I arrived, just before 9am in the mild temperature of São Paulo. At the far end of the hall, a breakfast buffet prepared by entrepreneurs from the periphery was positioned opposite the stage, and stalls selling books on

---

5   In 1996, the homicide rate in the district was 98 per 100,000 inhabitants, rising to 123 in 2001 (Monteiro Filho, 2006).
6   Júlio also mentions the Church's participation in the Grajaú Peace Movement, which in 2000 mobilised social actors and young 'protagonists' against violence in the district. Aged 71 at the time, Father Jaime classifies the 2000s as the 'years of individualism', as opposed to the community interest that had prevailed until the early 1990s (Fontes, 2018: 183).

organic food and tourism on the Billings reservoir shared the side wall. Neither registration for the event nor meals were charged. The first to arrive came from the other side of the bridge and began their networking, even though they're hindered by the loud sound and microphones. The opening speaker is an activist from A Banca, who abuses academic vocabulary and the term 'empowerment'. The tone, in general, is positive: as an event from the centre to the periphery, the idea is to engage new entrepreneurs and not discourage them with politics – there is practically no mention of the political and economic situation. The buzz doesn't stop as the work begins. The sound of a blender echoes and mobile phones are pulled out at every moment for a new photographic record. Throughout the day, with arrivals and departures, about half the auditorium is occupied, less than half by aspiring entrepreneurs, the target audience for social impact businesses. "The biggest enterprise in Brazil today is called *quebrada*," announces one of the participants.

The elective affinity between social entrepreneurship and some peripheral cultural collectives, in which the post-structuralist repertoire serves as an adhesive tape, is notable at events such as the NIP Forum.[7] There, hip hop was played in between activities, engaging speeches tried to motivate aspiring peripheral entrepreneurs and the dynamics of the corporate world were meant to identify 'privileges' among the participants. These situations of 'awareness', which are quite common at events of this type, are especially evident at specific moments of excitement, at the opening tables and during presentations of success stories.

This alchemy is completed by the speakers. How can one achieve success? A coach in the audience offered the answer: Keep your feet on the ground, don't quit your job at the call centre, study at night and do business on the weekends, and if 'your purpose is strong', your business will thrive. The profusion of uplifting phrases continues apace: "Ironing boards are surfboards who gave up their dreams for a boring job," says another. According to this mindset, the quest to generate income is no different from the adrenaline rush of a sport.[8] At the mention of the English term 'gig economy', someone bursts

---

7   Michael Löwy (2011: 139) interprets the Weberian use of the concept of elective affinity as the process by which two cultural forms – religious, intellectual, political or economic – "enter, on the basis of certain significant analogies, close kinships or affinities of meaning, into a relationship of reciprocal attraction and influence, mutual choice, active convergence and mutual reinforcement".

8   Alain Ehrenberg (2010: 174) associates entrepreneurial ideology with the culture present in sporting competitions, based on the logic of adventure, challenge and personal achievement, borrowed from the world of work and the rhetoric of companies and workers as an essential skill for the labour market. According to the author, in the new configuration erected by the 'cult of performance', everyone must, regardless of their origin, "accomplish the feat of

into laughter: "It's *frila*! It's *bico*!". Between one speech and another, tributes to Marielle Franco are lost in the bustle that takes over the lunch break, but the presentation of a craft beer produced by women gains a certain commotion. An anonymous question from the audience about what happens to the '*emprecariado*' ("the Uber driver who thinks he's an entrepreneur") gets a grimace and is quickly dismissed.

In specific sessions, experts and regulars on the social entrepreneurship circuit shared the microphone with entrepreneurs from various *quebradas* across the city, but there was also some time for participants to ask their questions. The panel I attended on the Creative Economy revealed a lowering of expectations. One of the speakers was Martin Dowle, the director of the British Council in Brazil and an Englishman with good fluency in Portuguese. He spoke about the noble motivation behind the creation of the British institute in 1934, when the rise of Nazi fascism instigated the defence of freedom against oppression through culture and education. About an hour later, the session would close with another speaker, who urged listeners distressed by the apparent contradiction between 'social responsibility' and the petty pursuit of profit not to be ashamed of making money. After all, "the rich aren't crooks, they just have a more structured business".

The disconnect between the speeches of these entrepreneurial ideologues and the expectations of the participants, who had generally signed up for the event in search of solutions to start their businesses, was revealed in the frustration of many who still didn't understand basic things like how to set a price for the products they make, distribute them, prepare a cost spreadsheet, etc. This discrepancy exposes one of the biggest flaws of these meetings: They are not designed to fulfil the role of practical training and guidance that characterises, for example, the purpose of SEBRAE (which, incidentally, does not usually appear on the list of supporters of these events). Rather, they aim to 'empower' attendees by overcoming the customs and practices that characterise the popular way of life.

In this endeavour, the therapeutic discourse is mobilised to convince people that the cure for suffering can be found in identity, but this process does

---

becoming someone". At the root of this new entrepreneurial understanding is the priority given to singularity as opposed to the 'disciplinary subjection' of Fordism, which transformed subjects into 'interchangeable numbers'. "Everyone should live their own life and succeed in it, since it is without a political or religious beyond," says Ehrenberg. Even in the 1970s, multilateral bodies such as the United Nations and the World Bank, and thinkers such as Alain Touraine, saw positive characteristics in this diagnosis, as it elevated individuals to the status of 'social actors' engaged in individual and 'realistic' projects (Souza, 2008).

not happen without provoking feelings of guilt in people who are new to the debates waged in decolonial tones. They express sincere doubts about, for example, whether it is right to sell Afro-centred products to white buyers and contemporary understandings of 'cultural appropriation'. Here, moreover, another source of suffering manifests. The budding entrepreneurs who take part in these circuits are looking for guidance so that their businesses can thrive, but they suffer from elusive and imprecise definitions. In these cases, they would like to be able to direct the fruits of their labour to the demonetised subjects with whom they share their peripheral neighbourhood. After all, they have been encouraged to make a social impact. However, it's usually the residents of the wealthy side of the bridge who do buy their products, and only in very specific situations, such as social entrepreneurship fairs.[9] The fact admitted by the speakers themselves, not without some annoyance, is that the vast majority of the time, for the peripheral entrepreneur, it is not possible to choose who they sell to. In this 'guilt world', to mediate their frustration, they try to assuage their feelings with the common practice of making the customer more conscientious.

Events like this have been quite common in the South of the city, with varying levels of professionalisation, but it was through cultural movements that entrepreneurship became part of the local grammar. Created in 1999 in Jardim Ângela itself, the production company A Banca began as "a youth movement organised to put on hip hop events as a way of gaining respect, having a voice and surviving the harsh local reality". In 2007, A Banca went through the Young Entrepreneurs Expedition promoted by the social impact accelerator Artemísia, established itself as a Civil Social Organisation of Public Interest (OSCIP) and became defined "as a social cultural producer with a positive impact, which uses music, hip hop culture, popular education and technology to promote inclusion, strengthen identity and peripheral entrepreneurship".[10]

Invariably repeated in the speeches of its members, the narratives of violence in the neighbourhood also head the 'Our Story' section of the production company's website. In November 2019, I visited its headquarters, a graffitied townhouse among houses, vacant lots, mechanic workshops and bars. The typical peripheral setting can be seen with the *favela* on the horizon and the lack of public facilities. I traveled there by bus, which from the city centre takes no less than an hour and a half (there are no train or underground stations nearby)

---

9   These fairs are very common in cities like London. But, in Brazil, this qualification differentiates them from the *feiras livres* (open-air market), which are very traditional and aimed to the popular audience.
10   Available at: https://www.abanca.org/nossahistoria.

and walked for a few more minutes in the heat and strong sun. In the pleasant office, where three people were working at the time, I looked at the walls decorated with old vinyl records, phrases by Paulo Freire and organisational charts, and waited for Leonardo, a 38-year-old member of A Banca and a DJ. His career has been marked by episodes of precarious work – he was a *motoboy* from 2001 to 2008, and from 1996 to 2000 he worked in a pharmacy making deliveries and tidying the shelves. Leonardo naturally explains the links between social entrepreneurship and a central element of peripheral culture. "Hip hop is the basis of the work we do. It was with this that I strengthened my identity, that I found an identity, it was with hip hop that I understood its values and carried that into my life."

The model of social pacification by outsourcing the state's social functions that marked the 1990s has been exhausted, a fact that emerges in the speeches of some of the social entrepreneurs as resentment. Having been part of the 'public policy laboratory', in the words of former PT mayor Marta Suplicy, for so long, they feel that the return was not what they wanted. One of the speakers at the opening table of the NIP Forum, Leonardo, was more forthcoming and animated at the event when I got to know him. Stern and short-sentenced in the interview, the executive director of A Banca expressed a recurring mistrust in this group of interlocutors, rooted in an unwillingness to engage with the third sector and 'academia'. Leonardo explains his point of view on that time period: "They were NGOs who thought they were going to save us because we were in 'this' situation, or they were journalists who wanted to know what had happened, people from university who wanted to do a thesis, all that sort of thing."[11]

His disdain doesn't just refer to those who are no longer authorities in the periphery. In the face of what is seen at A Banca events, he also describes his interlocutors and the conditions in which they will be received. "For a long time, Jardim Ângela experienced abuse, people coming to the *quebrada* and not being exchanged. So we brought a signature and a power, because we can't keep arming ourselves and going up against people. Because it doesn't work,

---

11 For Francisco de Oliveira (1988), the disproportionate ideological role played by the Brazilian middle class during the military dictatorship is explained by the regime's yoke on the working class, whose mediation of the oligarchical structures of state and private companies was stifled. Consequently, this role was taken on by the middle class, in a process of 'mediation without mediation', since there was no political weight on either side of the scales to make mediation necessary. This overvaluation of their political role naturally followed the structural tendency of peripheral capitalism, since the middle classes are central to the composition of demand in the durable goods industry.

and we're always the losers," emphasises Leonardo. In my case, I was treated kindly, but with little enthusiasm. By the way, my other contacts were more direct and asked me what my 'social counterpart' would be. My answer, which praised the public and accessible nature of the research, seemed unsatisfactory to them.[12]

The fatigue of the 'target audience' eventually turns to rebellion (Maciel, 2018). This is a kind of survivalism that ultimately re-signifies popular ways of life. Thus, says Christopher Lasch, "it should therefore not surprise us to find that although the narcissist conforms to social norms for fear of external retribution, he often thinks of himself an outlaw and sees others in the same way" (1991: 51). Entrepreneurship then becomes "a way of deconstructing this world that is given to us", as my interlocutor Leonardo puts it, so that the notion of a social counterpart (or 'exchange') applies here as a demand from the peripheral young people themselves, who thus respond to the emptying of their agency by the management model typical of the previous period, bluntly understood as an 'abuse'.

A few days before our conversation, Leonardo took his rap group to play at a seemingly unusual venue, the Lemann Foundation's Halloween party. As well as largely funding events in the periphery, the organisation has bet on the diversity of its 'collaborators', a fact that fills Leonardo with pride to be performing at its headquarters. The ecosystem that stimulates and builds social entrepreneurship from the ground up in the Zona Sul and in many other peripheries across Brazil is impressive because of the names that frequent the economic magazines and newspapers and that fill the national GDP. Until 2017, Jorge Paulo Lemann was the richest man in Brazil and one of the 20 richest in the world, leading, among other companies, the transnational brewery AB Imbev. As well as being considered a global model of entrepreneurship for thousands of business students around the world, Lemann turns the foundation that bears his name into a 'social impact agent' aligned with the most modern determinations of globalised philanthrocapitalism (Sklair; Glucksberg, 2021).

---

12   Sposito and Corrochano point to the idea of a quid pro quo as a recurring assumption in government actions to transfer resources, so that they escape a 'merely welfare' bias and a possible break with the logic of philanthropy. Within the crisis of the welfare state, they say, "the aim is to re-establish social solidarity through public action, constituting, in addition to the transfer of income, a kind of distribution of responsibilities that mobilises citizens for their effective integration into the national order". In practice, in programmes aimed at young people, quid pro quo can include compulsory school attendance, "but it can also include the necessary attendance at socio-educational activities and participation in community engagement actions, generally proposed by the partner institutions responsible for implementing the programme at local level" (2005: 160–161).

The counterpart to this model is much more tangible than any offered by NGOs and academia: financing a multitude of training events for entrepreneurship, an initiative that, with the fraying of public policies, takes on the appearance of a bet on a new form of pacification. In any case, the innovative proposal that combines assistance with entrepreneurship would only be possible with the active support of the people on the edge, who no longer see themselves as vulnerable in the face of institutions foreign to that world, but as people endowed with creative power and a strong sense of survival.

3   Two Sides of the Bridge

It was a rainy afternoon in the summer of 2019 in the Bela Vista neighbourhood, in central São Paulo, when I met João Vicente, a young black man in his 30s and a rising star in peripheral entrepreneurship. At a workshop he was taking part in as a speaker at the SESC Research and Training Centre, he was observed with curiosity by a non-specialist audience made up mostly of white ladies interested in healthy eating alternatives. The atmosphere was that of an afternoon tea, with tastings of organic tomatoes, carefree smiles and a concern for the environment. The first speaker, who co-ordinated an NGO in the Zona Oeste, seemed quite familiar and moved around fluently, but her successor had to work a little harder to bring the periphery into that self-centred world. Asked by one of the listeners with a certain sarcasm how he defined himself, João replied with open arms and an unexpected quip: 'I'm an alchemist!'.

Used to dealing with all kinds of characters who inhabit the world of entrepreneurship, from Avenida Faria Lima to the far reaches of the Zona Sul, João Vicente saw his career take a defining turn when he created his coworking centre in Campo Limpo, to which he dedicates himself entirely. His entrepreneurial *ethos* benefited from the cultural and economic dynamics there, which were given a decisive boost in the context of *Lulismo* and two concomitant federal government programmes. These were the Pontos de Cultura, an initiative by the Ministry of Culture to establish agreements with local cultural projects through public notices, and partnerships with the then National Secretariat for Solidarity Economy (SENAES). One of them gave birth to the Community Bank in Jardim Maria Sampaio, which, based on the principles defended by the secretariat, aimed to establish exchanges of services through its own social currency. The coworking space, transformed into a social entrepreneurship agency, was thus created from this experience, bringing together collectives and professionals from the local production and cultural circulation.

João is part of a context in which performance "is an invention, ideas emerge and are put into practice as new demands arise" (Bergamin, 2015: 150), a hallmark of social entrepreneurship. In fact, with its performance in the area of culture consolidated, the agency also began to dedicate itself to a concern that is rife in middle-class circles: healthy eating. They set up an organic store for local producers in the property's garage and later invested in the restaurant that João's mother would run after renovating the backyard, a project made possible by crowdfunding. By the way, the remodelling and metamorphosis of the house's uses suggest a different quality that it now displays (Cavalcanti, 2009).

Charismatic and fast-paced, João Vicente has already been featured in cult magazine *Piauí*, São Paulo's main newspapers, has appeared on Rede Globo TV programmes and was on the cover of popular *Veja SP* magazine with his mother. At the time, he had a queue of dozens of entrepreneurs waiting to join his coworking space – a strong indication of his relevance on the local scene. You're likely to find him wearing a shirt with Afro-inspired prints and trousers or shorts from the Fundão clothing brand, owned by entrepreneurs from the *favela* of the same name. Tall, he focuses on the person he's talking to, but is often interrupted by his mobile phone or by an acquaintance (or admirer), with whom he articulates ideas that have arisen at that moment, and almost always ends the conversation with variations on the phrase "do you have my WhatsApp?".

He didn't benefit from any public policy. He started a degree in Business at a private college but left when he ran out of money. In the Projeto Rede, João received formal education and became interested in entrepreneurship. In 2018, he was selected to take part in RenovaBR[13] with a scholarship that helped pay off the debt on the agency's headquarters, which he was in danger of losing to creditors.

His trademark is the relentless exhortation that economics is at the heart of young people's behaviour in the periphery. "We come from a very humble background, so from an early age young people from the periphery are ... how can I put it, provoked to generate income, you know." With a fierce disposition and patience, his objective at the SESC meeting, as well as in practically all the spaces in which he participates in the centre or in the neighbourhoods of the Zona Oeste, was, as he puts it, 'pragmatic'. He sought to gain supporters and people willing to bring resources to the other side of the bridge by consuming local food, honouring artists from the periphery and attending his events. The

---

13   A 'pro-political renewal' group, also known as a 'political start up', which grants scholarships to those who want to run for the legislature and is supported by donations from businesspeople.

main event is the Festival that the coworking centre organises every year in Campo Limpo, with dozens of entrepreneurs, from organic food producers to fashion designers, well-known chefs from the city's main restaurants and concerts with newcomers and famous artists from the periphery.

João Vicente's journey through the city's social entrepreneurship circuit began at the age of 15, when he went to Vila Madalena for the first time for an event on social impact businesses. Although his main memory of the occasion was of being 'framed' by a security guard on the street, he wasn't intimidated. João had already been attending the Projeto Rede for five years and excelled in the entrepreneurship classes. Around this time, he registered his first environmental education project and raised 20,000 dollars, which turned into a pioneering waste disposal programme focused on a local stream. In Rede's example, most of the teenagers looking for the courses on offer want a traditional qualification, because they 'arrive lost' and 'don't know their talents'. The information that I received from one of its managers is that the culture of families on the periphery is not yet 'entrepreneurial', and that they encourage their children to get a job as soon as possible, a remnant of the remote family project of social ascension (Zaluar, 1985; Durham, 1988).[14]

But João didn't live on mirages alone, and it's possible that without such perseverance his career would have taken him far from the magazine covers and closer to two other well-known destinations for him: precarious work and the world of crime, which ultimately marked his life and that of his entire family. He had his first job at the age of 11, working in an amusement park where his older sister also worked. "Manual labour, a very deplorable situation," he says of assembling and dismantling the rides. João left the 10 reais he earned each day with his mother, and at one point they managed to *bater a laje* (build the slab) of her house, when she still lived in the neighbouring municipality of Embu das Artes at the time. In fact, for João this was his first contact with the need to generate income, 'from a very early age', as he puts it, both for himself and for his family, who took different paths.

---

14 As Tommasi (2015: 101) says, "working with what you love and what you know how to do seemed, for many of those young people, to be synonymous with working with 'art and culture' and as a self-employed worker. Today, with the multiplication of public notices and training courses aimed at promoting 'young cultural entrepreneurs', it seems that the wishes of those young people are coming true. Becoming a 'cultural worker' seems to be an 'opportunity' that is opening up even for young people from working class backgrounds. It is an achievable alternative to escape unemployment or employment in subordinate roles – an alternative that is not subject to the need for a university degree in order to get a decent level of pay".

For the younger brother, it was the desire for consumption that shone through, and for whom precarious work gave no hope. In 2011, the boy was killed by the police after a bank robbery. He had already been involved in robberies for some years. "And, bro, the bullet passed close by, took my brother and passed me, you know? I was there at the Community Bank. *Saidinha de banco* and I was at the community bank! Did you get the picture?"[15] João's metaphor about the bullet that 'passed close by' points to the experiences that he and his brother, only a year younger, had in common. What saved him was a certain restraint in contrast to the younger brother's fascination with the world of consumption.

At that point, João was already involved in the Community Bank and reaping his first successes as a social entrepreneur, but he was far from a life of luxury. The cruelty of the police, who shot his brother eleven times, was followed by the cruelty of his brother's co-conspirators, who took the boy's belongings from his family home as 'reparations' for their unsuccessful work. João then moved with his mum for a while to a town in the countryside. Afraid of reprisals? I asked him, and, although he didn't answer in the negative, he claimed that he didn't want to share in the 'economic outcome'. "That's why we have an economic debate when we talk about the extermination of young people. He wanted to buy a motorbike, you know? He wanted to buy a lot of things and he wanted to take this quicker route."

In fact, especially from the 1990s onwards, the world of crime began to compete with work for the aspirations of poor young people. For Gabriel Feltran (2011), the attraction of rapid social ascension through crime is seen as a form of distinction from the generation of working parents.[16] Vera Telles and Daniel Hirata (2010: 46) analysed the "overlapping circuits of new, old or redefined illegalisms, between survival expedients, irregular work, small local enterprises and criminal businesses", which include illicit drug sales points, car dismantling, etc. Behind this is a new disposition towards the world of consumption among these young people who are strictly excluded from it (Pereira, 2014; Pinheiro-Machado, Scalco, 2018).

Both the experience and the courses at the Projeto Rede and the episode involving his brother 'turned a switch' in João Vicente's head, who today is

---

15   *Saidinha de banco* (bank robbery) is a slang term for robbing customers, usually after they have withdrawn their money from the bank.
16   Notable testimonies in this sense can be found in the documentary *Notícias de uma guerra particular*, by Kátia Lund and João Moreira Salles, and in the lyrics of the Racionais MC's, summarised in the verse "Time to think, do you want to stop / What do you want? / To live a little like a king or a lot like a Zé?" from *Vida Loka part 2*.

proud to have been the first young entrepreneur at Rede and of the activity he continues. But if the quicker path taken by his 'bandit' brother allowed him to 'live like a king' (Hirata, 2011) for a very brief period that would be abruptly interrupted, does the entrepreneurial brother's trajectory promise anything at least close to that? A former resident of Jardim Maria Sampaio, João moved to a condominium in Campo Limpo with his wife, one-year-old daughter and dog Martin, a choice in keeping with the new middle class on the periphery. He shares a moderate lifestyle, which encompasses his religiosity (non-practising Catholic) and his *habitus*, which in no way resembles that of a 'king'. Work and leisure are intertwined and he can be seen in the soirees of the Zona Sul shoring up partnerships while sharing a *cachaça* with lemon and exchanging messages on his mobile phone. He has a genuine ambition to become a reference in social entrepreneurship, but that doesn't turn into material ostentation. Everything he earns ends up invested in the agency, the restaurant and the bills to be paid.

Although he doesn't forget to mention the issues of 'structural racism' and the 'extermination of youth', his pragmatism drives him to, as he puts it, "make the economic debate", in other words, to understand the economic conditions of the youth he is part of by seeking alternatives for generating income that, in the last resort, will get them out of the sight of the police. Institutional reform would obviously be welcome, but is unexpected, so João chooses to act where the results can be concretised. These alternatives are, as is common in social entrepreneurship discourse, ambiguous. His dream of getting young people from the *favelas* out of the world of crime and drug addiction comes up against what João calls a lack of 'scale'. His coworking space can accommodate a few dozen candidates, which is not enough, in his opinion, and he makes a curious association with what he's aiming for, a kind of fast food for young entrepreneurs. "That's my dream, that's where I'll see that I'm really getting young people out of crime. But bro, we're a needle, we don't do anything, you know? Crime has something that seduces young people in such a way that they get into it." João shows himself to be absolutely aware of his limitations, just as he understands the contemporary world of work to be crossed by the world of crime, intertwined with it in the very subjectivity of these young people that he witnesses working in the *biqueira* in search of the consumer society, the 'by-product of capitalism' running at full speed.[17]

It's a cynical view, after all. João has seen violence knock on his door, enter his home and drive him away from his mother, to whom he is unconditionally

---

17   The expression indicates the act of literally working at a drug point (*biqueira*).

attached. At the same time, he had a revelation with the incipient entrepreneurship that presented itself to him through a social project on the outskirts of town. But personal experience is combined with careful observation of his *quebrada* and others, which he accesses through his contacts throughout the country and on social networks. In his Facebook contacts, he distinguishes between 'intellectuals' and friends from the periphery, saturated with violent sociability (Machado da Silva; Menezes, 2019), suggesting that he does this so as not to lose touch with the social ground.

João realises the need to show his interlocutors at least an appetiser of this 'by-product of capitalism'. Invited by him, I took part in a coworking *vivência* in summer 2019. Twelve people, all living in central neighbourhoods, took part in the activity, which began with breakfast at the agency itself.[18] João Vicente served us coffee, juices, sourdough bread and organic fruit, emphasising their peripheral origin and their availability in the healthy food store he created in his garage. Then, wearing a large black T-shirt emblazoned with actor Al Pacino in his Scarface role, his partner at the agency gave us a presentation about the Festival and we set off on a walk through Jardim Maria Sampaio, which neighbours the municipality of Taboão da Serra. At the gates of the *favela*, João proposes an awareness-raising activity that everyone naturally follows: We hold hands and close our eyes to 'connect' to the proposed objective, and then a PCC *disciplina* let us in. The rain that had fallen a few hours earlier emphasised the precariousness of the place, where a multitude of wet, squalid cats circulated among the shacks and the tangle of cables and wires.

The aestheticisation of precariousness is accompanied by a discourse of overcoming hardship. Next to the hostile local *piscinão*, a few years earlier there had been a severe flood, which had knocked down the retaining walls of the stream that runs through the area. Once rebuilt, the walls were decorated with graffiti, colouring the banks of the Pirajussara stream. Back at the agency, we went through a *descarrego* session – an exorcism ritual common in Pentecostal cults and which still causes astonishment among higher social strata – before eating the vegan *feijoada* prepared by his mother. The reference to Pentecostalism, however, is justified by its harmony with "the values dear to the professional ethics postulated by the free and post-social market that took hold in the country in the 1990s", according to Diana Lima (2007: 23). The

---

18 Leonardo, whose cultural production company in Jardim Ângela also promotes these experiences, described the public that the activity is aimed at as follows: "White people, upper middle class, who work in companies that give them a lot of money and who have never experienced a *quebrada*, they've never had that opportunity, they only know about it from newspapers, magazines, radio, all that stuff."

alchemy of symbolic elements characteristic of peripheral culture, but with a brief interruption that reveals their popular origin, is explained by the multiple references that make up the social entrepreneur, but which also fulfils the public's interest in the exotic.

The purpose of this type of activity, which is also promoted by other cultural collectives from the periphery, is to 'build bridges'. They are inspired by the Interdisciplinary Internships promoted by the Landless Rural Workers' Movement (MST) since 2003, usually in model settlements and with university students as the target audience. In fact, an MST flag decorated the agency's yard on my first visits. In this case, they are shorter, part-time activities on Saturdays, which do little to compromise the visitors' schedules. As we'll see below, these exchanges promoted by João also have significance for his individual behaviour in and out of the periphery.

As I've realised over the years of research, it's mainly on these weekends that bridges are built, starting with the Festival. João organises partnerships full-time, but the results can be seen when other people's time allows. I've been to the Festival for two consecutive years, which didn't happen again due to the COVID-19 pandemic. The Praça do Campo Limpo, very close to the bus station, is quite large and pleasant, and the exhibitors' stands are spread out in a well-coordinated manner, divided into food, fashion and craft aisles, photographic exhibitions, as well as children's tents, *samba* and rap circles and the main stage, where a big show is held in the evening. Also, that afternoon chef Bel Coelho was there, who is well-known on the São Paulo gastronomic circuit, as well as Greenpeace's volunteers.

It was interesting to note that in the 2018 edition, which took place in November, a mostly white, middle-class crowd enjoyed the sunny Sunday, giving the gathering a carefree, festive atmosphere. The following year, however, funding problems pushed the Festival into December, and the reduced attendance was noticeable, both visually and in the assessment of many local entrepreneurs. As night fell, the presence of local residents became more noticeable than the previous year. I was watching the action when a group of boys crossed my field of vision dressed as the Joker, the main villain of the Batman comics. Meanwhile, on stage, local graffiti artist Gamão entertained the audience waiting for rapper Rael's concert with phrases encouraging entrepreneurship.

The difficulty exposed in this case is that the absence of the public from wealthy neighbourhoods creates a vacuum in the Festival's sustainability. In fact, I heard from a qualified interlocutor that João needed to make his business sustainable every day of the week and not depend so much on events. Incidentally, it's when faced with the abyss of debt that he and his colleagues take their chances. But this is a clear symptom of the agency's strategic action, which is to sell the periphery to the capitalised circuits of the city that see it as a business or social marketing opportunity. Still in 2019, I witnessed him and his partner commenting on the difficulty of organising the next edition of the festival, as they still hadn't managed to close the bills for the previous ones and negotiate with the city hall about providing stages, chemical toilets, etc.: "2017 was so bad that we still owe a lot. God willing, this month we're going to pay the five *contos* (thousands) we still owe from 2017," João reiterated.

Despite his conviction about his vocation for entrepreneurship, these choices weren't easy for João, and they still aren't fully reassuring. Until age 18, he didn't know what he wanted to be professionally. His wife has a salaried job, which guarantees the upkeep of the house, but his very modern profile as a worker/entrepreneur confuses more than it clarifies. "People think you're not working, that *vivência* is *cachacinha*. It is too! But the art of my thing is there, you know?". Now, with his daughter still in the early years of childhood, subjects that aren't as light-hearted as what he shares in his meetings begin to weigh on his shoulders, creating dissonance in his narrative. At the time, a debate about a new pension reform was intensifying in public opinion, which seemed to bring out, to João's irritation, the unpredictable side of his choices, in this case the fact that a pension will not come smoothly for him. He says that he would only go to the CLT "if it was for a lot of money, like 10 thousand, 20 thousand a month", but he feels the pressure to have a higher education degree that he left by the wayside and which, with his responsibility as a father, now seems to be lacking for when he needs an occupation that pays at least enough.

He vehemently denounces the racism he has experienced on the entrepreneurial circuit, but he also responds in a restrained and, once again, pragmatic way. He lets out a nervous laugh when he tells of the times he was mistaken for a delivery man when he arrived for a meeting with businessmen, and with this another ambiguity appears: it's not 'those at the top' he directs his complaints to, but rather the petty powers of those who control the entrances and exits, i.e. workers who often live in the same *quebrada* as him. Sometimes, João feels a sense of revolt, of putting an end to situations that are truly humiliating. "It's just that I'm at a point in my life, with my daughter, that I can't go on playing the *vida loka*. Do you think I don't want to play Mano Brown?[19] But you can't, look at the bang we're involved in, bro. The bang we're involved in is very big. There's a calculation". But, in general, his response is to maintain

---

19   The expression indicates a confrontational attitude, like rapper Mano Brown, from the Racionais MC's.

his 'professionalism' and 'do his best', and his restraint has earned him the possibility of many other invitations, the result of the 'calculation' he makes between the radical denunciation of racism and the uncertainty about the consequences for these relationships.

There are times when João seems discouraged. His efforts to sell the periphery to the centre have their moments of frustration, especially when an event he organised doesn't get the 'other side of the bridge' support he had hoped for. João hopes to meet the expectations of those looking for the 'authentic' peripheral subject: A victim of state violence, politicised in their fight for recognition, but far removed from the 'old politics'. And, of course, the entrepreneurial and optimistic profile that, together with others like him, will promote the pacification of the *quebradas*. In fact, the way he refers to his peripheral neighbours and the university students who visit the periphery is curious. When asked about the social impact he brings to the neighbourhood, he uses the visitors as an example, who cross the bridge to get to know his social technology – a sign that his enterprise has reach – while the former are often labelled *zé povinho*, in the manner of the Racionais MC's. "So, when *zé povinho* see us [on Rede Globo], they don't call us vagabonds anymore, you know? They used to say it was bum stuff, that it was pothead stuff, that it was bandit stuff ... you went there, you saw it!".

His disdain for the *zé povinho*, as opposed to his tolerance for the actors in the social impact ecosystem, shows that his 'principle of justification' is based on a particular universe that may target the periphery, but whose determinations come from elsewhere. This principle predicts that, within the system, opinions and attitudes are adjusted, maintaining the 'natural' situation of that context in which only those who share the same nature are included and those who resist fitting in are threatened with exclusion (Boltanski; Thevénot, 2006). Studying one of these systems, called 'philanthrocapitalism' in their ethnography conducted in Brazil and the UK, Sklair and Glucksberg (2021: 10) observe an overlap between wealth management and philanthropic counselling.[20] Thus, in spaces like these, including social impact businesses, the demand for professionalisation is not restricted to managers and advisors, but affects social entrepreneurs from the peripheries with their jargon and, above all, their attitudes and lifestyles.

---

20 The objective in this case ranges from tax reduction to 'succession planning' strategies – philanthropy as a gateway to 'inclusive values', persuading disintegrated family members to unite around a project – as well as contributing to their good public reputation (Sklair; Glucksberg, 2021).

The impact that seems to be worthwhile for João is what is perceived on the other side of the bridge, but he himself recognises that the middle class that visits him in Campo Limpo is 'a bit *blasé*', that they aren't very impressed by important actions in the periphery like painting the wall of a school. He therefore suggests that in order to get them there, he needs to organise events that are interesting for them, and not necessarily for the periphery. The return for the periphery, he hopes, will come at another time and in the form of money and projects, or 'counterparts', as he prefers to say. João thus lives between two worlds, and his agency is located right in the middle. When he talks about the future of his enterprise, he expounds a utopian vision of a 'Woodstock' of the periphery, which is how everyone who was part of it will remember it.

Throughout the time I've followed João Vicente's work, I've witnessed his talent for forging partnerships and, with his unusual charisma, bringing well-known names in the entertainment world, including journalists, actors, and musicians, to the periphery. In December 2021 it was chef Alex Atala's turn to make an appearance. On the first weekend of the month, he and João's mother would prepare a menu of fish and vegan *moquecas* to raise funds for projects to fight hunger in the peripheries. The invitation stated that bookings were required and would be accepted until 5pm. Compared to my first visits, the professionalism of the staff was striking. I arrived around two hours early, and on my table was a handwritten note with the words 'Henrique Sociólogo' in blue pen, but the event wasn't full, despite the presence of the chef himself, who was smilingly walking around the place taking selfies. As the afternoon progressed and a *roda de samba* (*samba* circle) was organised, the event became emptier, with only João's bros, other entrepreneurs from the *quebradas*, remaining.

4   Spreading Wings

I got off the train that Sunday with a feeling of discomfort that went beyond my exhaustion from days of fieldwork. To make things a little more challenging, that day in the winter of 2019 was the coldest of the year in São Paulo, with drizzle and a temperature of around 12°C, but at the CPTM Grajaú station the intense agglomeration of *viradores* was the same as always and didn't allow me to complain too much. A few kilometres away was my destination on that gloomy day, the Amaphiko Festival, which featured one stage for concerts, one stage for the afternoon debates, and a large bar positioned at the entrance to the square selling Red Bull products, which sponsored the event. On a stand at the side, a mostly young and black crowd occupied the space, and as you moved around the square, the tone of political engagement could be seen in practically everything, except for that island of energy drinks that gave it a party face. The debate brought together some important figures from the entrepreneurial periphery, who denounced structural racism and urged us to confront it through ancestral inspiration. Incidentally, the expression 'Ancestral Future' was the event's slogan.

Amaphiko, in the Zulu language, means 'wings'. According to the festival's website, "it was through the inspiration of this word that Red Bull started a global programme with the aim of empowering the development of people and projects that can have a positive impact on society". Every year, the company selects a few dozen fellows, entrepreneurs who already have a project underway or in progress, and who stand out for the innovation of their proposals.[21] (Coincidence or not, the company's slogan is 'Red Bull gives you wings'). But at the other end of this relationship, the difficulty of accessing these spaces for the vast majority of entrepreneurs is evident. Relegated to corners and side streets, no more than twenty businesses, including handicrafts, fashion and gastronomy, were vying for the limelight, prompting protests from some of them.

Felipe, aged 31, was born in Bahia and graduated with a degree in graphic design after studying all his life in public schools. He moved to the Zona Leste of São Paulo as an adult and has been travelling across the city to visit social entrepreneurship fairs. Felipe makes handicrafts, which he sells in a collaborative shop aimed at Afro-entrepreneurs, while earning his main income from his *frilas*. He says that having a boss all his life 'is complicated', without disguising his sullen look. Sérgio, 27, didn't have his proposal selected by the festival organisers and was working as an attendant in another tent. With his partner, he makes handicrafts inspired by Afro aesthetics at their home in Grajaú, where he was born and raised, and at just nine years old he was already working at a street market. "I started out as entrepreneur since *de menor*,"[22] he jokes. He worked in a Burger King and after five years in various restaurants, he left the salaried life for entrepreneurship. He also became interested in recycling when he noticed the state of rubbish collection on the periphery. Sérgio now believes he's chasing his own dream: "A salaried job gives you more security, but you can't make a living working like this all day, every day, every day to

---

21   Available at: https://www.redbull.com/br-pt/projects/red-bull-amaphiko.
22   In Brazil, the expression *de menor* indicates legal minority, but it is usually attributed in a jocular tone to poor children and young people; in this case, the interlocutor used it as an ironic self-reflection.

support a dream that isn't yours ... it's kind of embarrassing". In the artisan's words, entrepreneurship is justified by what is 'political' about it.

It's not a question of escaping precariousness, but of pursuing 'a dream', says the discourse disseminated on the peripheral entrepreneurship circuit. But for some of the trajectories narrated here, it is the weight of the reality of wage labour that torments, and for which entrepreneurship brings a remedy that can be uncertain, inconsequential or imaginary; and so it injects the subject with hope for a future that at least frees them from situations of oppression and abuse. Ana Luiza, 34, and Carla, 38, have created a brand of accessories aimed at black people and at 'empowering children'. The former is a mother of three and lives in Guarulhos, while the latter lives in the North of the capital and has a son. Both are teachers, but Carla is also an educational coach. Her dream was once to do theatre arts, but she gave it up when she realised that 'it wasn't profitable'. She says that since she works with children with disabilities, she specialises in dealing with 'emotional intelligence'.

Ana Luiza is more sceptical about her profession. Unlike her partner, her dream was to become a teacher, but her experience in the classroom was not what she had hoped for. With a certain mystery and a shaky voice, Ana says she was depressed "because of processes in the classroom", which she prefers not to detail. Her husband was unemployed, and nothing seemed to work out. Thus, she decided to follow a slogan of the Brazilian crises – 'in the crisis, create', she says with a broad smile that expresses her optimism. Ana no longer saw a future as a teacher. She now has that expectation as an entrepreneur, even though she hasn't left school for good yet. Indifferent to the direction of the economy or institutional politics, Ana preaches that 'we have to survive'.

About a year later, Ana confidently and charismatically introduced herself as the 'founder and CEO' of her design brand in the *Shark Tank Brasil* studio. With a line of 'inclusive ethnic stationery' and functional bags, she argued that her entrepreneurship wasn't born out of necessity, but out of 'healing'. When asked to elaborate by one of the 'sharks', she described having been beaten up by a student in class, a fact that explained the depression she barely mentioned in her conversation with me. It wasn't for this reason, however, that Ana received an offer on the programme and sold 30% of her brand in exchange for an investment of 280 thousand reais. Rather, it was the perseverance that keeps the entrepreneurial utopia alive.

5 Powers

On a warm evening in late autumn, I went to Interlagos to meet Vitória, one of the organisers of the Amaphiko festival and a resident of Grajaú. The craft brewery she proposed belonged to some acquaintances who were part of her network and who, in turn, had introduced her to some Red Bull staff who look after the company's social impact businesses. She soon offers me her business card, a light brown one adorned with African motifs and indicating her activity as a 'cultural producer', 'sustainability designer', 'facilitator' and 'astrologer'. At 27, Vitória has many occupations, after all, she refuses to have a 'label'. But she is forced to accept, summing up our conversation, that of producer.[23] At the time of the interview, she was working and studying entirely from home and doing odd jobs as a photographer. A job which, incidentally, wasn't on her card.

In her own way, Vitória develops a lifestyle in line with contemporary management narratives in its exaltation of flexibility, where the aspirations of her generation and the demands of the market intersect. Her reasoning pares down and adapts professions that may require years or decades of training and practice. The 'know-how' that inspires pride in Geraldo sounds like a reductive identity to her. "I'll use your example. Sociologist, sociologist, sociologist … Everyone sees me like that, and if I want to change I can't, because everyone says that's who I am. So, I end up convincing myself that I am that. Just that," she explains without any condescension. Vitória doesn't show any desire for professional qualifications, and she relies on her interlocutors believing in her *potência* (power), shared with other young people from the periphery like her.

Taken by her mother, a retired civil servant who frequented Grajaú's *sambas*, Vitória ended up finding her 'tribe' at the Centre for Arts and Social Promotion (Caps), where she formed a local culture forum with partners and artists around 2012. At the entrepreneurship festival they organised the following year, she and a partner worked on the same craft and vegetarian food stall and discovered that they had 'the greatest power together'. (Vitória always refers to her fellow entrepreneurs as 'powers'). Her aim at the festival was to bring them together and make some money. "It grew, it took us a while to understand what we were doing, what we were producing, because we didn't have a theoretical basis, we had the will to do it and we also had the strength of the

---

23 Livia de Tommasi and Gabriel Silva (2020: 202) have noted that many individuals who circulate in peripheral culture end up taking on the labour occupation of producer, despite the "heterogeneity of the subjects who declared themselves cultural producers (some exclusively entrepreneurs or administrators, i.e. those who manage the calendar of shows, recordings, interviews, band activities; others also musicians, singers, partners)".

network," she says. With their goal realised, she and the others got excited: in 2017 they held a new instalment. With the support of Red Bull, the fairs grew from around ten entrepreneurs to twice as many. Her initial stimulus? "To see that the periphery has money," she says. Speaking about money, for Vitória, is a problem she claims to have overcome. Before, she felt she 'couldn't aim for money', and slowly she discovered ways to break this 'taboo'.

Despite her young age, Vitória has some unusual stories to tell. Her first job was with her father at his real estate agency. She worked for a few months as a telemarketer while pursuing a degree in Psychology at a private university, which she didn't complete. At the age of 22, she did some internships when, through the collective she was part of, she learned about agroecology and moved to an MST settlement in São José do Campos, in the interior. Shortly afterwards, back in Grajaú, she decided to become an entrepreneur with her father's encouragement. As an aside, Vitória's ambiguity in relation to entrepreneurship doesn't end with her conflictual relationship with her family, as we'll see below. She distinguishes the entrepreneurship she practises at her fairs, and in the company of other 'powers', from what companies do. Although she no longer sees the act of earning money as taboo, Vitoria doesn't shy away from criticising profit without 'counterpart'.

As much as Vitória holds certain expectations regarding business support for her initiatives, she also feels an urgency to make things happen. To do so, she mobilises networks that mobilise other networks. But her perspective belongs to someone who sometimes feels alone, and her desires are at odds with the real life of the 'modern *quilombo*', as she refers to the *quebrada*. She responds by insisting that the challenge now would be to 'awaken' people, "because the plan has been so well thought out that we end up killing our dreams". What plan? 'The plan of genocide,' she replies, which many of her peers on the periphery, pacified by the television, ignore. Vitória understands genocide in her own way, not just as the violent action of the state against subaltern segments, but also that of 'dreams', which the state's agent, the media, seeks to exterminate. That dream is autonomy, which she ends up associating with entrepreneurship.

Her father may have been her first entrepreneurial inspiration, but he won't be in the future that Vitória imagines. In 2018, she broke up with him, because he voted for Jair Bolsonaro for president. "Defending armaments. How do you dialogue with someone like that?". Quite a turnaround for this former PT activist, whom Vitória remembers well from the photos she kept of him carrying her on his shoulders and wearing red in past elections. "Man, it's hard to say, because my father didn't finish secondary school, but he's one of the most intelligent people I know, he reads a lot. Self-taught. I think it's because of the television." It's the subject of the military dictatorship that exposes the root of their disagreement, the opposition between her competent discourse and his concrete gaze. Her parents lived through the military period and passed through it without any known trauma – on the contrary, her mother became a civil servant and her grandmother managed to realise her desire for home ownership at that time. Meanwhile, her father doesn't renounce his opinions, minimising the repression that existed right outside his doorstep. "But I see it as ignorance. I think Brazil is a country that has lost its recent memory … There's a lot of television in people's heads too. So there's no way to compete with that, there isn't. So, what you can do is your 'micro-things' there, stimulating one by one, as you can." she concludes.

Relevant here are the 'micropolitics' celebrated by Michel Foucault and often mentioned in the activist context. However, it is remarkable how this interpretation of politics sometimes slips into a certain nihilism. Vitória says she has never voted for a candidate, whatever their proposal. In the first elections she participated in, she voted null or blank, and in 2018, when Bolsonaro was emerging, she didn't even leave the house, she didn't feel 'stimulated'. She has a certain fondness for Lula – who is also 'no saint' – and says she recognises his contribution to the underprivileged. She might have voted for him if he had been on the ballot. But, strictly speaking, her opinion is that "the system has already failed … I think it's been bankrupt for so long and we're alone … Because they're so attached to where they are, which has been ruined for a long time. Are you going to keep protecting this circus?", she says about the politicians.

What matters in this analysis is the set of ideas that she proposes as possible, and even desirable, in this moment, in which entrepreneurship, with or without a social purpose, saturates the structure of feelings in which we live. This is filled by the need for 'theory', which she says is necessary to run her business and which she absorbs through mentoring. Finally, she turns her back definitively on wage labour, which she considers 'modern slavery'. This pressure from the competent discourse ultimately affects Vitória's own subjectivity. She lists the degree courses she would like to do (continue with Psychology, start Philosophy or Pedagogy). It's not that this choice isn't important, or that it won't help her, one day, to be able to look for the salaried job that she is currently rejecting. It's more that she chooses to feel qualified for the world of social entrepreneurship in which she lives, "to make a better contribution, right? Society hears you differently. The fact that you have a degree. Unfortunately or fortunately."

Vitoria's dissatisfaction with wage labour is perceptible and reflects that of her colleagues, who took part in the Amaphiko Festival. What's more, it is key to understanding a kind of emancipatory vision of contemporary entrepreneurship – that is, the desire to have no boss. Pointing to the avenue, she notes that "people make a little house in order to become entrepreneurs, to become a business, so they don't have to work for others. Who likes working for other people, for God's sake?". What is new here is the eloquent purpose of *decommodification*. For social entrepreneurs on the periphery, this commitment is saturated with idealism, because the entrepreneurship dreamt up by Vitória must serve the construction of a utopian future.

It is with this motto that she gives talks at cultural centres in the city's middle-class neighbourhoods, where she proposes the following exercise of imagination: "When you think about the future, what do you think about? Then you think of various things. Within that future that you've thought about, do you see trans people? If you thought about it and didn't think about trans people, you're not very far into a future that is, you know, welcoming, participatory in general." It is to this future that Vitória orients her reflections, even if it seems so uncertain today, because "nature itself is already showing signs that it is no longer putting up with our irresponsibility, our ignorance". So this is a future that, for her, is entirely realised in the present: "I'm convinced of this, I don't know what it's going to be like, but I'm trying my best to do things now to honour the past and also to welcome the future. Because we can only change the future by doing it now."

Thus, Vitória has pinned her individual and collective hopes on her business, through which she wants to definitively overcome wage labour. Entrepreneurship, in turn, is 'new packaging for old interests', as the singer Criolo quote she likes to repeat so much goes. Even though it has lost the 'magic' it had when it first became fashionable, it is at the heart of her dream of "providing healthier environments for less privileged people". Vitória hopes for "peace of mind, prosperity, abundance and wealth" in the future, so that she can conquer her 'place in the sun' and "do entrepreneurship without guilt, just for the money". She doesn't rule out leaving the periphery for good and doesn't want to feel guilty about it, because she believes she will take the *quebradas* to other places. Because her victory, she explains, "is already an impact, because they don't want me to win".

6 Competence

Founded in 2001 by poet Sérgio Vaz, the Cooperativa Cultural da Periferia (Cooperifa) soiree takes place weekly in Jardim Guarujá. 'Silence is a prayer,' says the message given at the start of the performances, which are open to anyone willing to show their art to the crowds. Walking a few hundred metres uphill from the main avenue, past quiet residential streets, you arrive at Zé Batidão's bar, where I went for the first time for this research in July 2019. As the hot, dry night dawned, I settled into the still-deserted bar, with the stereo already set up and *forró* and *sertanejo* alternating on the bar's radio. Gradually, the place filled up and Vaz's presence was noticed, as he greeted everyone there. Attendees took selfies in front of the Cooperifa banner until the venue was completely full, even spilling onto the street and part of the small square in front.

The scenes were almost exactly the same on the other three occasions I was there in the following months. The performances followed one another with discipline, and sometimes affective themes and interpretations of classics from the national songbook emerged among the raps engaged with denunciations of racism, social inequality and police violence. On that first visit, as well as following the soiree, my aim was to interview João Vicente, which I only managed to do months later. The 'alchemist' moved between tables, always requested and well received. Over the course of the evening, I realised that the interview we had arranged wouldn't happen, but João, as a good host, introduced me to other colleagues, some of them entrepreneurs, and offered it to them.

In addition to the soirees, for the past twelve years the collective has promoted the Mostra Cultural with the support of state and federal public offices, SESC and private foundations. The exhibition began in 2007 with the Semana de Arte Moderna da Periferia. The name was a reference to the seminal modern art week of 1922, a pioneering event in the history of Brazilian modernism held in São Paulo. The peripheral version sought to be a counterpoint to it, which manifested itself in the choice of the event's title, the parody of the modernist week's poster, the appropriation of the concept of anthropophagy and the publication of the 'Manifesto da Antropofagia Periférica' (Nascimento, 2010). The 2018 event, which took place at various points in the Zona Sul, had a special panel on entrepreneurship, but the current relevance of the phenomenon was evident when we saw it permeate the other activities.

It was November when I sat with around 30 people in an auditorium at the Fábrica de Cultura Jardim São Luís to listen to Adriana Barbosa, founder of Feira Preta and a key reference when it comes to Afro-entrepreneurship. Born in the North of the city, Adriana travelled the country giving workshops on the subject, which I would attend twice afterwards, and on that Friday, she was dressed all in white, a tradition that refers to Afro-Brazilian religions. Adriana is the owner of several catchphrases, extolling 'entrepreneurial potential' and 'authenticity to overcome the competition'. She suggests that she fully understands how regulated citizenship works in practice, citing her great-grandmother, freed from slavery, as proof that "black people have been doing entrepreneurship for 130 years".

At Cooperifa's soirees, Adriana's words seem to resonate among the dozens of young people who circulate around the little square in front of Zé Batidão's bar, usually with a disposable glass of *cachaça*, honey and lemon in one hand and a mobile phone in the other. Both the square and the surrounding streets were filled with the buzz of people who had just met, and the formation of new networks. That's how João Vicente introduced me to Maria Rita, 27, an Afro-Indian journalist whose final course work at the private FMU college had been on peripheral entrepreneurship. With her incisive opinions and quick thinking, Maria balances fixed and freelance jobs, running her own newspaper with activism. She started at the age of 14 as a young apprentice administrative assistant at USP, where she worked for another six years. She graduated in social communication with Fies funding and worked as a reporter and press officer for a deputy in the São Paulo Legislative Assembly (Alesp). She also did collaborative stories on the daily life of the periphery for Mídia Ninja.[24]

She recently concluded that "Today, I wouldn't go to work so soon, because I think it's something that blocks a lot of other things". That 'something', in this case, is the labour market. About three years ago, Maria created her own online newspaper, which opened some doors for her in the world of media activism. She says that, 'all things considered', it was worth investing in freelance work, "without getting angry, without having to put up with the boss giving you a hard time". Her involvement with the political agenda at one of the newspapers where she worked as a trainee gave her some opportunities, including the advisory position she held at Alesp that ultimately paid her bills. Despite this being her first formal job, Maria absolutely rejects the idea of having a career in the conventional sense of the term, climbing the ranks and hoping to be recognised in the long term. In fact, she thinks that "we have to put an end to this culture that you must enter the labour market". She doesn't see any point in having a formal job and doesn't hesitate to define herself as an 'entrepreneur', which she associates with a better quality of life in which she can choose her own hours.

Maria Rita goes on to associate the labour market with a 'standard' imposed on them and entrepreneurship with an alternative way of generating income 'theoretically, outside the system'. Reflecting a structure of feelings that combines conventional work with mental illness, so common in contemporary

---

24 Mídia Ninja is a collective of journalists and cultural producers that came to prominence in 2013 with the June demonstrations. It's also an arm of the Coletivo Fora do Eixo.

therapeutic discourse, she adds that "there's your psychological involved, there's your health involved, and people don't have health today, in a common work environment". This is another interesting consequence of the entrepreneurial utopia of these interlocutors, since, on the contrary a position that condemns the rigidity of the formal labour contract is fully available for the accumulation of jobs. "Today I work as a reporter, press officer, I do cultural management, I do photography ... and even administration. So, look how much broader it is than just fulfilling a role there," exalting her ability to fulfil numerous tasks at the same time. Maria describes very precisely the emancipatory impulse that she and others from her peripheral generation see in entrepreneurship. In fact, it is a political appropriation of a set of precepts that are only exotic in appearance. Her career in the world of work is relatively short, but she perceives it as a prison. Beyond that, it is the 'system' itself that is a prison. Therefore, it becomes logical to reason that to be an entrepreneur is to be outside of it, to "go beyond what has been imposed".

To be outside the system, you need, as Vitória would say, 'theory'. Maria also emphasises financial education, which empowers popular subject to follow the path of autonomy, because today "economics in the *quebrada* is for paying bills". As a journalist who covers the daily life of the periphery, she is very sensitive to the economic pattern that accompanies its residents, between having to choose which bill will be paid and which will be postponed, the fault of an education that is not only insufficient but that planned for this. "Poor people's leisure is the shopping centre, so they go there to spend everything they've worked for all month. And understanding that there's something beyond that, understanding that you can spend in a place that will help someone else, is very important, very important indeed," she says, reflecting on the need to help other local entrepreneurs.

It's not surprising that such a perception exists and is widespread in the contemporary world. Throughout this book, we have seen the trajectories of people with different profiles in search of autonomy, excited at the prospect of not submitting to a boss and working exclusively in their own businesses, like one who has found an oasis and drowned in its waters. But Maria Rita, like the other interlocutors in this chapter, reveal very particular aspects of the peripheral experience. They are on average younger, the children of immigrants, but already born in São Paulo. They also started working later and in occupations that weren't as strenuous as a childhood spent in the fields, for example, and decided very early on that they didn't want a conventional career, with labour rights and a pension. They see the labour market as a conspiracy to keep them in thrall, suppressing their talents and dreams. So, any context in which they participate and where there is a situation of subjugation causes them great suffering, "because for me capitalism is no good at all. Oh, there's conscious capitalism ... Capitalism always oppresses someone. And I feel guilty that I'm oppressing someone".

Refusing situations of subordination, poorly paid jobs and humiliation can indicate very powerful alternatives to Brazil's structural precariousness. It is also admirable that such nonconformity intervenes in a traditional adaptation to suffering, so common in the working class saturated with popular Catholicism. In this sense, there is a relevant aspect to highlight: in this case, this remarkable politicisation has its origins in the discursive matrices that Eder Sader (1988) had already identified in the mid-1980s, namely the Catholic Church and Teologia da Libertação, trade unionism and academic Marxism. This is part of a residual culture that persists in the Zona Sul, as many of those 'new characters' have remained faithful enough to their causes to pass them on to their children. This is the case of Maria Rita, now a member of Umbanda, but who grew up in an Ecclesial Base Community (CEB) in Taboão da Serra. "Today it's normal, but at the time there was a super progressive priest, and then he brought the grassroots ecclesial movement into the church, and that's when I got involved with the MST, MTST. I started taking part in the Pastoral of Faith and Politics, understanding how it worked." Her father was a PT councillor and still follows politics, as does her mother. Maria, by the way, was a PSOL member, an enthusiastic Lula supporter and saw his government's social programmes, especially for education, as 'revolutionary' projects. "When did you see black people at Mackenzie?" she asked rhetorically, mentioning a traditional Presbyterian university of the city.

We can see from the stories highlighted here that a good portion of the social legitimacy gained by the discourse of entrepreneurship in the periphery comes from a sense of its own power, attributed to it by young people with some previous militancy in the family. Maria's early politicisation instils in her an insubordinate spirit, but she represents a residual culture within a much broader structure of feelings. In a national context of clashes with reactionaries, she has often found herself speaking among the few, realising that the plurality that exists in the periphery doesn't necessarily lean towards the side of peripheral culture. "Because culture in the periphery, despite being in the periphery, is elitist. Not everyone has access to it, and even when they do, people don't see it as culture, they don't see it as entertainment, they think it's boring to come to the soiree ... the soiree is in the *quebrada*, but people from the *quebrada* don't come to the soiree," she points out.

Maria Rita sees education, and not necessarily formal education, as having the power to reverse what she understands as the population's lack of political awareness. She feels similarly about journalism, which she sees as a 'tool for social transformation'. So much commitment has the side effect of reinforcing a competent discourse that also functions as a vector of social distinction. In the Brazil of the 2010s, she only saw 'calamity' and shame, and if she could, she would leave the country. Although she admits it's a cliché, she says she would actually go to Cuba. She's not surprised by the 2018 electoral tragedy because, as a militant, "we know what we encounter on the streets every day". Why did they vote for Bolsonaro? 'Because they're alienated,' Maria replies, in no uncertain terms. It's interesting to note that Maria claims tradition to a certain extent, but not the tradition practised by her parents and their generation, which combines in a contradictory way with peripheral culture's contempt for academia. "Knowledge doesn't just come from academia. It comes from experience, from living. From the ancestral." In the break with the space of experience, the absence of concrete references takes her back to a previous time, when there are no living witnesses; there are only fragments of memory collected by specialists. It is thus clear from her comments that, as people who exist in the interim of that time, it was her parents and relatives, in fact, who broke with their ancestry, and for this they must be judged.

Regarding the opposition to *Lulismo* that she finds on the streets, Maria Rita minimises the economic crises that the country has been going through since 2015, citing the US crash of 2008 as an example. Here it was 'very mild', she says. "It happens, that's economics. People have no concept of economics and think it's all nonsense. But if we had economic education, people would have that notion." Granted a certain caution, she tries to soften her judgements, but in practice she has broken off relations with relatives and friends "because they voted against my life. I'm black, I'm bisexual, and everything I am … I'm a journalist, everything I am is an attack on them". Finally, showing her nonconformity to her acquaintances, she believes that she has 'living', 'experience' and a 'journey', and that they don't listen to her out of bad faith. The identity aspects give her a basis, but what really annoys her is the disdain for her competence.

Her combative stance is explained by her background as a militant from an early age and an observer of the daily violence against minorities. Politics as a refuge certainly spares her from inconvenient company, but not everything is solved by this choice. Both PSOL and Mídia Ninja, despite ensuring visibility for her work, cause her the same discomfort, because "the majority are white, bourgeois. It's very easy … For example, several times they've asked me to cover stories and I didn't have the money to drive. And, like, they don't even ask, because it's not part of their reality." But even with all the adversity, from inside and outside of politics, she maintains her perseverance. This perseverance she finds above all in her community, peripheral entrepreneurs who distribute dreams around the square in front of the Cooperifa soirée, and who, in their most moving moments, make her believe it's possible to take the starry sky by storm. "I think peripheral culture is what's going to save this country," Maria concludes.

7 Peripheral Subject

The peripheral subject is often a suspicious subject. In almost all the interviews that form part of this chapter, I realised straight away, sometimes even before the first personal contact, that my position as a researcher had created some noise. This is because 'academia' doesn't seem to be at the height of its popularity among my interlocutors, in fact, it's quite the opposite. Just like other social institutions, such as media companies, which have been dragged into the mass grave of the popular imagination, public universities suffer from similar rejection among activists from the periphery. So, my search for these new 'characters' (in Sader's sense loosely applied here), when contact wasn't made in the fieldwork itself, often ended with an unanswered email or a call. In some cases, my patience was rewarded, not without some kind of excuse of a busy schedule followed by a warning about the 'social counterpart' of the research. This was, in fact, one of my first discoveries in the field.

In one of these successful attempts, a month and a half after the first contact and on that day in September 2019, I arrived at the headquarters of a 'journalism production company from the *quebrada*' run by three former university classmates who live on the outskirts of the Zona Sul, one of them the journalist Júlio, who welcomed me after some insistence at the door of the house. It was a cloudy day, and the house was not very close to the Grajaú CPTM station, about an hour and a half from the city centre, plus a 25-minute walk along Avenida Belmira Marin. Despite having the same fast-food outlets and well-known retail chains as those further north on the periphery, the avenue looked rundown, and had no housing developments. Vehicles in terrible condition spewed out tonnes of black smoke on every block.

The surroundings of the beige house, encircled by a high wall, look like a quiet residential neighbourhood, but my interlocutor prefers to stress the violence of the area. The district lies almost at the edge of the city, squeezed by the Guarapiranga and Billings reservoirs. It is the largest in the city, according to the Seade Population Projections System, with more than 390,000 people.[25] According to Júlio, the great exposure that Jardim Ângela and Capão Redondo

---

25 Available at: https://populacao.seade.gov.br/evolucao-populacional-msp/.

had in the 1990s helped to reduce the rates of violence in these districts, thus elevating Grajaú to the position of the most dangerous region. The perception of violence is perhaps greater than the coldness of the figures, which continue to show Capão and three other neighbouring districts as the capital's homicide champions.[26] Removing the idea that the periphery is just poverty and violence, but also 'culture and power' is a pillar of peripheral culture, but it contrasts with the reiteration of the periphery as a space of insecurity and precarity, which in any case is an important persuasive strategy.

Born and raised in Grajaú, Júlio, 32, studied social communication at Santo Amaro University (Unisa). He entered the world of work at the age of 14 as a packer and then a clerk in a supermarket. While still at university, he got an internship at a consumer protection NGO based in the Zona Oeste. He then worked as a newsroom intern, covering technology and finance for a property listings website; as a reporter for a technology and business magazine; and for a Latin American news website. About ten years ago, he and two other undergraduate friends decided to create a production company, dissatisfied with working in a journalism market where they didn't see themselves represented. Since then, Júlio has worked as a content manager at the production company and has done other freelance work.

He went to university on a grant from the shop workers' union and it was with this experience that he and his colleagues began to question the traditional media's representation of the periphery. "What is this media I'm working for? What imaginary am I helping to construct exactly?" He is also concerned about the university. He stresses how much university 'increased his repertoire' so that he could analyse his reality, but distanced him, for example, from his early activism in the Catholic Church. Familiar with the peripheral culture circuit in the Zona Sul, he refers to the poet Sérgio Vaz in his defence of 'de-elitised' and democratic communication, as well as the poetry that emanates from Cooperifa's soirees. "What we do isn't new, I think what's new is access to university, which has allowed us to acquire theory and other knowledge," but he also emphasises the impact of new technologies, such as the internet, which "has allowed us to connect, for example, with other communication collectives."

The ambiguity of the relationship between young people from the periphery and university gains depth in Júlio's account, as someone who had been alienated from academia and who, when he got in, went all the way. Because it

---

26 According to data from the São Paulo Public Security Secretariat, in 2017 the five districts with the most intentional homicides in the capital were, in that order, Capão Redondo, Parque Santo Antônio, Campo Limpo, Parelheiros and Jardim Herculano.

is a symbol of distinction for the traditional middle class, it is seen, on the one hand, as a means of social climbing; on the other hand, especially in the case of most valued public institutions, it also appears to be an exotic place that harbours knowledge only offered to a select few, pejoratively known as 'intellectuals' or the 'academy'. Both facets have been going through a deep crisis since the 1980s, but their responsibility for promoting inclusion and therefore social mobility has gained relevance in Brazil, becoming the object of *Lulismo*'s public policies.[27] It is precisely when this inclusion takes place that the opposition to academia seems to intensify. In any case, accessing that hidden knowledge (the 'theory') responds to the need to build self-sufficient peripheral knowledge, but its real importance, ironically, is on the same level as access to the internet and other public policies for culture.

Recognising the periphery as a place of belonging gave rise to peripheral culture, as we saw earlier, but in this section, I have called Júlio a 'peripheral subject' for a more specific reason. This is not an attribution given from outside: at one point in the interview, he uses the term to describe himself. When asked about it, the journalist doesn't elaborate on his subjectivity, but refers to D'Andrea's doctoral thesis, *A formação do sujeito periférico: cultura e política na periferia de São Paulo*, defended in 2013 at USP and already mentioned here.[28] I asked Júlio to give his definition, and his answer was "a person who comes from the peripheries and who, from understanding the place they occupy, begins to act politically to transform their reality". With his thesis, D'Andrea seems to have created a code that political subjects like Júlio can identify with. "We believe in our emancipation as peripheral subjects and we don't think this is going to happen in this system that is capitalist, racist, sexist, LGBT-phobic and has a series of divisions," he says.

It is curious, however, that this is a highly academic code accessible to those who know how to decipher it, in this case university students. Thus, Júlio combines two characteristics that are not necessarily contradictory, but which seem to come from two universes that are constantly in tension: the periphery and the university. In his *quebrada*, he admits that there is still a 'long way to go' for the production company to reach a wider audience; despite claiming a lack of structure and resources for this, it is in his militant language that the wall that separates him from his neighbours seems to be built. Júlio tries to convince (me or himself) that reaching "Mrs. Maria, who goes to church next

---

27 See Prandi (1982) and the entry on 'intellectuals' in Williams (1976).
28 Feltran (2011) had also noticed these characteristic "modulations" among some of his interviewees, many of whom were prepared to cite authors and theories when alerted that this was doctoral or post-doctoral research.

door" is merely a technical matter, of who has adequate internet service etc. However, the fact is that, even after overcoming these obstacles, "we speak to a very specific audience, which is an audience that is also from a movement, is from a collective, or is already politically engaged, or has had access to higher education or, in short, is a civil servant, there are many teachers who accompany us". With this, his concern for Mrs. Maria quickly fades and he finds his focus again on 'subjective issues', because "our struggle is to give back a humanity that are denied for us all the time".

For D'Andrea (2013: 136–142), the attribute 'peripheral' would have been superimposed on those of "suburban, poor, black, and fundamentally, worker", since the recognition of urban inequality from the 1990s onwards, in a context of growing unemployment and neoliberalism, would have eliminated work as a central identity category in the popular context. However, even for younger people who "entered a world that had already been turned upside down", as Vera Telles (2006) puts it, this superimposition is not an obvious one. For Júlio, 'peripheral subject' may be a cooler identity, but what really saturates his testimony is his identity as a conventional worker. Regarding his past with a formal labour contract, he still sees himself as someone lucky in a career marked by recent precariousness. He says he sees no disadvantage in the CLT and regrets that outside it he probably won't be entitled to a pension. Even so, he left by choice. Trying to maintain consistency, Júlio considers the epithet 'entrepreneur' to be deceptive, but his choice to leave the CLT and no longer work for a market that 'dehumanises' him and in which he doesn't see himself represented is part of the same utopian desire that makes entrepreneurship essential in this structure of feelings. "I don't consider myself an entrepreneur even though we … in our case, we created a business from scratch, but that's because we say that we created our work, we created our job," says the journalist, so that, realising the contradiction, he says he's not interested in profit.

It is also a symptom of scepticism to renounce the world around you, constructing a virtual reality in which recurring themes in the progressive agenda artificially become the norm. This is what seems to happen at times with Júlio and his fellow 'peripheral subjects', for whom politics, however well-intentioned, does not serve to dispute society (or even the periphery), but to create distinctions and labels suitable for echo chambers. In the tension between the theory he learned at university and the pragmatism that he tries to disguise, some critical element always escapes. "So, we have to bring this to this collective reflection, like, what's left for us, right? Again, what's left? There are always crumbs left over, right?" he says of the partnerships with companies that, after all, are the hallmark of social entrepreneurship.

The perception of violence in the periphery helps explain the behaviour of young people from the periphery in the 2020s. What they are aware of is that the outside world is very dangerous, and facing it is increasingly exhausting. Júlio shows signs of weariness, which is nothing new, given the growing hostility towards activism in the peripheries (Rocha, 2013). In this purgatory, they shrink and support each other, trying to fortify themselves with more than crumbs against the feeling shared with their readers that 'it seems like it's all over'. One of the projects Júlio is proud of at the production company has to do, once again, with 'subjective issues'. He tells the life stories of women who took part in movements to fight for rights in the Grajaú region, revealing their agency and resilience, searching somewhere in the past for the experience that his generation lacks. "People are fighting their battles in their homes to stay alive, to survive. So how do we move on from this question of here and now, but of extending this space of time? Bringing back the history of these women, for example, is for us to go back thirty, forty years, to show what they did back when it was all bush, literally, here."

PART 2

Structure of Feelings

∴

CHAPTER 4

Reconfigurations

What explains the recent success of speeches extolling entrepreneurship in Brazil? If there is more than one type, what do they align with, and what do they oppose? Is it possible to use the same expression for experiences as different as the ones I've reported in this book?[1] In this chapter, I try to discuss these questions by analysing the new ways of life that have been created on the margins of the city. With the growth of self-employment in Brazil in the 2010s, which was preceded by some social mobility, emerging cultural forms naturally consolidated in the interstices of a break with the space of popular experience, a much deeper and far-reaching process.

Between the 1970s and 1980s, the chaotic occupation that had begun around 30 years earlier by workers expelled from the central regions, paired with intense migration towards the city (the result of its robust but uneven and centrifugal economic development), began to take hold on the outskirts of São Paulo. It was through self-building on irregular plots of land that this dispossessed population settled in areas lacking urban infrastructure, basically provided with dirt roads at the time. Without financing or government aid, this was the pattern of peripheral expansion in the São Paulo State capital, where, driven by the dream of home ownership, thousands of workers used their free time and meagre savings to gradually consolidate a family project of citizenship (Holston, 2008).

At the root of this malaise, the end of the utopian wage society and national developmentalism at the turn of the 1990s was accompanied by the growing disappointment in the family project of social mobility through home ownership and formal education for children. Its replacement by the purely monetary mediation of social relations would be a consequence of this.[2] "When

---

1 However, it's important to point out, in line with Koselleck (2004), that these experiences don't occur at the same speed depending on other social factors such as the subjects' class position. Karl Mannheim (1993) uses the category of 'generational units' to describe individuals who develop different perspectives and reactions to the same generational context. I also addressed these cleavages in my master's dissertation, in which two groups of students receiving scholarships from the University for All Programme (Prouni) at the same university in São Paulo had opposite responses to and perspectives on access to a higher education degree (Costa, 2018).
2 According to Feltran (2007), the 'worker's project' was constituted and sustained by residents of these neighbourhoods during the 1970s and 1980s and consisted of social ascension through participation in social movements, constructing their own housing and factory work.

neither the law nor what is considered right can mediate the relationship between population groups and their progressively autonomous ways of conceiving of themselves and others, it is money that appears as the only objective way of mediating their relationships," points out Gabriel Feltran (2014: 14). In the collapse of those pillars and the consecration of Lula's project of inclusion through consumption, a virtually classless society appears, symbolised by the entrepreneur in its multiple versions, the result of a late cultural modernisation conducted in a public-private manner. Traditional social forms that are simply considered disposable are thus reincorporated on new bases, and precariousness, although not new in Brazil, reappears stripped of the previous project of citizenship.[3]

Important reconfigurations in wageless life have taken place in recent decades, adding new characters and reinserting others.[4] On the outskirts of large cities, Vera Telles (2006) observed that low wages and high turnover have blurred the boundaries between formal and informal and between permanent and temporary, especially for those who entered the labour market between 1995 and 2005. Francisco de Oliveira (2003: 136) interpreted informal labour at the turn of the century as a working population transformed "into an indeterminate sum of active and reserve army, who interchange not in business cycles, but on a daily basis". With the same premise, Cibele Rizek (2012: 41) saw a "more or less recent set of transformations, in which the experience of work – beyond factory work – and of the city – beyond dualised references such as centre and periphery, presence or absence of the state, place of work and place of residence – have become confused". Feltran (2007: 33) comments that for a

---

3   The expansion of citizenship through monetisation is not a new idea. Among the contractualists, it was already naturally present, because property, in capitalism, is the element that mediates social relations, subjecting men to each other and to the commodity fetish, and is therefore the basis for the modern concept of citizenship. In his *Philosophy of Money*, Georg Simmel speculated that money doesn't buy freedom, but rather allows for a freer relationship by decompressing the burdens imposed by immediate needs. However, in the urban peripheries, the entrepreneurial logic that runs through evangelicals, bandits and state actors – transforming all of them into market operators – universalises monetisation as the only possible language for managing social and urban conflict.

4   Liana Carleial and Christian Azaïs (2007) call this blurring between formal and informal, especially in the context of neoliberal deregulation, both in Brazil and France, 'hybridisation'. Azaïs also mentions the concept of 'grey zones', which is "one of the links in understanding the institutional change that the various forms of employment and work, whether emerging or not, are undergoing. Diversity of trajectories, entanglement, overlapping of formal and informal activities ... we are far from a uniform vision of the universe of employment and labour relations" (Costa et al., 2021: 982).

generation born and raised in the 1990s, lifestyles are already "mostly shaped by the permanence of these crises and their inescapability".

In this way, the popular world remakes itself and weaves new sociabilities in condominiums that strengthen bonds of family affection, but which take on the appearance of dependency as the outside world seems increasingly threatening. This reflects a housing model that Caldeira (2000) called 'fortified enclaves' and which, until the 1980s, was a characteristic pattern of elite gated communities that began to expand to other territories.[5] Concerns about children condition what is allowed and what is avoided, and reinforces the idealisation of the past in popular memory, when people played in the street and drugs and sexuality were restricted to a more private sphere. The result is the search for refuge precisely in over-protected spaces, where habits and customs are reinterpreted and recognition for competence fills the identity of this 'new middle class'.

These ways of life are constantly reinvigorated in the peripheries, where an endogenous circulation relates to the 'formal' market only by crossing the bridge. They appear in a subordinate way insofar as the popular economy is based on non-salaried activities and self-employment grows rapidly, stimulated by legislation aimed at facilitating forms of micro-entrepreneurship.[6] The high unemployment rates of recent years have also pushed many former employees into entrepreneurship out of necessity. This is not, however, the focus of this research, although it does address characters who had their first entrepreneurial impulse due to the need to obtain or supplement income. Through perseverance, some of these figures have prospered or are still trying to, and it is this aptitude that is of interest here. For others, however, there is no shortage of work. In fact, a lifetime of exploitation and abuse has long outstripped their ability to absorb suffering. "One day I'll start a restaurant, I don't know when, even if it's in my house," Estela told me, with 61 years of hardship behind her.

Symptomatically, the generational conflict also expands, as entrepreneurship promises younger people the ability to move between social classes through modern culture and the depreciation of customs. This seems to be

---

5   Symbols of this transformation are shopping malls, the former stronghold of the wealthier classes, which synthesised the offer of services combined with privileges and the paranoia for protection and security, and private universities located at major urban junctions, whose turnstiles sought to sell the feeling of security and exclusivity. See Caldeira (2000) and Costa (2018).
6   Self-employment reached 24.6 million Brazilians in the quarter ending in December 2019, according to data from the Continuous National Household Sample Survey (PNAD-Contínua).

an unexpected outcome for parents, who, when investing in their children's education, expected this development to continue the family's desired social mobility without realising the ambiguities that this process would bring to both family relationships and the sociability of these young people (Tomizaki, 2006; Beaud; Pialoux, 2009). Ownership of the self-constructed house, in turn, which is also fundamental to the family project, helped provide the material support for this. Today it is vital for many children and grandchildren to be able to postpone their entry into the labour market in a precarious situation, thus extending the parental home and gaining more space to advance.[7]

The rupture of the space of experience promotes the impulse towards constant transformations and a way of life to be lived entirely as a career, but with disdain for the stability represented by the Consolidation of Labour Laws (CLT) and the work card. This drive towards rationalisation belittles accumulated experience and practical knowledge and reforms one of the central elements of popular individualism by assuming that those who have acquired 'theory' have merit. This is measured in abstract terms in the form of certificates and diplomas, and no longer because of work done with discipline, dedication and know-how. Unaware of waged labour and the social rights associated with it, it breaks with the idea of expectation to enjoy the present, because 'the future can't wait', as the private higher education market advertising usually informs us. Thus, as Machado da Silva once said, it provides a 'new labour culture in the making'.[8]

Of course, this rationalisation can come with very good intentions. This can be mapped out, for example, and especially important for the Latin American context, in the work of Peruvian economist Hernando de Soto. In 1987, he published *El otro sendero* (The Other Path), a reference to the far-left political

---

7   As Cardoso (2008: 571) observes, "what characterises the contemporary world is the fact that youth unemployment slows down the trajectories of young people, pushing employment further and further back in the biography of individuals, thereby weakening the coincidence between adulthood and financial independence, and with it the responsibility for providing for oneself and one's family. As a result, the *débâcle of* developmentalism, which began in the 1990s and is still being consolidated, has not meant an end to the precariousness of the school-to-work transition process. On the contrary, it has greatly increased young people's uncertainties about their place in the social order."

8   "very different from that which corresponded to the history of the construction of wage labour," continues Machado da Silva (2018: 296–298), for whom it represented a 'virtuous combination' that generated the "expansion of accumulation and a positive self-image of the working population", while the employability/entrepreneurship pair "kills" the possibilities of social solidarity. This is a perspective with which I have attempted to critically engage in this book.

party and terrorist organisation Sendero Luminoso (Shining Path) and the alternative path that he and the Instituto Libertad y Democracia (IDL) proposed, that of property ownership by the poor and entrepreneurship, seeking to defeat Sendero 'in the world of ideas' (De Soto, 1989). Following the downfall of socialist alternatives in Latin America and beyond, including violent ones, in fact, 'the other way' had already flourished as an idea, bringing together typically progressive principles such as diversity and protagonism from below.

Society is not static, however, and these proposals can thrive in contradictory ways, depending on the structure of feelings in which they are embedded, and reorganise themselves in unexpected ways. For Williams, this is the practical consciousness of a moment. They fulfil feelings and tastes that "saturate the lifeworld in complex ways, such as mood, attitude, manners, emotions and so on" (Highmore, 2016: 149). Williams seeks to go beyond systematic beliefs and ideologies, emphasising meanings and values as they are actually lived and felt. It is therefore less about deliberate action by the ruling class or mere manipulation, and more about the production of common sense, implying a process that the historian, inspired by Gramsci, defines as the 'saturation' of consciousness at a given historical moment. Hegemony constitutes, in this case, "a sense of reality for most people in the society, a sense of absolute because experienced reality beyond which it is very difficult for most members of the society to move, in most areas of their lives" (Williams, 1973: 9).

In this part of the book, I extend the analysis of the trajectories presented in Part 1 in a transversal way, using the experiences of wageless life. These are individual behaviours that rework an *ethos* whose formation does not happen spontaneously but is transmitted by generations and the experiences of others, shaping what Koselleck (2004) calls the space of experience. It preserves accumulated customs and knowledge that has not been completely overcome by the advance of rationalism, residual cultural forms that are preserved with more or less vigour while maintaining their intelligibility in popular culture, forming a past insofar as it is present.

It is within this popular context in São Paulo (and in the country in general) that small traders, self-employed workers, former salaried workers or people with a formal contract who need to supplement their income with odd jobs mingle, reproducing wageless life, individualism and a certain discomfort with situations of subjection. The experience of formalisation, by the way, is often belittled by the countless situations of exhaustion and exploitation of a section of the population that is also very poorly paid. These forms of social reproduction also coexist within families, which accommodate individuals with and without a fixed occupation and, more intensely in the 1990s, those involved in the criminal world. In neighbourhood life, especially in the more remote regions, the self-employed and the small shopkeeper mix with the working class *stricto sensu,* sharing the same ways of life.

Thus, my interlocutors listed in Chapter 1 realistically understand their 'dreams' as family projects, as Eduardo told me. In their quest for autonomy, these working class people have ambitions that fall within a modest definition of material comfort, such as the possibility of enjoying one holiday a year. They don't allow themselves any illusions, because their experiences with work, which for most of them began in childhood or adolescence, bind them tightly to solid ground, implying calculated risks. Sueli, for example, talks about 'achievable goals', improving one step at a time and starting with small objectives. "I don't want to get rich, but I want to have a minimum of comfort, right? So I can survive well, so I don't have to be so tight. But I don't want to be a millionaire, it's good to keep your feet on the ground," she says, laughing at her own ambition.

The trajectories reported in chapters 1 and 2, together with participant observation, allowed me to guide the analysis from the micro to the macro, as Michael Burawoy (2009) teaches, and with the help of the relevant literature, I was able to add experiences in which, in their particularities, the *ethos* of autonomous work rooted in popular culture emerges. It is important to note that this is not simply a question of continuity, as if these characters could be found in any other time and place. On the contrary, the thesis I present here reflects on fundamental characteristics of the experience of wageless life in Brazil which, given the massification of therapeutic discourse and the evolution of technical means of self-management previously unavailable to a large part of the poorer population, could only deepen. A persistent reference to individual merit and a belief in hard work and honesty (and the grace of God) being rewarded remain a part of this *ethos*. This is still an ingrained culture that, along with practical knowledge, rationalisation seeks to disregard, strengthening the competent discourse, which I discussed especially in Chapter 3.

In popular contexts, opposition to the 'market', seen as the imposition of rationalisation and depersonalisation, finds in the same entrepreneurship a mechanism of resistance through the aspiration to non-subordinated work, because it is through a fictionalisation of autonomy that, by taking on a narrative form, allows subjects to establish connections between current uncertainties and future states (Beckert, 2013).

1 Family, Community and Social Classes

Popular individualism is characteristic of the wageless life, and as an ideal type, it is not absolute. Among my interlocutors who are over thirty and who live in the more peripheral areas – Vargem Grande being the best example – we can see a resilient community relationship, in which the small business owner is perceived and understood as a reference in the neighbourhood, as in the cases of Renato, Delei, Lígia, and others. They see their customers as friends, and nods between neighbours are common. Here, there is a recognisable value and a very organic relationship between them and the other workers. These are relations like those observed by Richard Hoggart (2009) among members of the English working class in the mid-20th century. On the other hand, Hoggart also had an intuition about the small shopkeepers who worked far from where they lived and observed how inferior and subaltern they felt when serving middle-class customers in their neighbourhoods. In the popular shopping area of Santo Amaro, I saw situations in which the distance from home to work frustrated community relations and made individuals more sceptical and suspicious.

In large neighbourhoods in the South, such as the Paraisópolis *favela*, the magnitude of the conflicts is proportional to their diversity, which mixes situations of vulnerability, regulation of entry and exit from certain points by the First Command of Capital (PCC) and their relevance in the imaginary position both inside and outside the *favela*. Closely related to the upper-middle class Morumbi neighbourhood, the obvious oppositions present in this relationship between the neighbourhoods often hide the way Paraisópolis residents see their own neighbours. For example, there is a certain hostility from those who live or do business near Morumbi, like my interlocutor Celso, towards those who hang out in the 'middle', around Rua Ernst Renan, where the vibrant local commerce even takes over the pavement. This is also where the Baile da Dz7 takes place, one of the city's biggest funk parties, where in December 2019 a police intervention caused panic and the deaths of nine young people.

Opinions on the tragedy reveal the ambiguity with which *flows* are perceived by the neighbours themselves: many interlocutors strike a balance between condemning the police action and vehemently rejecting the events, which takes place from Wednesday to Sunday and don't end until dawn. Between moral outrage and despair at the inescapable routine, the only positive point they see is the opportunity an influx of customers for some local businesses. An escape from realities seen as unbearable has stimulated, on the one hand, the proliferation of condominiums outside the area, where unpleasant situations can be avoided and class experiences can be re-enacted, and, on the other, generates reactions of incomprehension and internal conflict.

The combined elements of renewing the importance of the family and maintaining occupations based on practical and manual knowledge lead to an attachment to the concrete and lived reality of the social reproduction of wageless life. Faced with increasing uncertainty, it is in these areas that the individual becomes trapped. Thus, my interlocutors perceive a certain practical logic governing their actions, which are not limited to monetary calculations, but favour popular understandings of family well-being (De L'Estoile, 2020). These choices are not, as Marshall Sahlins (1976) would suggest, merely utilitarian, evoking a theory of praxis in which material comfort justifies a logic of means and ends. Often, this logic becomes more flexible and manifests itself in its opposite. In Sahlins' own terms, there are 'significant reasons' that govern them, hostile to the rationalisation imposed by the labour market, by companies and by the discourse of entrepreneurship, which is viewed with curiosity and at the same time suspicion.

The references to family among my interlocutors, who are between 30 and 40 years old, are not only repeated, but also perceived in field situations, where the presence of younger children created curious situations of affection mixed with attempts to curb behaviour considered erratic or excessive, such as stubbornness or hyperactivity. We also realise that family formation drives pragmatic decisions even among those who exalt social entrepreneurship as a principle. For example, João Vicente, who has a young daughter, moves between his position of a convinced entrepreneur (with an unstable income) and questioning whether he should pursue a degree that will put him in a position to eventually compete for more formal jobs. This contrasts with the women interlocutors who, in the same age bracket, end up choosing home, raising their children and, to supplement the family income, self-employment. As in the examples of Sueli and Keila, these situations can lead to committed entrepreneurship. In Carolina's case, there is also the criterion of proximity to home, which allows her to work in her shop in Paraisópolis and visit her young son just a few blocks away.

In their relationship with their parents, these interlocutors show great deference, out of respect for their humble origins, to the challenges of immigrating to São Paulo and the rigour with which they were raised. Contradictorily, this last aspect is emphasised above all when the interlocutor has children, which often leads them to reflect on their own childhood and adolescence, and see themselves in the position their parents were in. Keila, for example, repeats several times that the worsening conditions of sociability on the periphery are the result of the decline in relations of respect between parents and children. She herself was a mother at a very young age and, now with three children, feels the weight of this responsibility. A practical reason appears here in the very exaltation of rigour against the perversions of the contemporary world, which takes the form of the internet in Ronaldo's case, or, as Otávio commented, of the 'easy access' relating to drug use, which he sees as permissive in Paraisópolis, where he moved for the safety of his children. These considerations obviously have a strong moral charge and are emphasised when they refer to the funk parties. Yet, they are also based on the subjects' own experiences with crime, drug addiction or early pregnancy, situations they claim they don't want for their children. As they reach adolescence, these discourses become even more securitised, with the fear of being unprepared for adult life and the imminent feeling of losing control over them. Turning the wheel of social reproduction, this is where something that my younger interlocutors often complain about manifests. That is, the imposition of paid labour as a way of controlling them and repressing their desires.

Concern for the safety of children can also be seen in the growth in the number of condominiums, given a boost by the housing programme *My House My Life* (MCMV), which focused on the new middle class emerging on the outskirts of the metropolises as we saw in detail in Chapter 1. These fortified enclaves, as Caldeira (2000) puts it, have come to stand out in the landscape where informal structures used to predominate. These structures still exist in immense numbers, of course, but are beginning to disappear in districts like Campo Limpo. In the interpretation proposed in this book, the success of this process also restores the working class dream of acquiring home ownership and realising the family project, but the desire is here already adulterated by transformations in the structure of feelings. Something fundamental to mention is that it is precisely the stabilisation of the family institution in past decades that today allows many of these young people to postpone entering the labour market. The contradiction in this case is that, as Sader (1988: 113) observed, "with the goal achieved, one lives the history of progress". Once this stability has been reached, however, the priority for families is to maintain it, with all the moral and political repercussions this involves for the relationship between generations.

This renewed urban pattern is also reflected in the local standard of living and stimulates entrepreneurship in two directions. Products and services that were once considered elitist are now part of the peripheral menu, such as organic food, craft hamburgers and breweries, in the places I visited during my fieldwork and whose owners were important interlocutors. The second consequence of the proliferation of condominiums is the possibility they open up for intramural commerce, producing relationships of trust and community that have become scarce outside them. I've spoken to many residents of these places who embraced entrepreneurship initially out of necessity, but who found in this isolated city experience the very consumers of their homemade and delivery dishes. Again, the family appears here, sharing all the business tasks. For example, Eduardo cooks, his wife Raphaela takes care of the accounting, and their eldest daughter makes the deliveries within the condominium. Naturally, they set their sights on diversifying local tastes, a result of the increase in the local standard of living. So, with his CV filled with restaurants aimed at the upper-middle class in wealthier areas of the city, Eduardo reproduces this experience for his neighbours at a more affordable price.

In fact, both for his family and for a seemingly distant case (the burger restaurant in Paraisópolis), one can see the consecration of practical reason in the conviction with which they understand the demands of this new middle class, eager for the products and services available on the other side of the bridge, but with a much lower income. So, they reproduce these experiments within the periphery and have been successful, though not without some personal sacrifices typical of the entrepreneurial *ethos*, such as long working hours and, ironically, little attention to family.

These experiences are not reducible to a more comfortable standard of living; access to the 'traditional' middle class depends on other factors. These hard-working families who now live in condominiums set up their businesses, consume products and services that were previously unavailable on the peripheries and form an aspiring class whose upward mobility in recent years takes it away from the working class, but also brings them only halfway to the middle class, which lives in the city centre or in high-end condominiums and remain close to the cultural elite. This is not a trivial difference: the transition to the middle class still depends on the availability of other non-economic capital or even 'theory', as Paul Willis has already observed,[9] in which an important symbol of distinction, the university degree, is no longer enough. Increasingly, postgraduate courses, MBAs and, above all, international experience are becoming these differentiators, raising the bar for social distinction (Méndez, 2008).

---

9 Willis observed in the 'counter-school culture' of industrial England in the late 1970s, fundamentally influenced by the shopfloor, that there was a deep conviction among manual workers that practical skills and knowledge are a condition for other skills. Thus, "whereas in middle class culture knowledge and qualifications are seen as a way of shifting upwards the whole mode of practical alternatives open to an individual, in working class eyes theory is riveted to particular productive practices. If it cannot earn its keep there, it is to be rejected" (Willis, 1981: 56).

Back in 2014, as part of my research for my previous book, I received a glimpse from an interlocutor of someone deeply involved in this process, an Information Security student who was out of work after trying his luck at a failed startup. Aged 22 at the time, he is the son of parents from Pernambuco and a resident of Vila Mariana, a gentrified former working class neighbourhood on the Zona Sul. He had started working five years earlier as a stockist in a clothing shop. He attributed his relative economic stability to his work and his family's perseverance and said that without the University for All Programme (Prouni) scholarship he wouldn't have been able to go to university because he was unemployed and couldn't afford it. It was a trivial trajectory, but one that took on a distinctive shape in the way he perceived mobility between social classes, saturated with disbelief and a sense of warning.

> I had a friend who was middle class. He lived near Vila Mariana, he had an excellent flat, big, they were a family … we used to joke, 'you're the richest', but they were middle class. But there was a setback, and because of a slip-up today they are lower class. I'd say that if it's so flexible that you can change classes, then there's no such thing as the middle. You're either one or you're not. So if you're almost rich, you're poor, if you're almost poor, you're rich.
> COSTA, 2018: 204

The ambiguous relationship between the traditional middle class and the periphery is often illustrated by the metaphor of the 'bridge'. More than just a geographical coincidence due to the position of the Pinheiros River on the city map, the bridge is also the reinforced concrete reality of the division between classes in São Paulo. The city's other peripheries, especially the Zona Leste, have developed in the same 'logic of disorder' (Kowarick, 1980), but none of them have this explicit symbolism. While entrepreneurs import and adapt the middle class *habitus* to the periphery, for thousands of workers 'crossing the bridge' means entering spaces of subordination. This may be a factory or a shop, but could also refer to the houses and flats where many work as maids, doormen or drivers.

This is a dialectical relationship, however, made explicit by the interlocutor Aparecida, who is aware of the fact that the management of these traditional middle class spaces is done by female workers from the peripheral side of the bridge. What's more, she notes with great perspicacity that these subordinates are evangelicals like herself. Pentecostalism thus appears with an ambiguity all its own, because in the view of the Universal Church of the Kingdom of God (UCKG), as long as popular culture remains saturated by Catholicism and its option for humility, a poor population will never be able to enjoy the benefits of modernity. A break is therefore necessary, and despite the opposition it still provokes in other Pentecostal denominations,[10] the UCKG project is gaining adherence and power, instigating rebellion and non-conformity, a silent revolutionary project of self-realisation whose social and political consequences have yet to fully emerge.

One interlocutor, the manager of a social organisation in Campo Limpo, observed that the culture of families on the periphery 'is not yet entrepreneurial'. This remark suggests that this type of work goes beyond questions of training or education. In fact, it highlights families' insistence on preserving their popular customs, the weight that their know-how has for them, and the values that cover them. They seek to preserve a spartan way of life that guarantees them a minimum of comfort and minimises the risks of the future; insist that work doesn't significantly alter a family structure that exalts the masculinity of hard work and the providence of the woman who takes care of the house (even when she works outside); and finally – and this is very evident in the interviews with fathers and mothers of teenagers, such as Otávio, Mari and Ronaldo – emphasise keeping their children out of trouble, whether it's the world of crime and drugs or an unwanted pregnancy.

2   Social Entrepreneurship and the Classless Society

Over the last few decades, a tangled network has formed on the peripheries of São Paulo that includes business, social foundations and institutes, including business schools and social projects, some of them led by managers born on the outskirts themselves. It aims to bridge the gap between precariousness and entrepreneurship by 'teaching people how to fish'. This is not about creating more entrepreneurs in a super-competitive world, but about deconstructing and renewing the profile of the worker under a new entrepreneurial culture, in other words, directly affecting their ways of acting and thinking as a workforce. For the individual who enters the world of social entrepreneurship, taking on a proposal for innovation means seeing this corporate world as a promise of social ascension which, in any case, re-qualifies them for the labour market. This demand also often generates anxiety and suffering due to the search for

---

10   My interlocutor Estela is from the Assembly of God and a staunch Lula supporter, which suggests great ambiguities in the evangelical world. See Vinicius S. M. Valle (2019).

differentiation from the huge contingent of new entrepreneurs who emerge as the labour market degrades even further.

Generally associated with the traditional middle class, currently represented by the world of startups and Silicon Valley billionaires, the modern entrepreneur is increasingly a model that young people from the Brazilian peripheries aspire to. Escaping a 'worker's destiny'[11] and getting rich easily with some 'innovation', often disregarding the knowledge taught in schools and colleges, seems for many to be a dream to cling to in the face of the gruelling daily routine of precarious jobs, high turnover and low salaries, which is difficult to combine with university courses. The required higher education qualification, seen more as an obstacle than as a training, doesn't give them any guarantee of a promising career (Costa, 2019a).

The premise of modernisation are increasingly present in schools, in the merchandise of the cultural industry and in the speeches of businesspeople and politicians.[12] In the Brazilian peripheries, they captivate young people who have been through school, social organisations and university courses formatted in this business/pedagogical model, which, among other things, exalts common themes of the corporate narrative such as autonomy, flexibility and teamwork.[13] University students are particularly encouraged to engage, but younger students already have contact with entrepreneurship at school through the new Common National Curriculum Base (BNCC) and the restructuring of secondary education, approved between 2016 and 2018 and which includes the subject as one of its main axes. But the role that education

---

11   For Bourdieu (2012: 589–90), the question of inheritance is that of the son who, in order to 'make a life', must deny his father's path, "by simply refusing to inherit and be inherited and thus retrospectively cancelling the entire paternal enterprise, materialised in the rejected inheritance". This effect of limiting ambitions, says the sociologist, is all the more powerful when the father occupies "a dominated position, either from an economic and social point of view (worker, small employee) or from a symbolic point of view (member of a stigmatised group) and is therefore inclined to ambivalence with regard to his son's success and with regard to himself".

12   Tommasi (2013: 197) identified this turning point in the 'pacification' of Rio's favelas in the first half of the 2010s, where "a significant spread of programmes, courses and projects aimed at stimulating what we call 'community-based entrepreneurship'".

13   Boltanski and Chiapello (2009: 103) compare two periods of bibliographical production on business management, the 1960s and the 1990s. Both criticise bureaucracy, but the 1990s manuals radicalise the denunciation of hierarchy within companies, both in its moral aspect and reflecting the increase in workers' education. The aim would be to organise workers "into small multidisciplinary teams (because they are more competent, flexible, inventive and autonomous than the specialised sections of the 1960s), whose real boss is the customer, with a coordinator rather than a boss".

plays in sewing this contemporary popular culture together is not restricted to these obvious symbols, because "with socio-emotional skills, the business community intends to teach working youth, through practical exercises – of course, because theory is unattractive and less important in the new school function – things like kindness, 'emotional resilience' and self-management" (Catini, 2020: 57).

In the case of peripheral culture, its articulation with social impact businesses was mediated by socio-educational projects that were set up in the 2000s in neighbourhoods such as Jardim São Luís and Capão Redondo, or that had already existed for many years and modulated their portfolios to the new terms in vogue. Projeto Rede, for example, is a social organisation (OS) that has existed in Campo Limpo since 1968 and has its origins in the mothers' clubs of the Zona Sul and the work of Catholic activists. These mothers, according to an interlocutor who works with the project, took the demand for income generation and started their own sewing business. In his book, Sader (1988) mentions this story, which involved not only autonomy (the 'organisation by themselves'), but also an awareness that led them to swap welfare work for the fight against injustice, together with the work of pastoral agents. Their children were pioneers in early childhood education at Rede and other OSs, and with the succession of generations, these projects expanded. Through agreements with the municipal departments of Education and Social Services, the OS provides care for children and teenagers, as well as projects that are independent from public authorities and funded by private foundations. Around 800 children, teenagers and young people attend the centre, plus around 100 adults.

In 2006, the Projeto Rede created a social intervention area in which one social entrepreneurship incubator stands out.[14] However, it was in 2014 that the demand for a training space for entrepreneurship was noticed. At the time, a partnership with the Spanish Telefónica Foundation for the creation of social impact projects resulted in relative failure: young people from the periphery found it difficult to keep up with the pace of the lessons and the plethora of technical terms that permeate this universe. From this "mismatch between

---

14 According to Paulo Freire's conception of education, the incubation process "consists of permanent education, aimed at the autonomy and emancipation of the incubated groups, as well as the development of new production and labour relations". Available at: https://prceu.usp.br/programa/itcp-usp/. Henrique Wellen (2008: 112) presents a Marxist-inspired critique of the concept of solidarity economy. According to him, "the solidarity that is presented as a quality that distinguishes this proposal from capitalist companies actually serves much more as an added value to publicity than it represents a concrete practice".

the method and the public", in the words of Felipe, my interlocutor at OS, the agents came up with a working agenda. The agenda tasked the Foundation with the technical training of teachers that Rede itself, with its expertise in serving young people from the periphery, would provide. The experience of the first cycle taught them about what they considered to be a breach of expectations in relation to the target audience: high school students were not yet ready to develop their own business. The priority would then be university students, with partnerships with private teaching institutions in the areas of Business and Information Technology (IT).

Those who decide to become entrepreneurs are subsequently monitored in order to validate their product and insert it into the ecosystem. This is what they call 'pre-acceleration': 'prototyping' and experimenting with sales, so that after five months the business has been minimally tested to find an investor. In the acceleration itself, there is also an advisory service that accompanies the entrepreneur, as well as an investment to get the business off the ground. "To make these challenges possible, it uses active and creative education methodologies, such as: design thinking, maker, do it Yourself (DIY) and project-based pedagogy," says the institution's website.

This two-way street between the market demand mirrored by private universities – whose focus is employability, as Renata Macedo (2021) analysed – and the social project indicates a specific type of training for work. In Rede's example, most of the teenagers looking through the courses on offer want a traditional qualification, as they 'arrive lost' and 'don't know their talents', according to Felipe. The information I get from him is that families still want their children to study and get a job as soon as possible, working with discipline to grow in the company. This is the old utopia of the work card, after all. So, for my interlocutor, it's not the most sought-after technique, because "the most important thing at this time is to broaden their vision, recover their self-esteem and their ability to dream".

At first glance, what is surprising about the OS project is its understanding of these talents. For my interlocutor, young people from the periphery 'have an advantage' in this new labour market. Yet, they lag behind in learning other languages and in access to information and good teachers. So, the Rede's proposal is that the teenager who arrives there should acquire a 'vision' of how to boost their professional life and develop their creativity, or they will tend to remain 'at the bottom of the pyramid'.

Creativity, then, is directed by the OS towards a demand for 'innovative' products, fuelling entrepreneurial prospects for its target audience. In the food sector, vegan and gluten-free options are particularly appreciated as growing niches. But the exchange isn't just about who buys and who sells. With the not-so-recent social mobility changing the face of the neighbourhood, Projeto Rede has not only been surrounded by new condominiums, but has also been sought out by children and young people from the new middle class on the outskirts. For my interlocutor, therein lies the answer to both the continuity of the project and a utopia: that is, 'the overcoming of social classes'. Activities that mix young people from Campo Limpo and Morumbi have already been tested to see 'what they have in common'. Felipe also sees a 'light at the end of the tunnel' in the change in attitude of public schools, which have relaxed their staunch resistance to partnerships with oss. They are finally realising, he says, that the "closed scheme doesn't protect them from social violence". Many young people and adults have already been through Rede's courses, and of those who have succeeded with their businesses, some have kept in touch with the project. They tend to have their ventures on the other side of the bridge. This refers to a 'dichotomy', says my interlocutor, which they have broken with.

The precariousness of the world of work, which a few years ago was handled by public policies that are now withering away, is now managed by entrepreneurship, which is asserting itself in peripheral subjectivities. Even the traditional entities that contain precariousness and the violence associated with it are looking for ways to legitimise themselves by offering training courses for this new reality. In Jardim São Luís, one of the few spaces of inclusion is the Fábrica de Cultura. I had already visited the place, created by the State Secretariat for Culture, the Inter-American Development Bank (IDB) and managed by another os, on my first field trip for this research in September 2018. It is one of two units in the South (the other is in Capão Redondo) and stands out in the landscape, just a few metres from the alleyways dominated by crammed shops and indominable traffic that characterise the neighbourhood. On the façade of the building, near the entrance, a green and yellow banner announced a new class for the 'business training and management' course aimed at entrepreneurs aged 18 to 35 who already have a business 'or need support to grow'.

On the cloudy day, children and young people ran around and danced in the place, which houses classrooms, laboratories, a vegetable garden, an auditorium and a small library, containing some classic books and best sellers, comics, left-wing newspapers and magazines such as Le Monde Diplomatique Brasil and Caros Amigos, as well as Galileu, Atlas do Agronegócio, Fala Guerreira and Amarelinho, a popular newspaper about jobs and competitions. On the walls of the open spaces, graffiti and the message in the 'inclusive language' *bemvindxs* (welcome) stood out in front of some young people rehearsing dance moves.[15] As a social pacification technology, the programme follows the normative and evaluative trends that permeate the subjectivity of young people in the process of professional qualification, currently focused on their 'competences' and 'skills'.[16]

What we can see is that the citizenship market model proposed in the 1990s seems close to exhaustion. Even though the discourse still clings to the 'transformative' potential of culture, it is progressively moving towards becoming a vector for social entrepreneurship in the peripheries.[17] Another interlocutor, a cultural manager at Fábrica de Cultura for eight years, took over the cultural agenda of the centre at the age of 16 ("which had a lot of this issue of youth protagonism"). Twenty years on, he notes that the crossover between peripheral culture and entrepreneurship had been going on for ten years or so, "because of the need for self-sustainability, with the problems of being a CLT worker and having few resources". The manager also emphasises the significant creation of the individual microentrepreneur entity (MEI) and the opening of SESC Campo Limpo. "Where there's culture and art, it's proven that it keeps crime away, and even the people who sell drugs in the *quebrada* don't want to be near them and respect these places," he says.

At the heart of the relationship between young people from the periphery and institutions such as the Lehmann Foundation and the Via Varejo Foundation, the British Council and FGV, is the 'social counterpart', a topic in which they negotiate their interests. On the one hand, this is an affirmation of autonomy and awareness of the interest they arouse for the social marketing of companies. On the other hand, this counterpart is rationalised: in the calculation of these subjects, the use of their time and their peripheral identities has a value, in this case monetary, which is also converted into contacts and opportunities on the other side of the bridge. For the bloc of companies and accelerators, there are no illusions either, as they have the legitimacy to implement a powerful instrument of hegemony. Incidentally, the cultural industry

---

15   It is quite common in peripheral entrepreneurship events, such as the Amaphiko Festival, which in its visual programme also greeted the public with *'Bemvindxs'*, instead of the regular *Bem-vindos*.
16   Antônia Colbari (2007: 86) explains that "traditional qualification models are being replaced by another training matrix in which operative skills – attention, initiative, manual agility and precision – are not enough; what is required is a real qualification with multiple facets – technical, socio-motivational, behavioural and cognitive – capable of developing the capacity to learn (the perspective of continuous learning), the desire to grow professionally, flexibility and a taste for risks and challenges and for achievement."
17   As I heard from a speaker at the 2° NIP Forum, "'NGOsation' isn't over, it's evolved".

is also involved in this process, as we saw when analysing the reality TV show *Shark Tank Brasil*.

What my young (under the age of 30) interviewees have in common, except for Carolina and Letícia, is a history of cultural and political activism, in which soirees and cultural collectives stand out. From this rich context of activity in the Zona Sul, peripheral culture was formed, which from the 1990s onwards narrated the experiences of these young people in search for both recognition and opportunities to earn a living. Since then, peripheral culture has become institutionalised, public and private facilities have been set up in various corners of the region and, with the support of the public policies brought in during the Lula's period, many of these young people have started to 'live off culture', a phenomenon that was partly interrupted with the discontinuation of the PT in the federal government. It survives because of its activist discourse, because of its deepening affinities with companies, and because one of its main premises has been maintained in the context of the break with the space of experience: their importance as welcoming spaces for those who have lost their concrete references.

The affirmation of peripheral identity, always remembered in expressions such as 'from the bridge to here' and references to the Racionais MC's, inevitably comes up against these contradictions. At Mostra Cultural of Cooperifa I came across a certain debauchery with solutions that come from outside the periphery. The antagonism between the two sides of the bridge is quite evident, as it was already part of the narrative disseminated by hip hop. Elisângela and Maria Rita's nonconformity with their fellow middle class activists clearly demonstrates the chasm that separates them, and erects a barrier to the 'overcoming of social classes'. But it is undeniable that, for peripheral entrepreneurs, entrepreneurship, far from meaning a way of life that imposes economic degradation, competition between subalterns and business opportunities for the other side of the bridge (in the end, antagonised only in speeches), appears at this moment in its utopian dimension for subjects that don't conform with the old world of work. And yet, the critique of alienated labour is present in a very politicised way, giving an unexpected dialectical twist to thinking about political projects.

3   From Precarious Labour to Popular Entrepreneurship

In the working class of São Paulo, the changes in the world of work were already evident to ABC workers, who perceived that the demands for professional qualifications were increasing every year, causing them to invest as much as they could in their children's schooling and professional training.[18] Kimi Tomizaki (2006) observes that this investment carries a series of ambiguities: it is impossible to understand this relationship between parents and children and the way in which, through conflicts and alliances, they have built a project for the future of their family members, without considering the process of social mobility that has marked their journeys and transformed their ways of life. The young workers interviewed by the sociologist shared a common feeling about their condition. They see it as a temporary situation that they wanted to overcome by gaining more valued school credentials. Thus, the extension of their studies meant that they moved to the 'other side' of the barrier that divides, in Brazil, those who have access to schooling and those who have remained on the margins, like their parents.

In the experiences captured here, these tendencies were not only confirmed, but deepened with my younger interlocutors, highlighted in Chapter 3. But instead of bemoaning their misfortune, these self-styled entrepreneurs, most of whom are involved in social entrepreneurship, see autonomy as a revolution for themselves and their neighbourhoods. They view the labour market with great contempt, comparing it in some cases to a 'plan' to fit them into precarious occupations, and more than that, to suppress their dreams.

Consequently, these young people have a very negative view of the labour market, but not of work itself. Elis has reservations but admits that "within this society and within this ideology that is given, work is dignity". It's common for social entrepreneurs to carry out these activities full time, intertwining work with leisure. The difference is that they see it as entrepreneurship. For them, it means breaking away from a set of rules that include fixed working hours and submission to a boss. This desire to break away is expressed by all my interlocutors, but here there is a different ambition, not coincidentally expressed in the idea of the 'dream', that is, of work as a place to realise individual satisfaction. This ambition is also symptomatically reflected in the demand for the recognition of merit, the re-signification of which generates new forms of anxiety and suffering. In this case, this generation's delayed entry into the labour market can be seen as both a cause and a consequence of this contradiction. While the older generation started working in childhood or adolescence, making this

---

18 'ABC' is a reference to the cities of Santo André, São Bernando and Diadema, important industrial centres around the city of São Paulo and the cradle of the workers' union movement that gave rise to the PT.

experience positive and determining their social recognition, the demand for merit by the younger generation is based on much more subjective criteria.[19]

This fact leaves no doubt as to the public diagnosis of the unfeasibility of the labour society, which in practice is not very different from the expression 'unemployable', proclaimed in 1997 by former president Fernando Henrique Cardoso.[20] It is based on the assumption that there is a population that no longer has any prospects of integration into regulated citizenship, to be managed through social programmes of conditional cash transfer (Lavinas, 2013), or through self-management that 'emancipates' them from the hands of the state, focusing above all on the recent generation that has invested hopes in access to higher education. In fact, a considerable part of the efforts undertaken by the last few Brazilian governments have been made on this basis. In 2004, the Ministry of Labour, already under the PT administration, launched the Young Entrepreneur programme, developed with SEBRAE and aimed at encouraging young people to enter the labour market with the purpose of "offering training to access credit, draw up a business plan and post-credit follow-up" (Tommasi, 2015: 111).

The march of instrumental rationality is taking place on a peripheral capitalist basis. It is present in school curricula, but it is not resolved in the labour market, which creates low-skilled and low-paid jobs, in turn occupied by young people with more academic knowledge than the occupation requires, reproducing a dysfunctionality that also affects those who interrupted their studies at secondary school (Georges, 2009).[21] A portion of these, as I analysed here and in my previous book, evaluate their own education with ambiguity, sometimes with scepticism about the effort and investment they see as redundant,

---

19 This prompted the government to propose social inclusion mechanisms that could speed up this transition. Also in 2001, the São Paulo city government, under the Marta Suplicy administration, developed two categories of social programmes, which were innovative at the time: the 'Redistributive' programmes – minimum income programmes conditional on school attendance and placement in the labour market for 'vulnerable' groups, especially the unemployed; and the 'Emancipatory' programmes, of which one objectives was the formation of collective and self-managed enterprises. All programmes required a family income of less than half the minimum wage per capita.

20 That year, FHC used the term 'unemployable' to refer to a contingent of 40 million workers who, according to the former president, had been swallowed up by technological development and no longer had a natural place in the economy, and who would therefore no longer be able to integrate as citizens (Gielow, 1997).

21 As Castel (2015: 519) warned, raising the level of qualifications required prevents young people who "twenty years ago would have been integrated smoothly into production from finding themselves condemned to wander from apprenticeship to apprenticeship or from one small service to another".

sometimes with distress about the accumulation of responsibilities that come with adulthood, when having a higher education seems like a guarantee (Costa, 2019a). Thus, the contemporary world corrupts them on both sides: if there is no reason to acquire a degree, there is no reason to enter labour market.[22]

The period in which my younger interlocutors began to question their place in the world coincides with the favourable economic moment of the transition between Lula's and Dilma's mandates, which was one of low unemployment and low pay – 94.8% of the jobs created in the 2000s paid up to 1.5 minimum wages (Pochmann, 2012). This means that the country did not have quality jobs that absorbed the increase in schooling or created them unevenly. Here, incidentally, lies the detail of the contradiction present in the speeches of these politicised young people. It is inevitable for them to see Prouni and Fies as the great achievements of Lula's first governments and to justify their support for the president, someone who 'looked at the poor' and 'put the poor in university'. But what emerges is that these programmes had a major impact, above all on their self-esteem, after all, many of the young people from the periphery discussed here didn't finish their degrees, and only a small number of them had access to the benefits. "What happened isn't going to go back, that the guy who did Prouni isn't going to be 'deprounise'. It will continue, bro, and we'll just want more rights," João Vicente told me.

While precariousness remains within its historical framework, what has begun to change is the perception of this precariousness. The increase in schooling, above all through access to higher education and the massification of the technical means of self-management, had already been noticeable since the 1990s and has become brutally accentuated in the last decade. At the same time as universities were becoming proletariat, institutions were investing in teaching entrepreneurship, above all as a new type of workforce for companies. In the notion of human capital, the maintenance of employability by the worker himself is essential, and in various reports here we have seen this exchange. This is the case for Elis, a resident of Jardim São Luís, who at just 16 was already attending entrepreneurship workshops and who at the time of our conversation was trying to make it possible to dedicate herself definitively to her production company. In fact, if the labour market is barely able to absorb this generation, postponing their incorporation, the public authorities and the

---

22 When they experience entrepreneurship as a form of engagement, "the lack of formal education is not a hindrance; on the contrary, it generates recognition thanks to the accumulation of specific knowledge. Naming oneself a cultural producer is, in this context, a form of social legitimisation." Tommasi and Silva (2020: 203). By the way, the occupation 'cultural producer' is quite recurrent among my interlocutors in Chapter 3.

social impact business ecosystem are trying to make up for it by encouraging entrepreneurship, both as a way of managing these populations and of giving them some means of integration instead of practical experience, which they are unlikely to have.

There is an important generational component here. On the one hand, it is true that this absorption of a rational principles, as opposed to family and customs, guide perspectives more among interlocutors under 30. As the age decreases, the weight of the influence of training projects can be seen, which increasingly emphasise entrepreneurship and the negative perception of salaried work. The cases I presented in Chapter 3 show an exaltation of increasingly abstract forms of self-recognition, such as 'ancestry' and 'authenticity', which are less grounded in practical experience. For example, Maria Rita is angry with her family, who don't respect her 'journey'. João Vicente didn't have a degree, but he snubbed the *zé povinho* with his appearances on Rede Globo programmes. These are young people who don't see, at least at this stage of their lives, any rationality in striving for diplomas and certificates, but rather attempts to mould them. Contradictorily, this is precisely the rationalisation project instilled in entrepreneurship.[23]

The issue of training, by the way, seems to have taken a turn in the subjective expectations of these young people. In Erik Olin Wright's (1989) argument, the acquisition of certificates implies privileges that translate into credential rents, distinguishing strata within the working class. But in the reproduction of a labour market that demands few qualifications (despite requiring a diploma as a way of selecting candidates),[24] scepticism about training is widespread.

---

23   In the popular experience, the workplace shared with small businesses the fact that they were highly individualised, stable, predictable and with a clear demarcation between working and non-working time. This led to a common ethic that was interwoven with the ways of life shared in their families and neighbourhoods. In turn, the incorporation of flexibility into contemporary work processes has led to group or cell work, which is present not only in factory contexts. Contrary to the cooperation it claims to encourage, in the cell the worker is even more individualised, since it is precisely in self-management that the fate of a worker who is harming the cell's goal is hidden – due to an inability to keep up with the intense pace, for example. This is an imposition of the particularised collective (the cell) on the whole, since it eliminates the class experience in the name of productivity and brings the subjects closer to an entrepreneurial ethic (Mello e Silva, 2007).

24   According to Márcia Lima (2012) with regard to the relationship between the job performed and the qualification, access to a diploma does not guarantee placement in occupations that actually require this qualification. Among the factors she highlights are the poor quality of courses and institutions and the use of job retention strategies in which tertiary education works defensively, as a means of maintaining employment and perhaps career progression, but in less complex occupations that don't require specific qualifications. The research cites the example that in order for telemarketers to 'progress in

The search for qualifications has always been tortuous in Brazil and among workers in the São Paulo industry, the level of schooling remained low for many decades. Leôncio Martins Rodrigues (2009) observed that in relatively few cases, low schooling was compensated for by technical courses. In general, 'hands-on' learning was quite common. Nadya Araújo Guimarães noticed in the São Paulo chemical industry that identitarian attributes such as gender and age proved to be more effective in distributing job opportunities in the context of firm restructuring, rather than education, synthesising "social representations about the 'suitable' individual and/or the 'fair' remuneration for a job". Therefore, professional qualifications proved to be less important for remaining in occupational positions in the industry. As a result, "the youngest, the least educated, those with the least time in employment and females almost only remained employed in the worst parts of the chemical industries: the small ones" (2004: 163–165).

In fact, even though these observations don't refer directly to wageless life, they have certainly affected the prospects of many. It's no coincidence that younger people not only resent the unsatisfactory opportunities offered by the labour market, but also largely ignore the importance of qualifications, as in the case of interlocutor Vitória. These feelings appear above all among women, who see gender issues as 'disqualifying' them, as we saw in the case of Letícia, who was passed over for a senior position by a white man of the same age, but with inferior academic and professional performance. She maintains her interest in training, but out of a sense of vocation that she shares with her new occupation as an entrepreneur. The market 'sells' qualifications as a gateway, but closes the door based on unrelated criteria – gender, race, class, etc., reinforcing the scepticism expressed by these young people.

Thus, the theme of the 'fleeing from working class destiny' reappears, as Stéphane Beaud and Michel Pialoux have pointed out. The policy of massification of secondary education and the educational paradigm offered to French working class youth provoked a process of 'de-workfication', of generational confrontation with working class identity and imitation of aspects of bourgeois youth, reviving the conflict between these different *ethos*. According to the sociologists, "participation in adolescent culture, the discovery in high school of the illegitimacy of a certain number of popular practices and the adoption (under severe budgetary constraints) of a collegiate lifestyle led to a

---

their careers' and become telemarketing managers, they often need a degree. However, this degree can be in either administration or gerontology.

certain distancing from the environment of origin" (2009: 181),[25] even though this working class fate, in what remains of the European welfare state, is less repulsive than the reality of precarious work among Brazilians.[26]

In the popular areas of Brazil, the increase in schooling and access to university, while bringing new cultural perspectives of autonomy and politicisation for the younger generation, are not enough to guarantee upward mobility. These transformations, which are expanding and accelerating with technological development, disrupt the space of experience, because for the younger generations,[27] the demands of contemporary work and the dynamics that interact with it no longer find a reference in the immediate past.[28]

Some narratives defy statistics. João Vicente keeps up an intense schedule of talks, workshops and fairs in various parts of the city, even though this doesn't solve all his difficulties. This is a sign that he is also aware of what's going on around him, I've sometimes seen a registration tent for the MCMV programme installed on the slab at his agency. But here I'd like to highlight Letícia's case, which I included in the first chapter even though she positions herself in dialogue with the world of social impact businesses. Just 26 years old at the time of the interview, she is an economist with a postgraduate degree from a federal public university who already had a consolidated consultancy business aimed at black and peripheral people. Her innovative methodology, which

---

25 Stéphane Beaud and Michel Pialoux (2009: 181). I'm not talking specifically about workers' culture here, but, as I observed in this book, it does share certain ethical aspects with self-employment, including the value of practical experience and manual labour. I also worked on this topic during my master's research with Prouni scholarship holders (Costa, 2018). Braga (2009) describes similar situations in his research with telemarketers.

26 For those who undertake this flight, the obstacle becomes the dimension of social integration, insofar as the middle class itself, as Robert Kurz (2004) pointed out, depends on the existence of an expanding industrial economy – which demands qualified sectors and remunerates them by redistributing surplus value. With deindustrialisation on a growing scale, this reality also affects the state and its capacity/willingness to promote institutions that train and employ qualified sectors, leaving residual and extremely competitive spaces of social prestige.

27 Karl Mannheim (1975) pointed out that the constant emergence of new culture bearers is a frequent and even necessary phenomenon. On the other hand, the succession of generations implies the loss of accumulated cultural goods and, consequently, profound changes in the generational experience of individuals.

28 For Ruy Braga (2019), the frustration of those who went into debt in the 2010s, especially those with a family income of between two and five minimum wages, would be the source of subsequent political events, since such investments in training, encouraged by the PT administrations, exacerbated the feeling of 'meritocracy' among working families. The recent reality is that 40 per cent of Brazilian higher education graduates don't get qualified jobs (Lima; Gerbelli, 2020).

aims to talk about financial education using lyrics from the Racionais MC's, has successfully fulfilled its purpose of helping the periphery break through the barrier of the monetary economy. Her main slogan is the issue of debt, which immediately prevents any successful entrepreneurial initiative. She starts from her own experience of being blocked in her career development and decided early on to become autonomous. Letícia identified not just a demand, but a social problem, to which she responded by combining her expertise with entrepreneurial drive. She doesn't delude herself; she understands themes like *funk ostentação*, the music subgenre which preaches the flaunting of money, as a desire for access, but she sees in some consumerist excesses a symptom of capitalism itself.

She's not the only one extolling the economy on the periphery. Maria Rita, for example, is very convinced of the need for financial education that provides tools for autonomy. Elis knows what she needs to do to get her production company off the ground – she has well-defined objectives and a talent for fundraising. In her case, even her experience as a left-wing activist has helped her aim for tangible goals and, above all, to avoid problems. Ana Luiza was exhausted by teaching, started her business designing Afro-inspired stationery and, by taking part in *Shark Tank Brasil*, managed to secure an investment to dedicate herself fully to the company, of which she describes herself as 'CEO'. These are emblematic models of how entrepreneurship taps into the peripheral youth's desire for autonomy eventually creating remarkable stories.

On the other hand, there are contexts in which the entrepreneurial discourse, with or without the social veneer, is challenged by reality. Such situations occur precisely when they take on concrete dimensions in trades that ultimately require practical skills, as the examples of Celso and Keila indicate, who are eager for courses that teach them in a 'hands on' way. Maicon, who has ambitions to open a restaurant, expresses some disappointment with the gastronomy course he enrolled in, which had to cancel practical classes because of the COVID-19 pandemic. In these cases, certification is less important to them than the ability to competently run their businesses.

Popular entrepreneurship is born out of this context saturated with contradictions. In this context, popular culture is being blasted by the discourses in vogue, already consolidated in the universe of the middle class familiar with globalised culture, but only recently applied to the management of precarious work in the peripheries for people who are too young or too old, both of whom are experiencing their uncertainties and reacting with scepticism. Here I return in particular to the case of Geraldo, a bricklayer and *acarajés* cook, who, after 61 years of hard labour, is beginning to see his body decline. In social impact entrepreneurship he sees a way out to a less stressful job that will guarantee him an income for a more peaceful old age. Convinced by the teachers on his entrepreneurship course, he realised the feat of innovation, a vegan fritter that is itself the result of a therapeutic narrative that has expanded into more traditional cuisine. From the *acarajé* he used to make, first as an offering to the orishas and then as a *viração*, Geraldo now wants to try his hand at entrepreneurship, but he can't leave all the experience he carries on his back and in his memory by the wayside. He still needs the 'know-how'.

Faced with diminishing expectations, as Paulo Arantes (2014) observed, these 'self-managed' subjectivities find themselves in entrepreneurship, the final horizon of the utopia of autonomy and the end of subordination. Already conditioned by the therapeutic discourse, they eliminate the last doubts about the path to follow, and all others are seen as sources of suffering and scepticism.

Situations of exploitation and abuse experienced by workers of all ages have the necessary poignancy to challenge them to risk a belated quest for autonomy. This is not about applying a veneer to entrepreneurship and describing it in a romanticised way as a lasting political project of autonomy for the poorest. It is simply a matter of describing it in its concrete reality, where successful cases not only legitimise precarious situations disguised as autonomy, but rewrite stories marked by suffering.

It is to the structure of feelings that entrepreneurship refers.

CHAPTER 5

Utopia and Suffering

In a footnote to *Civilization and its Discontents*, Sigmund Freud observes that "no other technique for the conduct of life binds individuals so firmly to reality as an emphasis on work, which at least fits then securely in a portion of reality, into the human community" (2016: 59). This assumption sets the tone for what we saw among my interlocutors. In this chapter, I discuss the ideological and material aspects that permeate entrepreneurship and the effects on subjectivities. If being part of the human community depends on work, the crisis of the way of life based on its centrality has the power to create, on the contrary, desocialisation.[1] So, while in the previous chapter I tried to reconstitute the ways of life of wageless workers in the light of the socio-economic and spatial reconfigurations of the Zona Sul, here I focus on the psychological repercussions determined by the structure of feelings, with consequences ranging from self-management of suffering to self-management of survival, in which popular entrepreneurship is its main manifestation.

The phenomenon of the social devaluation of university degrees in Brazil, although not so recent (Prandi, 1982), gained shades of deep scepticism at the turn of the 2010s, when the feeling that knowledge acquired with effort and financial investment is wasted in a labour market that does not assimilate it accordingly, and often appears redundant in a hyperconnected world (Georges, 2009; Costa, 2018; Macedo, 2020). Frustrated expectations reinforce the move towards entrepreneurship, which does not appear in these cases as a necessity, but as an alternative for the individual valorisation of people who are no longer content with subjection without recognition of what they see as merit. In this way, the continuous increase in the number of self-employed workers reflects not only the individualist *ethos*, but also the situations of uncertainty and indeterminacy typical of this category. Particularly among those who are still in the formal labour market, or who have only recently found themselves unemployed, setting up new businesses requires not only entrepreneurial

---

1 According to Robert Kurz (1992), this process is caused by the collapse of modernisation, in which Western societies, due to the intensification of competition between capitalists, begin to increasingly neglect the workforce, replacing it with scientific advancement and investment in technical development. This 'logical crisis of capitalism' points to the collapse of the commodity production system by progressively eliminating living labour, which in turn is responsible for the formation of surplus value.

initiative, because know-how has not always been part of their trajectories, and without experience they have to expose themselves to challenges that are often impossible.

The acquiescence of the wageless worker to entrepreneurship, in its modern and rationalising terms, is only possible because of the promise of freedom it carries. All these experiences are balanced between the poles of utopia and suffering. Between them lies the reality of the contemporary world of work, which to a greater or lesser extent squeezes their bodies and consciences. However, beyond this opposition to the exhaustion and humiliation of wage labour, popular entrepreneurs have also found in wageless life a place of recognition in the community, a business opportunity, an identity and a longing for emancipation. It is in this ideal of freedom that entrepreneurship is anchored, promising a possible escape from the negative centrality of labour (Arantes, 2014).

This challenge has been made possible for certain sections of the population by the introduction of advanced technological means, in which the 1990s began to provide – while also eliminating jobs in industry – self-management resources that allowed, for example, the production and spread of hip hop beyond the peripheries long before the advent of the internet. Júlio, for example, is quite emphatic in stating the importance of access to these means for the formation of peripheral culture.[2] Means that also enabled the creation of an evangelical cultural industry, with its own studios and channels.[3] It's no coincidence that these phenomena took off at the same time in history.[4]

---

2   Hip hop began to gain national repercussions with the creation of its own consumer markets that challenged the hegemonic narratives produced by big broadcasting groups and the music industry. Felipe Campos (2020: 85) identified as central to the diffusion and expansion of hip hop "the conditions of *production* (computers, music production software, MPCs etc.), *circulation* (concerts, the possibility of internationalising careers, events and the internet) and *consumption* (increasing the possibility of access to income; and the internet – streaming services and digital platforms), of songs, albums, CDs (and also LPs), as well as products associated with the artists' 'brands'".

3   One of the milestones of the evangelical cultural industry was the founding in 1971 of the Voz da Libertação record label of the Deus é Amor Pentecostal Church in the centre of São Paulo. Mariana Côrtes (2014) identifies in this movement of multiplication of record companies, studios and shops the affirmation of a 'Pentecostal market of preaching and testimonies' where individuals in situations of extreme precariousness negotiate the only commodity that they have available, that is, their own more or less tragic life stories, prior to religious conversion. In the group she calls *ex-tudo* (ex-everything), Côrtes (2014) brings together mainly those preacher-mendicants who sell their own narrative prior to conversion, in this case highlighting aspects such as drug and alcohol addiction, homosexuality and links to African religions, as well as 'healing' and redemption.

4   Arjun Appadurai realises that ingrained *habitus* are quickly challenged in this context. Images that circulate through the mass media reverberate when a migrant takes their local culture

We have seen an incredible acceleration of this process in the last decade with the expansion of mobile telephones and the internet in the daily lives of the working classes. According to data from the IBGE's PNAD-Contínua, in 2019 the proportion of households with a mobile phone reached 94%; among the population aged 10 and over, 81% had a mobile phone for personal use. Home use of the internet reached 82.7%, and it was accessed in 98.6% of cases by mobile phone.[5]

Why is the data I've presented above important? Firstly, because the use of digital technology stands out frequently in the stories I've presented. Ronaldo is an employee, but he uses transport apps to supplement his insufficient income. Fernanda, Eduardo and Raphaela, Mercedes, the burger restaurant in Paraisópolis, Diego, Maicon and Geraldo, as well as all my interlocutors in Chapter 3, use social media as essential tools for their businesses – through social media they advertise their products, and recently also to fulfil delivery orders. It has also enabled Estela, aged 61, to sell her homemade cakes. But above all, it is important because technology needs a purpose, as Williams (2003) warned: just as with the advent of television, the internet and mobile telephones exist as a specific cultural form of social relations in certain places and historical moments.

Herbert Marcuse (1999: 74) said that technology "can promote both authoritarianism and freedom, both scarcity and abundance, both the increase and the abolition of hard labour". Social processes determine its function. It is therefore a question of avoiding technological determinism by understanding this purpose. Most of the inventions of modernity have been aimed at the self-management of individuals. For this to happen, it is not enough to have an appropriate technical means, but it is essential, as my interlocutors say, to have 'theory', in other words, knowledge and specialised literature to guide this self-management, in this case provided by psychology as a rational discipline and therapeutic technique.

Eva Illouz (2007) gives us a pertinent example. She saw in the spread of paperback books in the United States in 1934 the popularisation of the therapeutic discourse that Freud had inaugurated just a few years earlier. The father of psychoanalysis lamented the fact that his profession was aimed exclusive

---

with them to another, integrating different realities under similar narratives of deterritorialisation and overcoming. "It is the imagination, in its collective forms, that creates ideas of neighbourhood and nationhood, of moral economies and unjust rule, of higher wages and foreign labour prospects. The imagination is today a staging ground for action, and not only for escape" (1996: 7).

5   Available at: https://biblioteca.ibge.gov.br/visualizacao/livros/liv101794_informativo.pdf.

to the middle classes, who were able to afford the high costs of analysis sessions. Illouz shows how some of his followers succeeded in crossing the class boundaries of psychology by significantly broadening the field of pathologies and, moreover, reinforcing the role of the individual in solving their mental problems. This gave impetus to a huge market for both therapies and self-help literature. The result was that an innovation in the material conditions of dissemination turned out to be essential for a 'rescue' of the Self by the individual, a resource that is still widely used today and which accompanies the process of secularisation in the West.⁶

Illouz considers the therapeutic discourse to have a practical effect on psychological traumas and sufferings that occupy the centre of individual narratives, diagnosed by professional psychologists and managed in their simplest cases by resorting to self-help. As well as involving a series of actors (the state, psychologists and psychiatrists, the pharmaceutical industry, the cultural industry, etc.), the therapeutic discourse becomes part of everyday life, transforming individuals with more or less serious mental problems into functional people, prepared to face the exploitations and abuses of contemporary capitalism. My interlocutors Elis and Maria Rita, for example, repeatedly use the theme of mental health to explain their own situations or those of others. Above all, self-help focuses on individualisation, recognising 'problems' and selling solutions, i.e., possibilities for self-realisation.⁷

The evolution of technological resources deepens self-help techniques and expands the scope of self-management, where its purpose ultimately lies. Self-management is therefore a dimension of this self-realisation project. The success of self-help narratives certainly dialogues with an original individualism and plants deep within the subject the ambition for self-realisation. Just like the popularisation of paperback books in the 1930s, the introduction of mobile telephony is proving to be fundamental in strengthening these narratives. "When they live only in the mind, cultural ideas are weak," observes Illouz (2007), so they need to be embodied in the practices of everyday life.

---

6 According to the Book Retail Panel survey in Brazil, carried out by Nielsen BookScan for the National Book Publishers Union (SNEL), book sales in the country increased by 29.36% from 2020 to 2021. The two best-selling books of the year were Napoleon Hill's *Outwitting the Devil: The Secret to Freedom and Success* and Thiago Nigro's *Do mil a um milhão*, both self-help books. When analysing non-academic literature on entrepreneurship, Elaine Leite and Natália Melo (2008) observed "a set of ideal principles of good behaviour".

7 In this sense, the goal of 'demassification' that Wendy Brown (2019) attributes to the theorists of neoliberalism has more to do with the tremendous spread of therapeutic discourse – the fact that this discourse presents tangible results on an individual level reaffirms a type of individualistic behaviour.

In short, the evolution of technology has allowed therapeutic discourse to become a form of self-management. While the expansion of pathology modalities allowed for the spread of support groups and the individualisation of self-help techniques, this structure of feelings only lacked the appropriate technical means for self-realisation to become an entrepreneurial horizon. It does not only enable the necessary psychological stability at work, but also gives the individual the option of rejecting the labour market altogether. In this, we see the purpose of technological innovation: To allow the individual deprived of citizenship to act on their own, as in Rogerio's sagacious observation in Chapter 1.

In the research I have carried out here, obviously without pretending to cover the subject exhaustively, the therapeutic narrative appears in two forms, naturally integrated with the theme of entrepreneurship. First, it appears at events and workshops that publicise social entrepreneurship, especially with a focus on black and peripheral audiences. Second, it appears at prosperity services, especially those of the Universal Church of the Kingdom of God (UCKG). In the first case, these are welcoming spaces where people who aspire to have their own businesses don't primarily learn the practical and bureaucratic intricacies – although there is a demand for this – but rather seek to strengthen self-esteem, discuss trajectories and expose experiences of suffering and overcoming.[8] At the Periphery Impact Business Forum held in Jardim Ângela, which I describe in Chapter 3, the pauses between discussion tables were filled with stories like these, in which women entrepreneurs told their stories of overcoming and success, permeated by the therapeutic discourse of 'healing' and self-realisation, which some of my interlocutors also expressed during the interviews. This link can be seen, for example, in the words of Vitória, who left university out of concern for her mental health (as well as seeing the labour market as a source of suffering), and Ana Luiza, who saw entrepreneurship as a cure for the depression brought on by working at school.

These are programmes that compete for hegemony in the popular world, which is why they assert themselves in the imagination as ethics, sets of "beliefs associated with the capitalist order that contribute to justifying and sustaining that order, legitimising the modes of action and dispositions that are consistent with it" (Boltanski; Chiapello, 2009: 42). These are ethics that presuppose adherence and freely made sacrifices, because it is not the salary that provokes

---

8   Gleicy Silva (2019) provides several accounts of these activities, in which the making of a product (clothes, accessories, etc.) seeks to deconstruct 'beauty paradigms and feelings of inadequacy' with the aim of empowerment – in one of the cases mentioned, an entrepreneur defines her studio as a 'dream factory'.

the enthusiasm needed to fulfil the tasks, but the commitment that only maintaining one's own life can offer.

1   Self-Management and Therapeutic Narrative in Two Exemplary Cases

It is possible to see the practical application of the expansion of self-management provided by the technique in the two examples highlighted in this book. 'Crossing the bridge' here takes on the connotation of conversion to entrepreneurship for those whose conscience is saturated, either by exhaustion or by nonconformity with the devaluation of their school knowledge in the formal market. To manage anxieties and suffering, there are Pentecostal churches and their services aimed at 'freeing' workers from the yoke of subordination, on the one hand, and an art and culture apparatus, run by a myriad of social organisations, on the other. In the first case, the stimulus is orientated in a more 'traditional' way, i.e., towards the success of the individual and their family, reinforcing insubordination guidelines contained above all in the Old Testament. In the UCKG, financial success is inseparable from popular individualism in the emphasis on family planning. In the second case, there is a desire to reformat the workforce by encouraging self-management according to the latest social technology, targeting both young people and adults who are exasperated by a lack of prospects. This is an effort to modernise popular and peripheral practices, which I have witnessed at dozens of social entrepreneurship events on the periphery of Zona Sul.

The UCKG's slogan is 'Stop Suffering', which does indeed mobilise its followers, who, by reviewing their trajectories of humiliation, seek to recover their self-esteem.[9] Catering to a very diverse audience, the church has succeeded in finding this common denominator. It is also notable for its efforts to eliminate the traces of submission present in popular Catholicism, firstly by welcoming it (as it is still a pillar of popular culture), but also by deconstructing it through the entrepreneurial initiative it seeks to induce. In dialogue with popular culture (but differing from Catholicism in its exaltation of the simple and the humble (Lehmann, 1996), which reflects the stance of the local Catholic clergy, often made up of foreigners), the UCKG promotes the idea of

---

9   In the words of Taniele Rui (2010: 60), "it's about evoking the intolerable threshold of pain: the final point of destruction, of physical, moral, dignity and ethical pain that makes it possible to 'accept the programme'. Only through pain is it possible to accept that control of life has been lost and that help is needed."

the 'differentiated' individual, who doesn't accept humiliation, revolts against injustice and places himself below only God. By the way, these services stand out precisely for their self-help tone, bringing to the altar believers who have overcome personal dramas and who, by putting themselves first (but at the service of the divine), have set up successful businesses. The pastor acts as a lecturer, and as a sign of the effectiveness of his therapeutic discourse, he displays long queues of people who have paid off their debts, recovered their marriages, etc.

Clara Mafra et al. analysed Edir Macedo's originality and ability to transform a North American evangelical theology with strongly liberal tendencies, whose roots rest on an affluent economy and a consolidated individualistic *ethos*, into a popular pastoral project adapted to the conditions of a peripheral country in a post-colonial context. According to them, Macedo offers the lower classes "a bold composition of entrepreneurship, revolt and restlessness" (2012: 88), managing expectations and anxieties and stimulating access to the consumer goods of a modernity that has always been neglected for the poorest, but imposing limits on narcissism in the name of the evangelical 'common good' – the grace of God.

In both neo-Pentecostalism and social entrepreneurship, there is almost always a tacit rejection of the previous generation – yet another essential difference with popular Catholicism. In the UCKG, the exalted defence of the family rarely refers to the (moral and financial) parental heritage, usually of Catholic affiliation. This is also noticeably absent in entrepreneurship events as an aspect of the therapeutic discourse. In this case, it suggests blaming the previous generation for the interruption of ancestral experience. Thus, the search for the constitution of a way of life based on self-recognition and self-help must go back to time immemorial, far removed from concrete experience, which is why the basis of the discourse is, in the first case, the Old Testament, and in the second, African ancestry. However, in its own way, the success of neo-Pentecostalism lies in embracing the popular by re-signifying it, while the strategy of social impact businesses to create a peripheral elite involves deconstructing it.

2   The Guiltless World and Its Deconstruction

In the rationalising impulse that determines cultural forms of conduct and sociability, contradictory movements challenge individuals to adapt or burn out. If individualism is reinvigorated by therapeutic discourse, enabling the individual to self-manage, a feeling of inadequacy or fleeing forward resurfaces in the wageless worker. Their opposition is not to be found in individualism itself, but in the therapeutic discourse in which it is packaged. This is not primarily aimed at the small traders or self-employed workers, who value the individualism they have experienced and learned in the concrete battle to maintain their modest standard of living, and which implies both their view of merit as recognition for hard, honest work, and the minimisation of pain and suffering, which they try to keep secret, restricted to the private domain.

In residual popular culture, suffering at work is often seen with a certain pride. For example, what has become a commonplace of therapeutic discourse, that of 'resilience', is seen in its concreteness in the trajectories I have discussed in this book. Reports of child labour are common here, especially among immigrants: Sueli, Toni, Delei, Mari, Geraldo, Estela and Aparecida worked in the fields, migrated as teenagers to São Paulo and, in order to settle down, faced precarious work, difficulties in adapting, violence and struggle. They keep in their bodies and in their memories what they had to go through, which not by chance has 'struggle' as its main characteristic. Tássio, who also migrated with his family to Paraisópolis at a young age, gets emotional when he remembers how his parents arrived in the city, built their first shack and then their brick house. Thus, they see in their eventual rise or simple survival the merit of individual effort and efforts that were not in vain.

Increasingly exposed to therapeutic discourse, the working classes and other subjects rejected by society find both a way out and a commodity by re-evaluating their biographies, sometimes the only one they have, like the preachers in the centre of São Paulo, the protagonists of Mariana Côrtes' story (2014). One outsider character in pop culture portrays the relationship between suffering and success particularly well – this is the Joker, who appeared in graffiti and the make-up of peripheral kids during a festival I attended in Campo Limpo in 2019. A few weeks before that, the film inspired by the character opened in cinemas. The feature film directed by Todd Phillips became a box-office hit, telling the story of a failed comedian with poor mental health who, exhausted by humiliation, lashes out with extreme violence against his abusers. The film's success seems to indicate that suffering is now an element that accompanies the randomness of wageless life. More than that, it suggests that outbursts of 'regenerative' violence is therapeutic in itself (Pavez, 2015).

Like the defiant tone of Leonardo's account, Vitória's phrase about the impact of her success ("because they don't want me to win") and the resentment expressed by Aparecida, as well as her reasons for joining the UCKG, these feelings indicate a type of survival narcissism. Christopher Lasch understood that certain social arrangements survive in the individual even after they have become objectively undesirable. The ethic of self-preservation and psychic survival is rooted, he says, "not merely in objective conditions of economic warfare, rising rates of crime and social chaos, but in the subjective experience of emptiness and isolation" (1991: 51). This reflects the conviction that envy and exploitation dominate even the most intimate relationships as a projection of inner anxieties and an unshakeable perception of reality. In the perception of the world as a dangerous place, backed by a realistic awareness of the insecurity of social life, the narcissistic projection turns against the outside, embodying an absolute inability to feel part of something bigger, such as society or history. The lack of cohesion over time atrophies their desire for recognition.

However, we can see that Aparecida, even though she is an outsider, seems to find elements of recognition in popular entrepreneurship with other people like her. Incidentally, Norbert Elias (2000) pointed to a 'counter-stigmatisation' of the outsider group. As inequalities with the established group were reduced, their cohesion strengthened and the power distance to which they were subjected lessened. Thus, ambiguous signs of change began to appear with the success of *Lulismo*. The rise of the new middle class and inclusion through consumption in those years, together with the policies of scholarships and student finance (Prouni and Fies), would be fundamental for a renewed look at the population itself. It wasn't just about access to products and services, but a profound change in the structure of feelings: the popular world, with its new contradictions, finally promoted its process of counter-stigmatisation. For perhaps unusual reasons, the policies of the Lula period, by reducing the distance between the traditional middle class and the new middle class, brought the latter to a new level – travelling, university education, microcredit and financed cars came together with the vertiginous growth of Pentecostalism from below and entrepreneurship from above, two phenomena that feed each other.[10]

Unlike Estela, an evangelical member of the Assembly of God, for whom the account of her suffering eventually reaches the point of interpreting her terrible episodes almost as banal events, therapeutic discourse especially saturates the testimonies of younger people. They have entered the world of work late and have absorbed a consolidated culture, strongly present in their immediate

---

10 However, I notice that my younger interlocutors, on the contrary, reject this possible cohesion between outsiders, reflected in their own families, but seek to cross the bridge to the side of the established. If the incorporation of hip hop into the market took place without the knowledge of its first representatives, a new generation in tune with it has repaginated the genre into a new aesthetic that has absorbed both the market (through entrepreneurial ethics) and the state (through public policies). For Felipe Campos (2020), its main organiser is the rapper Emicida. Campos sees the rapper's project as an 'aesthetic of entrepreneurial overcoming'.

environments of the cultural industry and education, in which the concept of 'emotional intelligence' is exalted in teaching materials for children and young people (Catini, 2020).[11] With it, the poor and disillusioned young person learns to 'control' their emotions, reorganise their life narrative and become a worker ready to face the anguish of the present and the future once again.

The therapeutic discourse, as Illouz (2007, 2008) explains, preaches the opposite of safeguarding wageless workers. The sociologist observes that in order to pathologise more situations, even characteristics that used to be socially valued are now seen as inconvenient. In therapeutic narratives, negative feelings such as shame, guilt, fear or inadequacy come to the fore. These feelings must be dealt with publicly, discussed and debated, and this is how the subject participates in the public sphere. Therapeutic narratives are always written retrospectively, rewriting past traumas, and are devoid of moral self-judgement, as the 'blame' is always attributed to a third party. The commitment to work, above all, is reinterpreted as 'compulsive' and justified by some as trauma, making it amenable to self-help.

My younger interlocutors, born in São Paulo, who do not have stable jobs or children and are committed activists, spoke out against this 'compulsion'. Performative narratives are then developed in which suffering is highlighted and self-realisation becomes the goal of the life story. The therapeutic narrative deconstructs the guiltless world in order to apply its own treatments.

---

11   There are hundreds of examples, but one interesting case is that of psycho-pedagogue Leo Fraiman (2021) and his OPEE Methodology, which "helps children and young people to reach the best version of themselves, building noble and transformative life projects". In Fraiman's collection, aimed at children (4 to 5 years old), the author emphasises the theme "Discovering feelings" as the first topic. In the collection for the early years of primary school, the focus is on financial life. The aim of the collection is the 'development of socio-emotional competences'.

Conclusion: the Moral Economy of Brazilian Wageless Lives

An observation that could be adapted from George Simmel (2005), who wrote about a context quite different from the one reported in this book, would say that the deepest problems of contemporary life arise from the pretension of the popular individual to preserve the autonomy and peculiarity of his existence in the face of the impositions of society, globalised culture and the rationalisation of life. Certain elements of the popular experience, rooted in an individualistic ethic of social reproduction, make up the un-submissive basis of popular Brazil, in which the memory of remote times of escape from misery and violence perpetrated by the state are reaffirmed at every moment for its wageless workers, while the march of progress advances in spite of them. For or against progress, entrepreneurship is a structure of feelings that reaches everyone, and the success of entrepreneurship is its contemporary utopia.

This popular appropriation of entrepreneurship is done in a specific and, of course, contradictory way. On the one hand, the entrepreneurial discourse is modernising and seeks to de-traditionalise work relations and production processes through rationalisation (Roy, 2010; Beck, 1992). Contemporary entrepreneurship thus incorporates a series of prescriptions for rational individual conduct, namely innovation, protagonism and self-management (Illouz, 2008; Souza, 2008; Tommasi, 2015). In popular contexts, opposition to the 'market', seen as imposing rationalisation and depersonalisation, finds in entrepreneurship itself a mechanism of resistance through the aspiration to non-subordinated work, because it is through a fictionalisation of autonomy that, by taking on a narrative form, allows subjects to establish connections between current uncertainties and future states (Beckert, 2013).

In popular culture, tradition often takes the form of resistance to modernity. In the context studied by E. P. Thompson (1993), the advance of the market economy among 18th century English peasant labourers generated, as it were, a 'moral economy' of the plebs, the way in which customs were mobilised in this attempt to halt the advance of rationalisation, which after all came from the upper echelons of society as productive impositions. Paul Willis (1981) also realised that, in the counter-school culture and the subsequent choice of manual factory work by secondary school students in England, there was a powerful form of resistance to the way in which school tried to turn them into domesticated workers. Thompson perceived a paradox, that of a culture that was traditional and rebellious at the same time:

> The conservative culture of the plebs as often as not resists, in the name of custom, those economic rationalizations and innovations (such as enclosure, work-discipline, unregulated "free" markets in grain) which rulers, dealers, or employers seek to impose. Innovation is more evident at the top of society than below, but since this innovation is not some normless and neutral technological/sociological process ("modernization", "rationalization") but is the innovation of capitalist process, it is most often experienced by the plebs in the form of exploitation, or the expropriation of customary use-rights, or the violent disruption of valued patterns of work and leisure. Hence the plebian culture is rebellious, but rebellious in defence of custom.
>
> THOMPSON, 1993: 23

Similarly, in Brazil, the dissatisfaction of a segment of the population deprived of their sense of collective existence is mobilised by the threat to their individual and family stability – a family undoubtedly still marked by patriarchal relations, even with significant changes since the 1950s.[1] The clashes within families are the result of the accumulation of tension that exists between the attachment to the parents' experience and the children's contempt for it. It refers to the influence on young people of a bourgeois culture transmitted by school and by the technical means of globalisation, which lead them to reject the culture of a working class that is almost always manual in nature, and which in its heart is counter-education, as analysed by Bourdieu (2012), Beaud and Pialoux (2009), Willis (1981) and Tomizaki (2006). Of course, there are deep contradictions in this conservative rebellion, and this applies to both Thompson's study and this research.

In the popular culture that I've tried to describe from the periphery of São Paulo, the technical means that speed up the advance of rationalisation are the same ones that allow self-management by wageless workers. But it is specifically in politics that the clash between custom and innovation becomes visible, and in which a popular appropriation of technical means created for psychic and labour self-management is updated. The internet, created for

---

[1] This aspect was mutually reinforced within the labour market. Elisabeth Souza-Lobo (2011: 65) saw hierarchisation within the factory as a "complex cultural mechanism" that obeys non-technical criteria that assign qualifications to tasks and performers. Thus, it is arbitrarily defined that there are, for example, "women's [technical] courses" and, in addition, "different hierarchical and quality relations between the sexes, representations of responsibilities and suitability, which in turn refer to power relations based on technical knowledge".

self-management, also 'replaces' specialised or established knowledge, offering the possibility for individual self-realisation.

Such conflicts become more intense when young activists find themselves at one of the poles of the conflict. This applies especially to references to the military dictatorship. While young people like Vitória, Júlio and Maria Rita learned about the violations committed by the regime at school, the older ones not only attended the institution during the military dictatorship (1964–1985), but also lived on the outskirts, which were not the focus of political repression. With information limited by the cultural industry of the time, they knew little about it. And it's safe to say that some don't complain, as Vitória says about her family's achievements. They bought their own house through the old National Housing Bank (BNH), her father ran a real estate agency, and her mother was a civil servant during that time. In fact, among the interlocutors over 30, the military period is largely ignored or relativised.

These memories act as driving forces for new activism, a prism through which current collective action is conceived.[2] So the conflict becomes insoluble when the children deliberately break with the space of experience in which their parents are guided and replace it with 'theory'. While the tradition they defend comes from an intangible ancestry, a negation of both the previous generation and customs persists. On the other side of the relationship, parents often refuse to re-evaluate their experiences in the light of historiography and the ethical and humanitarian precepts that were affirmed after re-democratisation. As a result, my younger and more engaged interlocutors accuse not only their fathers, but also their uncles and cousins of ignorance, stubbornness and disrespect towards their trajectories. They symbolise these differences, especially in the political clash that became more radical with Jair Bolsonaro's victory in 2018. Many claim to have broken off relations with family members, or to have them very strained.

It's a specific type of narcissism that appears here, pragmatic, survivalist and busy with their 'micro-things', as interlocutor Vitória told me. It's striking that most of them, despite being viscerally opposed to the far-right former president, barely got involved in the electoral process that year, and some didn't even leave the house to vote. Elis says she 'gave up' after the election, and Vitória is very critical of politicians: "Are you going to keep protecting this circus?" she accuses, rhetorically. The disenchantment of young people from the periphery with traditional politics is noticeable in interviews and at social

---

[2] Activists from the black movement in Bahia, for example, directly link present-day police violence with repression by the military regime (Iamamoto et al., 2022).

entrepreneurship events, where mentions of the Bolsonaro government, for or against, were seldom.

The ecosystem that brings together social impact businesses sees itself as a world apart from political parties and parliaments, a sign that the expectation of regulated citizenship has been exhausted. Although they don't close their doors to councillors and members of parliament who might want to support their initiatives, politics is all about pragmatism. This is the case even when they take on militant overtones, as in the case of João Vicente, who keeps an MST flag and a *wiphala*[3] decorating different parts of his agency. Vitória has even had more affinity with left-wing movements, but she summarises her relationship in the following sentence: "When I met the MST, I really believed in it. But I was young, new to everything, I didn't know much about things." The point is that these young people from the periphery have been investing more and more in micro-politics, while some of them, even 'ready to shine', in Elis' words, fall hopelessly into precarious work, formalised or not. The world around them is perhaps no more oppressive than it was for the previous generation, but the perception of this reality is now almost unbearable. The moment, in fact, is one of 'sinister carnage capitalism', as João Vicente reflected. As reality always lets something get out of hand, these young people also have previously unknown implications, a desire to decommodify relationships that sounds auspicious, and perhaps a side effect of the therapeutic discourse. Elis doesn't agree to take part in this 'mega-billing of life'.

In the 1990s, Roberto Schwarz (1999: 220) questioned whether "we were becoming a classless society under the sign of delinquency", at a time when democratic participation was still in vogue.[4] The violent sociability that took on ungovernable proportions during that decade, the proliferation of fortified enclaves even on the peripheries, and disillusionment with the labour market permeated popular daily life, establishing what psychoanalyst Jurandir Freire Costa called a 'narcissistic culture of violence'. Thus, under the umbrella of therapeutic discourse, individualism is not only reinvigorated but reaffirmed as the correct behaviour in the face of the dangers posed by society. With limited

---

3 Flag of Inca origin representing the indigenous peoples of Bolivia.
4 From another perspective, Evelina Dagnino (2004: 151) believes that the "reframing of participation follows the same direction as the reconfiguration of civil society, with the emergence of so-called 'solidarity participation' and the emphasis on voluntary work and 'social responsibility', for both individuals and companies. The basic principle here seems to be the adoption of a privatised and individualistic perspective, capable of replacing and redefining the collective meaning of social participation. The very idea of 'solidarity', the great 'banner' of this redefined participation, is stripped of its political and collective meaning, and begins to rely on the private terrain of morality."

prospects for the future, "the way out is the immediate enjoyment of the present; submission to the *status quo* and systematic, methodical opposition to any project for change that involves social co-operation and non-violent negotiation of particular interests" (1988: s/p). *Bolsonarismo* has been a deliberate effort to transform this depoliticising alignment into a power project, and to this end it has the support of popular individuals who are indifferent to regulated citizenship, but eager to 'de-bureaucratise' and pay less taxes. They are in search of exclusive middle-class products and services, even without the status and credentials; seek to impose security and ostentatious policing; and, finally, are willing to reject society in its essentially political, participatory sense.

Responding to the subject's introspection, therapeutic techniques, through pocketbooks or mobile phones, are evolving and accelerating the possibilities of self-management. These techniques reach young and old, regardless of class, race and gender, democratically distributing the hope of eliminating suffering through autonomy. I analysed how these discourses materialise in books, lectures, courses and television programmes, from coaches to multilateral institutions. They are, in turn, techniques and discourses that work, i.e., they soothe consciences and make them available for work again. On the other hand, the obstacle to the acceptance of entrepreneurship programmes continues to be precisely the family, with its own contradictions. Fundamental to the narrative of Teologia da Prosperidade, there is no answer when the family itself is the anchor of the individual. For peripheral entrepreneurship and those engaged in struggles for recognition, the family institution remains a safe haven of human relationships against the excesses of rationalisation. It matters little to this analysis whether or not the family still represents the 'norm', because it is not dissociated from the objective conditions of existence.

In light of the research that I have presented here, I maintain that this diagnosis has only deepened with the expansion of entrepreneurial alternatives. Those who, out of conviction, embrace self-management, even from a popular place where 'knowing how to do things' prevails, ignite the flame of entrepreneurship with their ambition for the stability of their new class identity, even if they are prevented by *habitus* from accessing the physical and symbolic spaces of the traditional middle class. Those who seek entrepreneurship out of necessity and to escape suffering, anxiety about the present and uncertainty about the future, see the relatively few success stories as concrete examples that yes, it is possible to live a worthwhile life through autonomy. Popular entrepreneurship is the space that both characters inhabit.

As a phenomenon that reformats aspects of popular individualism in degenerate terms by mirroring the structure of feelings, popular entrepreneurship responds to feelings of social disintegration. If spasmodic reactions are present throughout history, it is because a significant number of people decide to react to what they see as a threat, something that Karl Polanyi interpreted as a 'self-protection movement of society'. For Polanyi (2000), the generalisation of mercantile self-regulation would result in the collapse of society, placing it at the mercy of the 'satanic mill' represented by the unrestricted administration of the market, and jeopardising harmony between individuals, nature, security and food production. By making unlimited use of the labour force, the system would also make use of the physical, psychological and moral entity of the subject.

Unlike the European context of the early 20th century, the ambiguous resistance of customs does not now find its enemy in the dichotomy between the poor and the rich. On the 'micro' level of popular daily life, it is directed at children and neighbours who are in the process of breaking with the space of experience, keeping latent advances and retreats in the process of rationalisation. It is therefore a conflict that takes place at the heart of popular culture, in which, faced with hegemonic discourses, the 'classes that live off work' (Antunes, 2015) lose any kind of internal cohesion. This conflict revolves around conservation versus rationalisation, but it is not expressed in the form of a class struggle, which would thus forge a class consciousness, as Thompson would hope. It is a conflict that tears the popular world apart from the inside, between a reluctant attachment to individualism and the family of those who look inwards, on the one hand, and young people who seek to cross the bridge, and in doing so push ahead with rationalisation in search of a typically bourgeois way of life, on the other.

However, Koselleck (2004: 259) observes that "expectation also takes place in the today; it is the future made present; it directs itself to the not-yet, to the inexperienced, to that which is to be revealed". Expectations include "hope and fear, wishes and desires, cares and rational analysis, receptive display and curiosity: all enter into expectation and constitute it". Thus, there is still a space of possibilities for consensus that does not appeal to the elimination of others. In this case, a still-timid awareness of the power of the popular economy and aspirations of decommodification offer a glimpse of autonomy, but on a solidarity basis.

References

Abílio, L.C. (2020) Uberização: A era do trabalhador *just-in-time*? *Estudos Avançados* 34(98): 111–126.

Alencar, G. (2010) *Assembleias de Deus: origem, implantação e militância (1911–1946)*. São Paulo: Arte Editorial.

Almeida, R. (2004) Religião na metrópole paulista. *Revista Brasileira de Ciências Sociais* 19(56): 15–27.

Almeida, R. (2009) *A Igreja Universal e seus demônios: um estudo etnográfico*. São Paulo: Editora Terceiro Nome.

Amaral, A.I. (2018) Identity, work, and mobility amongst Bolivian market vendors in El Alto and São Paulo. PhD Dissertation. University of Essex.

Antunes, R. (2015) *Adeus ao trabalho?* São Paulo: Cortez.

Appadurai, A. (1996) *Modernity at large: Cultural dimensions of globalization*. Minneapolis: University of Minnesota Press.

Arantes, P. (2014) *O novo tempo do mundo*. São Paulo: Boitempo.

Beaud, S. and Pialoux, M. (2009) *Retorno à condição operária: investigação em fábricas da Peugeot na França*. São Paulo: Boitempo.

Beck, U. (2014) *The brave new world of work*. Cambridge: Polity Press.

Beck, U. (1992) *Risk society: towards a new modernity*. London: Sage.

Beckert, J. (2013) Imagined futures: fictional expectations in the economy. *Theory and Society*, 42(3): 219–240.

Bergamin, M. (2015) Juventude, trabalho e cultura periférica: a experiência da Agência Popular de Cultura Solano Trindade. *Cadernos Adenauer XVI* 1: 141–159.

Bernardo, J. and Santos, C. (2021) Paraisópolis faz 100 anos e aposta no comércio local para se recuperar da pandemia. *Folha de S. Paulo* (15 September 2021). Available (consulted 30 April 2024) at: https://www1.folha.uol.com.br/cotidiano/2021/09/paraisopolis-faz-100-anos-e-aposta-no-comercio-local-para-se-recuperar-da-pandemia.shtml.

Biondi, K. (2019) *Junto e misturado: uma etnografia do PCC*. São Paulo: Terceiro Nome.

Birman, P. (2019) Narrativas seculares e religiosas sobre a violência: as fronteiras do humano no governo dos pobres. *Sociologia & Antropologia* 9(1): 111–134.

Blokland, T. (2003) *Urban Bonds*. Cambridge: Polity.

Boltanski, L. and Chiapello, E. (2009) *O novo espírito do capitalismo*. São Paulo: WMF Martins Fontes.

Boltanski, L. and Thévenot, L. (2006) *On justification: economies of worth*. Princeton: Princeton University Press.

Botto, C. (2015) I Love Paraisópolis chega ao fim com recorde de audiência no horário. *Correio* (1 November 2015). Available (consulted 13 October 2021) at:

https://www.correio24horas.com.br/noticia/nid/i-love-paraisopolis-chega-ao-fim-com-recorde-de-audiencia-no-horario/.

Bourdieu, P. (2012) As contradições da herança. In: *A miséria do mundo*. Petrópolis: Vozes.

Braga, R. (2009) A vingança de Braverman: o infotaylorismo como contratempo. In: Antunes, R. and Braga, R. *Infoproletários: degradação real do trabalho virtual*. São Paulo: Boitempo, 59–88.

Braga, R. (2012) *A política do precariado*. São Paulo: Boitempo.

Braga, R. (2019) From the Union Hall to the Church. *Jacobin* (4 July 2019). Available at (consulted at 10 June 2021): https://www.jacobinmag.com/2019/04/bolsonaro-election-unions-labor-evangelical-churches.

Braverman, H. (1980) *Trabalho e capital monopolista*. Rio de Janeiro: Zahar.

Brown, W. (2019) *Nas ruínas do neoliberalismo*. São Paulo: Politeia.

Burawoy, M. (2009) *The extended case method: Four countries, four decades, four great transformations and one theoretical tradition*. Berkeley: University of California Press.

Caldeira, T.P.R (1984) *A política dos outros: cotidiano dos moradores da periferia e o que pensam do poder e dos poderosos*. São Paulo: Brasiliense.

Caldeira, T.P.R (2000) *Cidade de muros: crime, segregação e cidadania em São Paulo*. São Paulo: Editora 34; Edusp.

Caldeira, T.P.R (2017) Peripheral urbanization: Autoconstruction, transversal logics, and politics in cities of the global south. *Environment and Planning D: Society and Space* 35(1): 3–20.

Campos, F. (2020) *Rap, cultura e política: Batalha da Matrix e a estética da superação empreendedora*. São Paulo: Hucitec.

Candido, A. (1970) Dialética da malandragem. *Revista do Instituto de Estudos Brasileiros* 8: 67–89.

Candido, A. (2017) *Os parceiros do Rio Bonito*. Rio de Janeiro and São Paulo: Ouro sobre azul; Edusp.

Cardoso, A. (2008) Transições da escola para o trabalho no Brasil: persistência da desigualdade e frustração de expectativas. *Dados* 51(3): 569–616.

Cardoso, A. (2019) *A construção da sociedade do trabalho no Brasil: uma investigação sobre a persistência secular das desigualdades*. Rio de Janeiro: Amazon.

Carleial, L. and Azaïs, C. (2007) Mercados de trabalho e hibridização: uniformidade e diferenças entre França e Brasil. *Caderno CRH*, 20(51): 401–417.

Castel, R. (2015) *As metamorfoses da questão social*. Petrópolis: Vozes.

Catini, C. (2020) Empreendedorismo, privatização e o trabalho sujo da educação. *Revista USP* 127: 53–68.

Cavalcanti, M. (2009) Do barraco à casa: Tempo, espaço e valor(es) em uma favela consolidada. *Revista Brasileira de Ciências Sociais* 24(69): 69–80.

Cesar, M. (2021) G10 Favelas procura empreendedores. *Valor Econômico* (2 August 2021). Available (consulted 21 October 2021) at: https://valor.globo.com/empresas/noticia/2021/08/02/g10-favelas-procura-empreendedores.ghtml.

Chapus, Q. (2020) L'émergence des "startuppers" au Maroc: institutions, trajectoires, réseaux sociaux. PhD dissertation. HESAM Université.

Chauí, M. (2001) *Cultura e democracia*. São Paulo: Cortez.

Colbari, A. (2007) A retórica do empreendedorismo e a formação para o trabalho na sociedade brasileira. *Sinais* 1(1): 75–111.

Côrtes, M. (2014) O mercado pentecostal de pregações e testemunhos: formas de gestão do sofrimento. *Religião e Sociedade* 34(2): 184–209.

Côrtes, M. (2017) *Diabo e fluoxetina: pentecostalismo e psiquiatria na gestão da diferença*. Curitiba: Appris.

Costa, H. (2018) *Entre o lulismo e o ceticismo: um estudo com bolsistas do Prouni de São Paulo*. São Paulo: Alameda.

Costa, H. (2019a) Estudantes do Prouni na crise do lulismo. *Plural* 26(1): 289–311.

Costa, H. (2019b) Fascismo na sociedade sem classes: uma interpretação do bolsonarismo. *Le Monde Diplomatique* (22 March 2019). Available at: https://diplomatique.org.br/fascismo-na-sociedade-sem-classes.

Costa, H., Leite, M., and Lindôso, R. (2021) A ressignificação do trabalho autônomo e a retórica empreendedora na França e no Marrocos: Entrevista com Christian Azaïs e Quentin Chapus. *Contemporânea* 11(3): 971–987.

Costa, J.F. (1988) Narcisismo em tempos sombrios. In: Birman, J. (ed.) *Recursos na História da Psicanálise*. Rio de Janeiro: Taurus.

D'Andrea, T. (2013) A formação dos sujeitos periféricos: cultura e política na periferia de São Paulo. PhD Dissertation. Universidade de São Paulo.

Dagnino, E. (2004) Construção democrática, neoliberalismo e participação: os dilemas da confluência perversa. *Política & Sociedade* 5: 139–164.

Das, V. (2004) The signature of the State: the paradox of illegibility. In: Das, V. and Poole, D. *Anthropology in the Margins of the State*. Santa Fé and Oxford: School of American Research Press/James Currey.

De L'Estoile, B. (2020) 'El dinero es bueno, pero un amigo es mejor': Incertidumbre, orientación al futuro y 'la Economía'. *Cuadernos de Antropología Social* 51: 49–69.

De Soto, H. (1989) *The other path*. New York: Basic Books.

Dejours, C. (1999) *A banalização da injustiça social*. Rio de Janeiro: FGV.

Denning, M. (2010) Wageless life. *New Left Review* 66: 79–97.

Dunker, C. (2009) A lógica do condomínio ou: o síndico e seus descontentes. *Revista Leitura Flutuante* 1(1): 1–8.

Durham, E. (1988) A sociedade vista da periferia. In: Kowarick, L. (ed.). *As lutas sociais e a cidade*. Rio de Janeiro: Paz e Terra.

Edington, J. (2015) *50 tons para o sucesso: conselhos para uma vida próspera*. Rio de Janeiro: Unipro, 2015.

Ehrenberg, A. (2010) *O culto da performance: da aventura empreendedora à depressão nervosa*. Aparecida: Ideias & Letras.

Elias, N. and Scotson, J. (2000) *Os estabelecidos e os outsiders*. Rio de Janeiro: Zahar.

Escobar, A. (1995) *Encountering development*. New Jersey: Princeton University Press.

Feltran, G. (2007) Vinte anos depois: a construção democrática brasileira vista da periferia de São Paulo. *Lua Nova* 72: 83–114.

Feltran, G. (2011) *Fronteiras de tensão*. São Paulo: Editora da UNESP.

Feltran, G. (2014) O valor dos pobres: a aposta no dinheiro como mediação para o conflito social contemporâneo. *Caderno CRH* 27(72): 495–512.

Ferrasoli, D. (2018) Condomínios com mais de uma torre se destacam no Campo Limpo, em SP. *Folha de S. Paulo* (25 February 2018). Available (consulted 10 December 2021) at https://www1.folha.uol.com.br/sobretudo/morar/2018/02/1957973-condominios-com-mais-de-uma-torre-se-destacam-no-campo-limpo-em-sp.shtml.

Fonseca, M. (2019) Este é o bairro de São Paulo que tem mais microempreendedores (MEIs). *Exame* (6 August 2019). Available (consulted 18 August 2020) at: https://exame.com/pme/este-e-o-bairro-de-sao-paulo-que-tem-mais-microempreededores-meis/.

Fontes, L. (2018) O direito à periferia: experiências de mobilidade social e luta por cidadania entre trabalhadores periféricos de São Paulo. PhD Dissertation. IESP-UERJ.

Fontes, L. (2022) Histórias de quem quer fugir e de quem quer ficar: laços comunitários nas cambiantes periferias de São Paulo. *Revista Brasileira de Ciências Sociais* 37(109): e3710902.

Foucault, M. (2004) *Microfísica do poder*. São Paulo: Graal.

Fraiman, L. (2021) *Projeto de vida e atitude empreendedora*. São Paulo: Editora FTD.

Freud, S. (2016) *Civilization and its discountents*. Peterborough: Broadview Press.

Gago, V. (2015) *La razón neoliberal: economias barrocas y pragmática popular*. Buenos Aires: Tinta Limón.

Georges, I. (2009) Trajetórias profissionais e saberes escolares: o caso do telemarketing no Brasil. In: Antunes, R. and Braga, R. *Infoproletários: degradação real do trabalho virtual*. São Paulo: Boitempo.

Gielow, I. (1997) Economia cria 'inempregáveis', diz FHC. *Folha de S. Paulo* (8 April 1997). Available (consulted 30 April 2024) at: https://www1.folha.uol.com.br/fsp/brasil/fc080427.htm#:~:text=A%20realidade%20econ%C3%B4mica%20do%20chamado,"%20aqueles%20que%20o%20criticam.

Global Entrepreneurship Monitor (GEM) (2021) 2020/2021 Global Report. London.

Gregori, M. (2000) *Viração: experiências de meninos de rua*. São Paulo: Companhia das Letras.

Guimarães, N.A. (2004) *Caminhos cruzados: estratégias de empresas e trajetórias de trabalhadores.* São Paulo: Editora 34.

Hall, S. (1981) Notes on deconstructing 'the popular'. In: Samuel, R. *People's history and socialist theory.* New York: Routledge.

Hamburger, E. (1998) Diluindo fronteiras: a televisão e as novelas no cotidiano. In: *História da vida privada no Brasil: contrastes da intimidade contemporânea, vol. 4.* São Paulo: Companhia das Letras.

Highmore, B. (2016) Formations of feelings, constellations of things. *Cultural Studies Review* 22(1): 144–167.

Hirata, D. (2011) Vida loka. In: Cabanes, R., Georges, I., Rizek, C. and Telles, V. *Saídas de Emergência.* São Paulo: Boitempo.

Hochschild, A.R. (2018) *Strangers in their own land: anger and mourning on the American right.* New York: The New Press.

Hoggart, R. (2009) *The uses of literacy.* London: Penguin.

Holston, J. (2008) *Insurgent Citizenship: Disjunctions of Democracy and Modernity in Brazil.* Princeton, NJ: Princeton University Press.

Iamamoto, S., Teles, R., and Santos, L. (2022) The authoritarian prism: the impact of memories of the dictatorship on young activists in contemporary Brazil. In: Lima, V., Pannain, R.N. and Martins, G.P. *The consequences of the social movements in Brazil.* Londres: Routledge.

Illouz, E. (2007) *Cold intimacies: The making of emotional capitalism.* Cambridge: Polity Press.

Illouz, E. (2008) *Saving the modern soul: therapy, emotions, and the culture of self-help.* Berkeley: University of California Press.

Jameson, F. (1974) *Marxism and form: twentieth-century dialectical theories of literature.* Princeton: Princeton University Press.

Jameson, F. (1992) Reification and utopia in mass culture. In: *Signatures of the visible.* New York: Routledge.

Jesus, C.M. (2014) *Quarto de despejo: diário de uma favelada.* São Paulo: Ática.

Koselleck, R. (2004) *Futures past: on the semantics of historical time.* New York: Columbia University Press.

Kowarick, L. (1980) *A espoliação urbana.* São Paulo: Paz e Terra.

Krastev, I. (2017) Majoritarian futures. In: Geiselberger, H. (ed.). *The great regression.* Cambridge: Polity Press.

Kurz, R. (1992) *O colapso da modernização.* São Paulo: Paz e Terra.

Kurz, R. (2004) O declínio da classe média. *Folha de S. Paulo* (19 September 2004). Available at (consulted at 30 April 2024): https://www1.folha.uol.com.br/fsp/mais/fs1909200408.htm.

Lasch, C. (1991) *The culture of narcissism.* New York: ww Norton.

Laval, C., Dardot, P. (2013) *La nueva razón del mundo: ensayo sobre la sociedad neoliberal*. Barcelona: Gedisa.

Lavinas, L. (2013) 21st century Welfare. *New Left Review* 84: 5–40.

Lehmann, D. (1996) *Struggle for the Spirit: Religious Transformation and Popular Culture in Brazil and Latin America*. Cambridge: Polity Press.

Leite, E.S. and Melo, N.M. (2008) Uma nova noção de empresário: a naturalização do 'empreendedor'. *Revista de Sociologia e Política* 16(31): 35–47.

Lima, B. and Gerbelli, L.G. (2020) No Brasil, 40% dos jovens com ensino superior não têm emprego qualificado. *G1* (11 August 2020) Available (consulted 6 September 2020) at: https://g1.globo.com/economia/concursos-e-emprego/noticia/2020/08/11/no-brasil-40percent-dos-jovens-com-ensino-superior-nao-tem-emprego-qualificado.ghtml.

Lima, D. (2007) "Trabalho", "mudança de vida" e "prosperidade" entre fiéis da Igreja Universal do Reino de Deus. *Religião e Sociedade* 27(1): 132–155.

Lima, M. (2012) Acesso à universidade e mercado de trabalho: o desafio das políticas de inclusão. In: Martins, H. and Collado, P. (eds.). *Trabalho e sindicalismo no Brasil e Argentina*. São Paulo and Mendoza: Hucitec; Universidad Nacional de Cuyo.

Löwy, M. (2011) Sobre o conceito de 'afinidade eletiva' em Max Weber. *Plural* 17(2): 129–142.

Löwy, M. (2014) *A jaula de aço: Max Weber e o marxismo weberiano*. São Paulo: Boitempo.

Macedo, R. (2020) "Agora quer ser rica?": negociações cotidianas sobre classe e mobilidade social entre estudantes universitárias. *Revista Antropolítica* 50: 197–223.

Macedo, R. (2021) Imagens de estudantes na publicidade do ensino superior privado: marcadores sociais da diferença em articulação. *Revista Brasileira de Sociologia* 9(21): 181–205.

Machado da Silva, L.A. (2018) Da informalidade à empregabilidade (reorganizando a dominação no mundo do trabalho). In: Cavalcanti, M., Motta, E. and Araujo, M. (eds.). *O mundo popular: trabalho e condições de vida*. Rio de Janeiro: Papeis Selvagens.

Machado da Silva, L.A. and Menezes, P.V. (2019) (Des)continuidades na experiência de 'vida sob cerco' e na 'sociabilidade violenta'. *Novos estudos* 38(3): 529–551.

Maciel, D. (2018) *A rebelião do público-alvo e a crise da tecnologia social de pacificação: luta no Programa Fábricas de Cultura*. PhD Dissertation. Universidade de São Paulo.

Mafra, C. (2002) *Na posse da palavra: religião, conversão e liberdade pessoal em dois contextos nacionais*. Lisboa: Instituto de Ciências Sociais da Universidade de Lisboa.

Mafra, C., Swatowiski, C. and Sampaio, C. (2012) O projeto pastoral de Edir Macedo: uma igreja benevolente para indivíduos ambiciosos? *Revista Brasileira de Ciências Sociais* 27(78): 81–96.

Mannheim, K. (1975) Funções das gerações novas. In: Foracchi, M. and Pereira, L. *Educação e sociedade*. São Paulo: Cia. Editora Nacional.
Mannheim, K. (1993). El problema de las generaciones. *Reis* 62: 193–242.
Marcuse, H. (1999) *Tecnologia, guerra e fascismo*. São Paulo: Editora da UNESP.
Mariano, R. (2004) Expansão pentecostal no Brasil: o caso da Igreja Universal. *Estudos Avançados* 18(52): 121–138.
Mariz, C. (1997) O demônio e os pentecostais no Brasil. In: Birman, P. et al. (eds.). *O mal à brasileira*. Rio de Janeiro: EdUERJ.
Martelli, C.G. (2010) Autoajuda e o 'espírito de nossa época'. *Perspectivas* 38: 195–220.
Mello e Silva, L. (2007) Trabalho e reestruturação produtiva: o desmanche da classe. In: Oliveira, F. and Rizek, C. (eds.) *A era da indeterminação*. São Paulo: Boitempo.
Mello, J.M.C. and Novais, F. (1998) Capitalismo tardio e sociabilidade moderna. In: Schwarcz, L.M. (ed.) *História da vida privada no Brasil: contrastes da intimidade contemporânea, vol. 4*. São Paulo: Companhia das Letras.
Méndez, M.L. (2008) Middle class identities in a neoliberal age: tensions between contested authenticities. *The Sociological Review* 56(2): 220–237.
Monteiro Filho, M. (2006) Das manchetes policiais para a revolução social. *Repórter Brasil* (12 January 2006). Available (consulted 22 January 2022) at: https://reporterbrasil.org.br/2006/01/das-manchetes-policiais-para-a-revolucao-social/.
Nascimento, E.P. (2010) A periferia de São Paulo: revendo discursos, atualizando o debate. *Revista RUA* 16(2): 112–128.
Neri, M.C. (2010) *A nova classe média: o lado brilhante dos pobres*. Rio de Janeiro: FGV/IBRE, CPS.
Öberg, B (2018) O segredo da 'cozinha afetiva': nostalgia e bom tino para negócios. *Veja SP* (21 May 2018). Available (consulted 15 December 2021) at: https://vejasp.abril.com.br/blog/vida-boa/comida-afetiva/.
Oliveira, A.S. (2018) O evangelho marginal dos Racionais MC's. In: Racionais MC'S. *Sobrevivendo no inferno*. São Paulo: Companhia das Letras.
Oliveira, F. (1988) Medusa ou as classes médias e a consolidação democrática. In: Reis, F.W. and O'Donnell, G. *A democracia no Brasil: dilemas e perspectivas*. São Paulo: Vértice.
Oliveira, F. (2003) *Crítica à razão dualista / O ornitorrinco*. São Paulo: Boitempo.
Pardo, I. (1996) *Managing existence in Naples: morality, action, and structure*. Cambridge: Cambridge University Press.
Pavez, T. (2015) Crime, trabalho e política: um estudo de caso entre jovens da periferia de São Paulo. PhD Dissertation. Universidade de São Paulo. de doutorado.
Pereira, A.B. (2014) Rolezinho no shopping: aproximação etnográfica e política. *Revista Pensata* 3(2): 8–16.
Pierucci, A.F. (1988) A direita mora do outro lado da cidade. *Revista Brasileira de Ciências Sociais* 4(10): 44–64.

Pinheiro-Machado, R. (2008) China-Paraguai-Brasil: uma rota para pensar a economia informal. *Revista Brasileira de Ciências Sociais* 23(67): 117–133.

Pinheiro-Machado, R. and Scalco, L. (2018) Da esperança ao ódio: juventude, política e pobreza do lulismo ao bolsonarismo. *Cadernos IHU Ideias* 16(278): 1–24.

Pochmann, M. (2012) *Nova classe média? O trabalho na base da pirâmide social brasileira.* São Paulo: Boitempo.

Polanyi, K. (2000) *A grande transformação.* Rio de Janeiro: Campus.

Prandi, R. (1982) *Os favoritos degradados: ensino superior e profissões de nível universitário no Brasil hoje.* São Paulo: Edições Loyola.

Prandi, R. (2004) O Brasil com axé: candomblé e umbanda no mercado religioso. *Estudos Avançados* 18 (52): 223–238.

Rizek, C.S. (2012) Trabalho, moradia e cidade: zonas de indiferenciação? *Revista Brasileira de Ciências Sociais* 27(78): 41–49.

Rocha, C. (2013) Encontros e desencontros entre petismo e lulismo: classe, ideologia e voto na periferia de São Paulo. Master thesis. Universidade de São Paulo.

Rodrigues, L.M. (2009) *Industrialização e atitudes operárias: estudo de um grupo de trabalhadores.* Rio de Janeiro: Centro Edelstein de Pesquisas Sociais.

Rossi, M. and Oliveira, R. (2021) A corrida pelo primeiro unicórnio da favela atrai políticos e empresários a Paraisópolis. *El País* (22 November 2021). Available (consulted 13 December 2021) at: https://brasil.elpais.com/economia/2021-11-22/a-corrida-pelo-primeiro-unicornio-da-favela-atrai-politicos-e-empresarios-a-paraisopolis.html.

Roy, A. (2010) *Poverty capital.* New York: Routledge.

Rui, T.C. (2010) A inconstância do tratamento: no interior de uma comunidade terapêutica. *Dilemas* 3(8): 45–73.

Sader, E. (1988) *Quando novos personagens entraram em cena.* Rio de Janeiro: Paz e Terra.

Sahlins, M. (1976) *Culture and practical reasons.* Chicago: University of Chicago Press.

Sant'ana, R. (2017) A nação cujo Deus é o senhor: a imaginação de uma coletividade "evangélica" a partir da Marcha para Jesus. PhD Dissertation. Universidade Federal do Rio de Janeiro.

Santos, W.G. (1979) *Cidadania e Justiça.* Rio de Janeiro: Campus.

Schwarz, R. (1999) *Sequências brasileiras.* São Paulo: Companhia da Letras.

Schwarz, R. (2002) Pressupostos, salvo engano, de 'Dialética da malandragem'. In: *Que horas são?* São Paulo: Companhia das Letras.

Scinocca, A.P. (2006) Lula elege Casas Bahia como modelo de desenvolvimento para o Brasil. *O Estado de S. Paulo* (29 April 2006). Available (consulted 30 April 2024) at: https://www2.senado.leg.br/bdsf/handle/id/319150.

Sennett, R. (2012) *A corrosão do caráter.* Rio de Janeiro: Record.

Silva, G. (2019) Corpo, política e emoção: feminismos, estética e consumo entre mulheres negras. *Horizontes antropológicos* 25(54): 173–201.

Simmel, G. (2005) As grandes cidades e a vida do espírito. *Mana* 11(2): 577–591.
Simone, A. (2004) *For the City Yet to Come – Changing African Life in Four Cities*. Durham, NC: Duke.
Singer, A. (2012) *Os sentidos do lulismo*. São Paulo: Companhia das Letras.
Sklair, J., Glucksberg, L. (2021) Philanthrocapitalism as wealth management strategy: Philanthropy, inheritance and succession planning among the global elite. *The Sociological Review* 69(2): 314–329.
Souza, J. (2010) *Os batalhadores brasileiros*. Belo Horizonte: Editora UFMG.
Souza, R.M. (2008) *O discurso do protagonismo juvenil*. São Paulo: Paulus.
Souza-Lobo, E. (2011) *A classe operária tem dois sexos: trabalho, dominação e resistência*. São Paulo: Editora Fundação Perseu Abramo.
Sposito, M. and Corrochano, M.C. (2005) A face oculta da transferência de renda para jovens no Brasil. *Tempo Social* 17(2): 141–172.
Teixeira, J.M. (2016) *A mulher universal: corpo, gênero e pedagogia da prosperidade*. São Paulo: Mar de Ideias.
Telles, V.S. (2006) Mutações do trabalho e experiência urbana. *Tempo Social* 18(1): 173–195.
Telles, V.S. and Hirata, D. (2010) Ilegalismos e jogos de poder em São Paulo. *Tempo Social* 22(2): 39–59.
Thompson, E.P. (1993) *Customs in common: studies in traditional popular culture*. New York: The New Press.
Tocqueville, A. (2002) *Democracy in America, vol 2*. Pennsylvania State University, Electronic Classics Series.
Tomizaki, K. (2006) A herança operária entre a fábrica e a escola. *Tempo social* 18(1): 153–171.
Tommasi, L. (2013) Culturas de periferia: entre o mercado, os dispositivos de gestão e o agir político. *Política & Sociedade* 12(23): 11–34.
Tommasi, L. (2015) Culto da performance e performance da cultura: os produtores culturais periféricos e seus múltiplos agenciamentos. *Crítica e sociedade* 5(2): 100–126.
Tommasi, L. and Silva, G.M. (2020) Empreendedor e precário: a carreira 'correria' dos trabalhadores da cultura entre sonhos, precariedades e resistências. *Política & Trabalho* 52: 196–211.
Valle, V.S.M. (2019) *Entre a religião e o lulismo: um estudo com pentecostais em São Paulo*. São Paulo: Recriar.
Vianna, S. (2013) *Rituais de sofrimento*. São Paulo: Boitempo.
Weber, M. (2004) *A ética protestante e o "espírito" do capitalismo*. São Paulo: Companhia das Letras.
Wellen, H. (2008) Contribuição à crítica da 'economia solidária'. *Revista Katál* 11(1): 105–115.

Wheatley, J. (2008) Popular retailer moves into Brazilian favela. *Financial Times* (14 November 2008). Available (consulted 7 November 2021) at: https://www.ft.com/content/58425fc0-b1cd-11dd-b97a-0000779fd18c.

Williams, R. (1973) Base and superstructure in Marxist cultural theory. *New Left Review* 1(82): 3–16.

Williams, R. (1976) *Keywords: a vocabulary of culture and society*. Oxford: Oxford University Press.

Williams, R. (1977) *Marxism and literature*. Oxford: Oxford University Press.

Williams, R. (1989) Culture is ordinary. In: *Resources of hope: culture, democracy, socialism*. London: Verso.

Williams, R. (2003) *Television: technology and cultural form*. New York: Routledge.

Willis, P. (1981) *Learning to labor*. New York: Columbia University Press.

Willis, P. and Trondman, M. (2008) Manifesto pela etnografia. *Educação, Sociedade & Culturas* 27: 211–220.

Wright, E.O. (1989) Rethinking, once again, the concept of class structure. In: Wright, E.O. et al. *The debate on classes*. London: Verso.

Zaluar, A. (1985) *A máquina e a revolta: as organizações populares e o significado da pobreza*. São Paulo: Brasiliense.

Index

addiction   3, 90n11, 106, 132, 165, 184n3
Almeida, Ronaldo   86, 87, 99
ancestral   14, 138, 148, 189
Apostolic Church of Faith   106
Arantes, Paulo   11, 11n15, 182, 184
Assembly of God   73, 99, 99n15, 99n15, 168n10, 191
autoconstruction   29, 30, 31, 32, 38, 103, 114
autonomy   1, 8, 63, 64, 66, 94, 122, 141, 146, 162, 169, 170, 170n14, 173, 175, 180, 181, 182, 193, 197, 198

Bahia   12, 28, 30, 45, 46, 71, 72, 108, 109, 138, 195n2
Barbosa, Adriana   144
Beaud, Stéphane   160, 179, 194
Beck, Ulrich   34, 193
Beckert, Jens   162, 193
Biondi, Karina   19n24
Birman, Patrícia   88
Bolsa Família   22n28
Bolsonaro, Jair   17, 50, 57, 82, 83, 104, 120, 121, 141, 142, 148, 195, 196
   Bolsonarismo   197
Boltanski, Luc   136, 169n13, 187
Braga, Ruy   38n13, 180n28
Brás   75, 119
Brasilândia   79
Braverman, Harry   40
Brazilian Micro and Small Business Support Service (SEBRAE)   44, 44n16, 52, 114, 124, 176
Brown, Wendy   2, 8n8, 66, 186n7
Burawoy, Michael   162
bureaucracy   56, 57, 82, 169n13

calculation   7, 8n8, 44, 136, 173
Caldeira, Teresa   2, 8, 20, 21, 30, 68, 69, 79, 159n5, 165
Campo Limpo   12, 13, 15, 16, 17, 30, 51, 53, 54, 59, 61, 63, 64, 110, 111, 114, 117, 128, 130, 132, 134, 137, 150n26, 165, 168, 170, 172, 173, 190
Candido, Antonio   8, 8n9, 9, 12, 97
Candomblé   109, 109n17
   Candomblecistas   20

Capão Redondo   16, 30, 54, 62, 118, 150, 150n26, 170, 172
capitalism   1, 8n8, 9, 16, 17, 42, 61n20, 97, 105, 126n11, 133, 147, 158n3, 181, 183n1, 186, 196
Cardoso, Adalberto   4, 8, 160n7
Cardoso, Fernando Henrique   176
Castel, Robert   3, 176n21
Catholicism   9, 20, 40, 45, 50, 61, 74, 99, 109, 122, 132, 147, 150, 170, 188, 189
Catini, Carolina   119, 170, 192
Chácara Santo Antônio   61, 63, 64
Chauí, Marilena   7n7
Chiapello, Ève   169n13, 187
class struggle   198
classless society   115, 158, 196
community   7, 28, 32, 33, 34, 35n9, 37, 39, 40, 41, 42, 43, 51, 54, 66, 72, 73, 75, 79, 80n4, 81, 83, 85, 105, 108, 118, 122n6, 127n12, 136, 148, 162, 163, 166, 169n12, 170, 183, 184
competence   3, 148, 159
condominium   16, 53, 54, 55, 56, 71, 81, 132, 166
Congress for Success   85, 88, 89, 90, 95, 96
Consolidation of Labour Laws (CLT)   4, 44, 48, 49, 58, 63, 78, 81, 83, 85, 118, 120, 135, 152, 160, 173
consumption   4, 29, 38n12, 39, 51, 184n2
   inclusion through consumption   22, 64, 83, 158, 191
Cooperifa   16, 143, 145, 148, 150, 174
Côrtes, Mariana   184n3, 190
Costa, Henrique   16, 40, 59, 83, 157n1, 158n4, 159n5, 167, 169, 177, 180n25, 183
Costa, Jurandir Freire   80, 196
counter-stigmatisation   191
COVID-19   12, 18, 19, 20n26, 38, 47, 49, 51, 53, 53n18, 69, 82, 84, 85, 99, 104, 107, 134, 181
   pandemic   18, 20n26, 38, 47, 49, 50, 51, 52, 53, 54, 55, 56, 56n19, 57, 58, 60, 61, 63, 68, 69, 73, 78, 80, 83, 84, 85, 93, 99, 104, 107, 111, 134, 181
Cratera de Colônia   16, 42
crime   2, 3, 6n5, 9, 19, 77, 78, 80, 82, 100, 114, 130, 131, 132, 165, 168, 173, 191

culture 1, 5, 5n4, 6n5, 8n9, 10n12, 11, 11n14, 12, 17n22, 20, 21, 63, 124, 129, 130, 130n14, 140, 145, 147, 150, 151, 159, 162, 166n9, 168, 173, 179, 180n25, 180n27, 185n4, 188, 190, 191, 193, 194, 196
   conservative culture 194
   globalised culture 181, 193
   peripheral culture 14n19, 18, 115, 116, 120, 126, 134, 140n23, 147, 148, 149, 150, 151, 170, 173, 174, 184
   popular culture 1, 2, 6, 10, 12, 18, 31, 47, 84, 97, 161, 162, 167, 170, 181, 188, 190, 193, 194, 198
culture industry 97
customs 2, 3, 4, 12, 87n9, 93, 125, 159, 161, 168, 178, 193, 195, 198

D'Andrea, Tiarajú 115, 116, 151, 152
Das, Veena 50, 79
De Soto, Hernando 160
Dejours, Christophe 3
Denning, Michael 6
Diadema 106
domestic work 12, 92, 98, 99, 100
Durham, Eunice 130

economy
   popular economy 8n8, 66, 159, 198
Elias, Norbert 87
empowerment 41, 64n22, 65, 66, 115, 123, 187n8
entertainment 97, 137, 147
entrepreneurship 33, 56, 70, 83, 98, 107, 183
   peripheral entrepreneurship 125, 128, 139, 145, 173n15, 197
   popular entrepreneurship 3, 11, 20, 57, 111, 112, 114, 174, 183, 191, 197
   social entrepreneurship 3, 13, 14, 16, 17, 17n22, 18, 115, 116, 117, 119, 123, 124, 125, 126, 127, 129, 130, 132, 138, 142, 152, 164, 168, 170, 173, 175, 187, 188, 189, 196
Escobar, Arturo 115
ethnography 3, 16, 20, 21, 136
ethos 10, 18, 31, 47, 63, 64, 82, 128, 161, 162, 166, 179, 183, 189
evangelical churches 1, 16, 18, 30, 103, 188
experience
   popular experience 3, 8, 42, 97, 111, 114, 117, 157, 178n23, 193

Fábrica de Cultura 16, 144, 172, 173
family 2, 4, 7, 8n8, 9n10, 11, 18, 20, 30, 31, 33, 40n14, 41, 43, 44, 46, 48, 49, 51, 52, 55, 57, 59, 60, 61, 63, 69, 70, 71, 74, 77, 78, 80, 80n4, 81, 82, 83, 84, 86, 87n7, 92, 93, 94, 95, 96, 98, 101, 102, 106, 109, 110, 116, 130, 131, 136n20, 141, 147, 157, 159, 160, 160n7, 162, 164, 165, 166, 167, 168, 175, 176n19, 178, 180n28, 188, 189, 190, 194, 195, 197, 198
favela 2, 16, 19, 28, 29, 30, 32, 33, 34, 34n9, 35, 36, 37, 38, 39, 41, 43, 46, 64, 66, 67, 74, 75, 78, 79, 80, 81, 95, 97, 120, 121, 126, 129, 132, 133, 163
Feltran, Gabriel 29, 131, 151n28, 157n2, 158
fiado 44
financial education 63, 146, 181
First Command of Capital (PCC) 19, 19n24, 19n25, 30, 133, 163
flow 19, 21, 30, 78, 79, 80, 163
forró 71, 99, 144
fortified enclaves 51, 54, 58, 159, 165, 196
Foucault, Michel 8n8, 142
Freud, Sigmund 183, 185

G10 Favelas 34, 34n9
gastronomy 59
Georges, Isabel 176, 183
Glucksberg, Luna 114, 128, 136
governmentality 8n8
Grajaú 16, 29n3, 30, 73, 122n6, 137, 138, 140, 141, 149, 150, 153
guiltless world 9, 12, 77, 192
Guimarães, Nadya Araújo 179

habitus 39, 132, 167, 184n4, 197
Hall, Stuart 10, 12
hegemony 161, 173, 187
Heliópolis 35n9, 46, 75
higher education 5, 7, 40, 58, 59, 81, 135, 152, 157n1, 160, 169, 176, 177, 180n28, 191
hip hop 16, 116, 123, 125, 126, 174, 184, 184n2, 191n10
Hirata, Daniel 9, 132
Hochschild, Arlie 2, 19
Hoggart, Richard 69, 72, 79, 163
Holston, James 30, 157
Holy Bonfire 93, 93n12, 95, 96
housework 2, 48, 49

INDEX 211

Housing and Urban Development Company (CDHU) 46
human rights 17n21, 40

Illouz, Eva 10, 11n14, 58, 185, 186, 192, 193
individual microentrepreneur (MEI) 16, 46, 55, 63, 173
individualism 1, 3, 9n10, 31, 47, 69, 83, 105, 122n6, 160, 161, 163, 186, 188, 189, 196, 197, 198
innovation 60, 194
Interlagos 51, 65, 92, 94, 140

Jameson, Fredric 1, 12, 31
Jardim Ângela 15, 16, 29n3, 57, 58, 98, 122, 125, 127, 133n18, 149, 187
Jardim Maria Sampaio 30, 114, 129, 132, 133
Jardim São Luís 30, 118, 119, 144, 170, 172, 177
Jesus, Carolina Maria de 97
Joker 37, 134, 190

Koselleck, Reinhart 6, 157n1, 161, 198
Kowarick, Lúcio 30, 167

L'Estoile, Benoît de 8
labour 2, 3, 4, 4n2, 4n3, 11, 12, 18, 36n10, 38n12, 39n13, 46, 48, 57, 59, 68, 84, 102, 125, 130, 140n23, 152, 158n4, 165, 170n14, 174, 176, 180n25, 181, 183n1, 185, 185n4, 190, 194, 198
  market 3, 36n10, 38n12, 65, 66, 81, 115, 122, 124n8, 145, 146, 158, 160, 164, 165, 168, 169, 171, 175, 176, 176n19, 177, 178, 179, 183, 187, 194n1, 196
  wage labour 55, 96, 121, 139, 142, 143, 160n8, 184
Largo Treze 16, 58, 83
Lasch, Christopher 11, 61, 61n20, 127, 190
legal entities (PJ) 45, 56n19, 74, 119
Lima, Diana 128, 134, 178n24, 180n28
Löwy, Michael 9, 123n7
Lula da Silva, Luiz Inácio 29n2, 32, 43, 51, 82, 104, 120, 147, 158, 174, 177, 191
  Lulismo 23n28, 64, 83, 128, 148, 151, 191

Macedo, Edir 86, 96, 96n13, 189
Machado da Silva, Luiz Antonio 7n7, 44, 133, 160, 160n8
Mafra, Clara 70, 86, 88, 89, 95, 96n13, 189

Mano Brown 136, 136n19
Marcuse, Herbert 185
market 4, 7, 13n18, 17n21, 31, 37, 47, 47n17, 52, 55, 59, 73, 77, 80, 81, 91, 108, 121, 125n9, 134, 140, 150, 152, 158n3, 159, 160, 162, 164, 171, 173, 179, 184n3, 186, 188, 191n10, 193, 198
media 13, 18, 38, 86, 141, 145, 149, 150, 184n4
merit 2, 56, 57, 64, 74, 160, 162, 175, 183, 190
meritocracy 3
microcredit 4, 16n21, 32, 33, 115, 191
middle class 13, 32, 38, 39, 40, 51, 63, 69, 72, 75, 81, 87, 92, 93, 99, 114, 119, 120, 126n11, 129, 133n18, 134, 137, 143, 151, 163, 166, 166n9, 167, 169, 174, 180n26, 181, 197
  new middle class 33, 34, 38, 39, 51, 132, 159, 165, 166, 172, 191
  traditional middle class 191, 197
Military Police (PM) 79
modernity 2, 11n15, 12, 168, 185, 189, 193
Morumbi 32, 33, 65, 74, 78, 163, 172
motoboy 39, 45, 126
My House My Life (MCMV) 51, 165

narcissism 11, 61, 101, 189, 190, 195
narcissistic 59, 191, 196
National Commercial Apprenticeship Service (SENAC) 54
neoliberalism 8n8, 18, 115, 152, 186n7
  neoliberal reason 8, 115
  neoliberalism from below 8n8
Neri, Marcelo Côrtes 38
non-governmental organizations (NGO) 32, 82, 128, 150
Northeast 8n9, 37, 40, 41, 57, 72, 101, 109
Northeastern 2, 20, 32, 71, 92, 100, 108
nostalgia 106
Novais, Fernando 8, 9n9

obreiros 88, 89, 90, 91
Oliveira, Acauam 115
Oliveira, Francisco de 66, 126n11, 158
organic food 16, 114, 123, 130, 165
outsiders 2, 87, 191n10

Paraisópolis 16, 19, 28, 29, 30, 32, 33, 34, 35n9, 36, 37, 38, 39, 40, 41, 41n15, 74, 77, 78, 79, 80, 80n4, 81, 82, 83, 163, 164, 165, 166, 185, 190

Paraná   43, 84
Pardo, Ítalo   5
Parelheiros   29n3, 42, 43, 103, 150n26
Parque Ipê   99
Partner Salon Law   45
Pentecostalism   20
    evangelicals   70, 74, 97, 158n3, 167
    neo-Pentecostalism   2, 61, 70, 95, 101, 134, 167, 189, 191
peripheral subject   12, 14, 116, 136, 149, 151, 152
periphery   1, 15, 59, 87, 127, 128, 132, 133, 134, 135, 136, 137, 138, 139, 140, 141, 143, 145, 146, 147, 149, 150, 151, 152, 153, 158, 164, 166, 167, 168, 170, 171, 173, 174, 177, 181, 188, 194, 195, 196
Pernambuco   92, 93, 98, 100, 101, 167
Pialoux, Michel   160, 179, 194
Pinheiro-Machado, Rosana   70, 132
Pochmann, Márcio   38n13, 177
Polanyi, Karl   198
poverty   9n9, 13, 17n21, 43, 50, 93, 95, 100, 115, 150
power   11, 31, 44n16, 50, 59, 82, 96, 99n15, 115, 120, 127, 128, 140, 147, 150, 183, 191, 194n1, 197
precarity   18, 30, 34, 69, 70, 115, 116, 133, 139, 147, 152, 158, 160n7, 168, 172, 177, 184n3
progressive   17, 121, 122, 147, 152, 161
Projeto Rede   13, 32, 33, 60, 80n4, 96, 107, 108, 110, 111, 112, 119, 129, 130, 132, 136, 170, 171, 172, 178

quebrada   13, 15, 16, 19, 37, 38, 118, 123, 124, 127, 133, 133n18, 135, 136, 137, 141, 143, 146, 147, 149, 151, 173

Racionais MC's   9, 16, 64, 66, 131n16, 136, 136n19, 174, 181
rapa   33, 34, 72
rationalisation   2, 7, 160, 162, 164, 178, 193, 194, 197, 198
reality show   35, 37, 39, 42
recognition   7, 11, 12, 44, 63, 64, 85, 115, 136, 148, 152, 159, 174, 175, 177n22, 178, 183, 184, 189, 190, 191, 197
regulated citizenship   4, 4n3, 144, 176, 196, 197
religion   2, 109, 109n17, 184n3

resentment   64, 97, 121, 126, 190
resilience   98
ride apps   38, 52, 104, 105, 106, 124, 185
    99   104
    driver   103, 105
    drivers   114
    Uber   104
Rio de Janeiro   34, 86, 98, 100, 103
Rizek, Cibele   158
Rodrigues, Leôncio Martins   179
Rousseff, Dilma   38, 43
Roy, Ananya   17n21, 193
Rui, Taniele   90n11, 106, 188n9

Sader, Eder   30, 147, 149
Sahlins, Marshall   164
Santo Amaro   57, 58, 71, 72, 83, 84, 85, 150, 163
Santos, Wanderley Guilherme dos   4n3
São Paulo Metropolitan Railway Company (CPTM)   15
São Paulo State   15, 54, 91, 157
scepticism   xiii, 2, 3, 11, 18, 48, 57, 69, 82, 83, 84, 101, 105, 117, 152, 176, 178, 179, 181, 182, 183
scholarship   40n14, 41, 41n15, 59, 65, 81, 83, 99n15, 119, 129, 167, 180n25
Schwarz, Roberto   196
self-employment   3, 31, 49, 72, 74, 157, 159, 164, 180n25
    self-employed workers   3, 8, 15, 20, 47, 53, 114, 161, 183, 190
self-help   11, 11n14, 13, 33, 86, 90, 92, 96, 98, 186, 186n6, 187, 189, 192
self-management   2, 11, 31, 70, 162, 170, 176, 177, 178n23, 183, 184, 185, 186, 187, 188, 193, 194, 197
Sennett, Richard   61n20, 63
sertanejo   47, 64n22, 78, 144
SESC   16, 117, 128, 129, 144, 173
shopping streets   18, 38, 57, 70, 72
Simmel, George   158n3, 193
Singer, André   22n28, 38n13
Sklair, Jessica   114, 136, 136n20
small businesses   3, 21, 29, 32, 41, 46, 69, 163, 178n23
small traders   3, 15, 20, 105, 161, 190
social ascension   2, 3, 4, 7, 58, 80, 100, 130, 131, 157n2, 168

social impact businesses   17, 17*n*22, 34*n*9, 35, 111, 114, 123, 125, 128, 130, 136, 137, 140, 170, 178, 180, 181, 189, 196
social media   15, 37, 59, 98, 104, 106, 114, 185
social mobility   6*n*4, 45, 63, 81, 83, 114, 151, 157, 160, 172, 175
Socialism and Freedom Party (PSOL)   43, 119, 147, 148
soirees   1, 16, 116, 117, 120, 132, 144, 145, 150, 174
Souza, Jessé   38*n*13
Souza, Regina Magalhães de   193
Sposito, Marilia Pontes   127*n*12
street vendor   34, 55, 71, 72, 101, 108
structure of feelings   11, 29, 39, 64, 115, 116, 120, 122, 142, 145, 147, 152, 161, 165, 182, 183, 187, 191, 193, 197
struggle   3, 9, 50, 97, 100, 101, 109, 152, 190
suffering   1, 3, 70, 88, 92, 97, 98, 101, 111, 111*n*18, 114, 125, 147, 159, 168, 175, 182, 183, 184, 187, 188, 190, 191, 192, 197
symbolic violence   4, 14

Taboão da Serra   16, 30, 64, 81, 109, 133, 147
Telles, Vera   115, 152, 158
Temer, Michel   83
Teologia da Libertação   147
Teologia da Prosperidade   86, 87*n*8, 92, 197
therapeutic discourse   3, 11, 116, 122, 125, 146, 162, 182, 185, 186, 186*n*7, 187, 189, 190, 191, 192, 196
Thompson, E. P.   2, 6*n*5, 193, 194, 198
tithe   86, 89, 91, 92
Tocqueville, Alexis de   9*n*10
Tomizaki, Kimi   160, 175, 194
Tommasi, Livia de   52, 130*n*14, 169*n*12, 176, 193

Umbanda   61, 109*n*17, 147
unemployment   3, 6, 28, 33, 53*n*18, 84, 96*n*14, 104, 107, 130*n*14, 152, 159, 160*n*7, 177
Unified Health System (SUS)   84
Union of Residents and Commerce of Paraisópolis (UMCP)   34
Universal Church of the Kingdom of God (UCKG)   70, 85, 85*n*5, 86, 87*n*7, 87*n*9, 88, 92, 93, 93*n*12, 95, 96, 99, 167, 168, 187, 188, 189, 190

University for All Programme (Prouni)   22*n*28, 40, 40*n*14, 59, 65, 83, 157*n*1, 167, 177, 180*n*25, 191
utopia   3, 4, 12, 79, 97, 100*n*16, 114, 117, 120, 121, 122, 137, 139, 143, 146, 152, 157, 171, 172, 174, 182, 184, 193

Valo Velho   54, 55
Vargas, Getúlio   4
Vargem Grande   42, 44, 71, 73, 76, 85, 103, 106, 163
vida loka   10, 136
viração   7, 14, 33, 45, 114, 182
vivência   15, 133, 135

wageless life   3, 5, 6, 10, 18, 34, 44, 46, 69, 72, 75, 85, 110, 158, 161, 162, 163, 164, 179, 184, 190
way of life   5, 7, 8*n*9, 39, 53, 69, 79, 114, 121, 125, 160, 168, 174, 183, 189, 198
Williams, Raymond   5, 10*n*13, 11, 20, 151*n*27, 161, 185
Willis, Paul   10*n*12, 21, 166, 166*n*9, 193, 194
work card   4, 107, 160, 171
Worker's Party (PT)   23*n*28, 33, 43, 82, 103, 120, 126, 141, 147, 174, 175*n*18, 176, 180*n*28
workers   1, 2, 4, 8*n*8, 29, 30, 32, 44, 49, 50, 53, 53*n*18, 61, 69, 80, 90, 105, 111*n*18, 124*n*8, 135, 150, 157, 163, 166*n*9, 167, 169*n*13, 174, 175*n*18, 176*n*20, 179, 180*n*25, 182, 188, 193
   wageless workers   14, 183, 184, 190, 192, 193, 194
working class   4, 7, 21, 33, 39*n*13, 57, 69, 79, 116, 126*n*11, 130*n*14, 147, 162, 163, 165, 166, 166*n*9, 167, 174, 178, 179, 194
   limits   99, 107
World Bank   17*n*21, 114, 115, 124*n*8
Wright, Erik Olin   178

Yunus, Muhammad   16*n*21

Zaluar, Alba   130
zé povinho   10, 136, 178
Zona Leste   45, 83, 138, 167
Zona Oeste   13, 39, 114, 128, 130, 150
Zona Sul   1, 12, 16, 17, 18, 20, 29, 43, 54, 70, 75, 78, 114, 115, 127, 128, 132, 144, 147, 149, 150, 167, 170, 174, 183, 188

www.ingramcontent.com/pod-product-compliance
Lightning Source LLC
Chambersburg PA
CBHW070619030426
42337CB00020B/3854